The Tracks North

CMAS BORDER & MIGRATION STUDIES SERIES
Series Editor: Gilberto Cárdenas

OTHER TITLES IN THE SERIES

The Border Guide: Institutions and Organizations of the United States–Mexico Borderlands, by Milton H. Jamail and Margo Gutiérrez, 1992

The Militarization of the U.S.–Mexico Border, 1978–1992: Low-Intensity Conflict Doctrine Comes Home, by Timothy J. Dunn, 1996

The Terror of the Machine: Technology, Work, Gender, and Ecology on the U.S.–Mexico Border, by Devon G. Peña, 1997

Health and Social Services among International Labor Migrants: A Comparative Perspective, edited by Antonio Ugalde and Gilberto Cárdenas, 1997

The Tracks North

The Railroad Bracero Program of World War II

BARBARA A. DRISCOLL

CMAS Books
The Center for Mexican American Studies
The University of Texas at Austin

A CMAS BOOK

Editor: Víctor J. Guerra
Editorial Assistant: Olga L. Mejía

The publication of this book was assisted by a grant from the
Inter-University Program for Latino Research.

Library of Congress Cataloging-in-Publication Data
Driscoll, Barbara A.
    The tracks north : the railroad bracero program of World War II /
Barbara A. Driscoll. — 1st ed.
        p. cm. — (CMAS border & migration studies series)
        Includes bibliographical references (p.   ) and index.
        ISBN 0–292–71593–5 (alk. paper). — ISBN 0–292–71592–7 (pbk. :
alk. paper)
        1. Railroad workers—United States—History—20th century.
2. Alien labor, Mexican—United States—History—20th century.
3. United States—Emigration and immigration—Government policy—
History—20th century.   4. Mexico—Emigration and immigration—
Government policy—History—20th century.   5. World War, 1939–1945—
Economic aspects—United States.   I. Title.   II. Series.
HD8039.R12U6244   1998
331.6′272073—dc21   97-49865

A Spanish translation of an earlier version of this book was published as
*Me voy pa' Pensilvania por no andar en la vagancia: Los ferrocarrileros mexi-
canos en Estados Unidos durante la Segunda Guerra Mundial.* Translated by
Lauro Medina. Mexico City: Consejo Nacional para la Cultura y las Artes
and Universidad Nacional Autónoma de México, 1996.

The stanzas on the part-title pages are from the *corrido* "La Pensilvania,"
from *A Texas-Mexican* Cancionero: *Folksongs of the Lower Border,* by
Américo Paredes (Austin: University of Texas Press, 1995).

♻ ∞ This book is printed on recycled, acid-free paper that conforms
to the American National Standard of permanence for printed library
materials, as approved by the American National Standards Institute.

Printed and bound in the United States of America.

First edition. First impression, March 1999.

Contents

Acknowledgments

The completion of this book would not have been possible without the support of many individuals and institutions during the long process of research and analysis. This publication affords me the opportunity to thank them publicly.

Since my doctoral dissertation forms the nucleus of this study, it is an honor to thank my two advisors. Dr. Philip Gleason of the Department of History of the University of Notre Dame shared his comprehensive experience in U.S. immigration history with me. Likewise, the late Dr. Julián Samora of the Department of Sociology of the same university, and the director of its Mexican American Graduate Studies Program, brought the significance of Mexican immigration into focus for me.

I conducted a preliminary revision of my thesis during my appointment to the Colegio de la Frontera Norte in Tijuana, Baja California. The support that Dr. Jorge Bustamante and the Colegio personnel extended in identifying additional sources in Mexico was crucial in fully understanding the importance of the railroad bracero program.

Moreover, other Mexican colleagues have helped in finding information in state archives that have been overlooked for the history of immigration. Dr. Gustavo del Castillo connected me with the state archive in San Luis Potosí, and Dr. Rafael Loyola helped me locate unusual documents in the state archive of Querétaro.

I would like to thank Mónica Verea Campos, the director of the North American Studies Center at the National Autonomous University of Mexico for her support in the final preparation and publication of the manuscript. Mónica's leadership of the center established a space for all of us to fully explore many crucial issues for Mexico in the increasingly complex context of economic integration. Likewise, the personnel of the center, particularly Dolores Latapí, the head of our editorial department, and our administrative support staff, Alicia García and Norberta Álvarez, graciously tolerated my neuroses during the final stages of preparing the manuscript.

Finally, the publication series on migration that the Center for Mexican American Studies sponsors under the leadership of Dr. Gilberto Cárdenas constitutes an important public space to discuss questions vital to the complex issue of Mexican immigration to the United States. Even the helpful comments of the reviewers reflect the center's commitment to produce the highest quality research possible. Likewise, Víctor Guerra, the editor of CMAS Books, has been most generous and supportive throughout the publication process.

Lastly, this research would not have been possible without the support, unfailing understanding, and constant sense of humor of my husband, Arturo Alvarado, and our son, Patrick José Alvarado. Thank you both.

— *Barbara A. Driscoll*
Mexico City, June 1997

Introduction

The greatest employment of Mexican immigrants, both legal and undocumented, in the United States since the end of the nineteenth century has generally been assumed to be in agricultural work. While agricultural employment has been and continues to be an important source of work for immigrants, nonagricultural jobs have proved significant, sometimes equally so. Both mines and some services, particularly in the U.S. Southwest, have traditionally sought Mexican immigrants. Nonetheless, the most significant nonagricultural employers have undoubtedly been the railroads.

This traditional recruitment of Mexican workers for the railroads enabled the railroad industry during World War II, when workers were scarce, to lobby successfully for railroad braceros. While the railroad bracero program did not survive the termination of the war, and was not quite as large as the infamous agricultural bracero program, it represents a singular and pivotal, albeit largely unknown, chapter of Mexican immigration to the United States. In a period of almost two and a half years—from 1943 to 1945—over 100,000 Mexican workers were recruited to work all over the United States for more than thirty railroads.

The project originated essentially as a rider to the agricultural program to contract a few hundred workers to be assigned to the railroads, but the railroad bracero program soon proved so popular that it acquired autonomy and became quite large. Indeed, the railroad braceros came to form a significant segment of the unskilled track labor in the United States during the war and contributed substantially to the railroads' participation in the war effort. Moreover, the railroad bracero program was implemented in spite of the presence of large and powerful railroad unions in both Mexico and the United States, a factor usually responsible for protecting domestic labor markets from temporary contract labor programs.

Like its larger and better known counterpart, the wartime agricultural program, railroad recruitment was governed by binational agreements and administered by representatives from both countries. And like the agricultural program, the employers were so pleased with the workers they were able to contract through the program that the number of braceros requested increased dramatically. Likewise, in spite of the protections for workers that negotiators tried to build into the program, many complaints surfaced about working and living conditions. Unlike the agricultural program, however, the recruitment of Mexican railroad workers was phased out at war's end, in accordance with the original arrangements and in spite of attempts by the railroads to continue it.

That such a program could be formally organized reflects the convergence of several disparate historical phenomena that are not usually associated. The tradition of Mexican employment on U.S. railroads in the Southwest and the Midwest provided the justification for the railroads to make the unusual request that the government recruit them. That the railroads could even make such a request reflects the longstanding relationship between the industry and the federal government. Finally, the extraordinary conditions of World War II made it possible for the United States to elicit such support from a Mexican government, which ordinarily was quite reluctant to send its workers to the United States.

One of the most intriguing aspects of the railroad bracero program is the agreement establishing this brief program: it is the only migration agreement between Mexico and the United States in which both governments were able to establish their priorities and realize them. The United States wanted unskilled workers for the railroads; Mexico was willing to supply them, but only through a binational program that protected the workers and had a well-defined end. The desperation of the United States to find workers during the war, coupled with an abundance of suitable labor in Mexico, created the basis for an equal relationship between Mexico and the United States.

In many respects, the railroad bracero program during World War II stands out as the only successful binational immigration project implemented by the U.S. and Mexican governments. It is the only instance in which the Mexican government was able to stand up to the U.S. government in order to protect its workers, and it is the only instance of a temporary contract labor program that was formally negotiated by both governments and respected according to the conditions established through bilateral discussions.

This is in stark contrast to the agricultural bracero program, which also originated during the domestic labor crisis of World War II. The agricultural program was to have ended with the termination of World

War II as well, but complicity between large growers, particularly in California, and parts of the U.S. government, along with a weakening of the Mexican government's position after the war, created conditions that led to its extension until 1964.

With the end of the two bracero programs, the hiring of undocumented workers became a prevalent practice among an increased number of U.S. companies. Yet many U.S. industries—agriculture, service, and others—would today avail themselves of a temporary labor program with Mexico if it were possible. Further, given the present controversy over undocumented immigration from Mexico, some policymakers would consider a temporary contract program a viable solution. Although limited numbers of temporary unskilled workers from Mexico continue to be admitted to the United States through H-2 visas, this is not an alternative to the bracero program. Moreover, the introduction of employer sanctions in the Immigration Reform and Control Act of 1986 has forced some employers to reconsider their practice of hiring undocumented immigrants.

Would another binational temporary contract labor program, supervised by both Mexico and the United States, provide a more equitable channel to connect Mexican immigrants with prospective employers? A government-to-government agreement provides a line of communication to discuss problems that worker-employer contracts cannot have. A formal government-to-government agreement may not be, and perhaps cannot be, a perfect solution to regulating and monitoring the employment of Mexican immigrants, but it does provide a point of departure for considering policy alternatives.

The Literature

The body of literature on Mexican immigration to the United States by Mexican and U.S. authors is enormous; certainly an extensive critical review is a study in itself. The range of research and writing just about the agricultural bracero program is impressive—from specialized scholarly studies to overviews for general audiences to personal accounts. But few references are found anywhere to the railroad bracero program, and in fact almost no published descriptions or analyses exist—even the employment of Mexicans on the railroads has been relatively ignored. Most of the literature about braceros deals with the agricultural program, focusing on the 1950s and 1960s from a regional perspective, at the expense of analyses of its national or international impact and its formative years during

World War II when the agricultural program was contemporaneous with the railroad program. Here I will review the few extant references to the railroad bracero program and the literature about the agricultural program helpful in documenting and analyzing the railroad program.

Shortly after the railroad bracero program began in 1942, the Pan American Union commissioned Robert ("Cuba") Jones to write a descriptive account of the agricultural bracero program. Published in both English and Spanish in 1945, *Mexican War Workers in the United States* constitutes an important contemporary description by an informed observer of both programs during the war. Since Jones, writing in 1944, could not anticipate the fate of either program, his perception of the railroad program provides a relatively accurate picture of its role within the entire wartime project. Using interviews, observations, and data provided by official sources, Jones devotes almost half of the study to the railroad program. Although the tone Jones adopts seems overly optimistic and paternalistic for those studying the program after the fact—for example, he does not discuss workers' complaints—the author provides an invaluable contemporary overview of the program from 1942 to the end of 1944.[1]

Obviously the bracero programs of World War II cannot be discussed without mentioning the classic work of Ernesto Galarza. The *Merchants of Labor* studies the course of the agricultural bracero program in its formative years from 1942 to 1947, mostly in the state of California. Although Galarza only mentions the recruitment of Mexican workers for the railroads in passing, *Merchants* constitutes a basic point of reference for the agricultural program during the war, which is essential for an understanding of the railroad bracero program.[2]

Richard Craig's pioneering work *The Bracero Program* emphasizes the lobbies and pressure groups influential in implementing the agricultural program and extending it until the 1960s. His periodization is useful in understanding the maturation and decline of the agricultural bracero program, and in appreciating its national impact. Moreover, Craig's research clearly demonstrates that for a long time the agricultural bracero program functioned for U.S. agriculture as a vehicle for obtaining inexpensive, plentiful Mexican immigrant labor.[3]

Peter Kirstein, in *Anglo over Bracero: A History of the Mexican Workers in the United States from Roosevelt to Nixon,* studies both the agricultural and railroad programs during World War II and the agricultural program for a time thereafter. Based principally on sources at the Truman Library in Missouri, Kirstein's work describes the bracero program of

World War II, including the railroad component, and its aftermath, including the President's Commission on Migratory Labor established in 1950. Even though the study is narrow in focus and sources of information, Kirstein's is the only study done after both programs ended that attempts a comparison of the railroad program with the agricultural one.[4]

A recent study by Erasmo Gamboa about the impact of the bracero program on agriculture in the Northwest during World War II, *Mexican Labor and World War II,* is the only one to date to emphasize a region outside the Southwest and one of a handful to concentrate on the agricultural program's formative phase during World War II. While certain characteristics of agriculture are unique to the Northwest, Gamboa's research shows that the agricultural bracero program was remarkably flexible in its application to varying circumstances. The study also demonstrates that the structure of the agricultural program was inexorably given to abuses and that workers had little recourse to legal protection, despite some bureaucrats' best efforts. Unlike California farmers, northwestern farmers after World War II turned to Mexican American farmworkers for their farm labor needs, since they proved less problematic.[5]

Primary documents are also of great value for a historical analysis of the railroad bracero program. Among those hitherto not applied to the study of Mexican immigration are documents housed in the National Archives in Washington, D.C., in the Railroad Retirement Board in Chicago, in the Archivo General de la Nación in Mexico City, and in the state archives of Querétaro. Another valuable primary source is an internal report of the Southern Pacific Railroad, "Historical Data in Connection with Employment of Mexican National Laborers Imported from Mexico."[6]

Objectives

The present study documents the seemingly incongruent factors and the negotiations that led to the creation of the railroad bracero program, and provides a historical overview of the program in Mexico and the United States. It also highlights the international character of the program, and the remarkable fact that this short-lived program remains the only binational migration agreement between Mexico and the United States that both parties respected in its original form.

Abbreviations

AFL   American Federation of Labor
CIO   Congress of Industrial Organizations
CTM   Confederación de Trabajadores Mexicanos
         (Mexican Workers' Union)
FEPC Fair Employment Practices Commission
FSA   Farm Security Administration
ICC   Interstate Commerce Commission
INS   Immigration and Naturalization Service
ODT   Office of Defense Transportation
OPA   Office of Price Administration
RFC   Reconstruction Finance Corporation
RRB   Railroad Retirement Board
SRE   Secretaría de Relaciones Exteriores
         (Secretariat of Foreign Affairs)
STPS Secretaría de Trabajo y Previsión Social
         (Secretariat of Labor and Social Security)
USDA United States Department of Agriculture
WARE Western Association of Railroad Executives
WMC   War Manpower Commission

The Tracks North

Part One

BACKGROUND

Adiós estado de Texas,
con toda su plantación;
ya me voy pa' Pensilvania
por no pizcar algodón.

1

The U.S. Government and the Railroad Industry

That the railroads, a powerful and diversified industry in the 1940s, pressed the federal government along with agribusiness in a time of crisis to locate workers in Mexico on their behalf might seem extraordinary as we approach the end of the twentieth century. It is akin to the airline industry today insisting that the Department of Labor hire temporary foreign contract workers to do airport maintenance work. Yet the railroads' attitude and their campaign to extend the bracero program were entirely consistent with a long and largely symbiotic relationship between the two. The development of the railroads as the first modern transcontinental transportation system was realized in large part through extensive support from Washington, D.C., and the state governments. A detailed, multifaceted analysis of the relationship between the railroads and the government would require much more space than is available for the present endeavor, but it is necessary in any discussion of the railroad bracero program to establish that the railroads were justified in their expectation that the federal government would help them find workers. Therefore this chapter will briefly delineate the development of the railroads from their beginnings to World War II, focusing on the relationship of the railroads with the federal government.

The Early Railroads

Generous post–Civil War subsidies and land grants from the public sector enabled private entrepreneurs to assume the challenge of joining the Atlantic and Pacific with the iron horse. Government support was pivotal in promoting the railroads as the first significant expression of a nascent continental U.S. economic nationalism. Railroad companies and the public sector became partners in defining the United States, economically and politically. Indeed, the United States owes much of its spectacular economic growth since the Civil War to advanced and integrated transportation systems, mostly the railroads.

In the early years, the railroads' priorities, of course, centered on acquiring land, labor, and raw materials at a good price. Lack of regulation regarding labor allowed the railroads to use questionable tactics to recruit workers and gain possession of land. Above all, the railroads were never reticent about using their relationship with the government to their advantage.

The major western roads acquired the bulk of the land upon which they built their tracks after the Civil War through land grants from the government, both federal and state. A railroad system, tentatively called the National Railroad, that would join the East Coast with the West Coast had been discussed for many years, but the Civil War made it patently clear that such a project was imperative for further national economic development. Since the area between the Mississippi River and California was inhabited mostly by seminomadic Native American groups, private initiative was cautious about investing the huge sums required for the construction of a railroad. The federal government soon understood that an incentive for railroad investors was in order. In fact, the symbolic laying of the Golden Spike at Ogden, Utah, in 1869 when the Central Pacific and the Union Pacific met to form the first transcontinental railroad can be attributed to that collaboration between railroad entrepreneurs and the government.

Although some eastern states had previously facilitated local railroad construction through subsidies and other support for railroads such as the Baltimore and Ohio, the federal government did not issue land grants until 1850, when it granted land for and authorized the construction of a railroad connecting the Lake Michigan Canal and the mouth of the Ohio River. Normally, such land grants entitled the railroad companies to lay track and benefit from tax breaks, while they enabled the federal government to control the routes covered by railroads. Similar grants were made until 1871, when Congress ended the practice because abuses by the railroads aroused so much public criticism. Settlers, for example, near railroad land complained of excessive property taxes and liberties taken by the companies. However, the federal government continued its assistance to the industry by delegating land to state governments, who made land grants to railroad developers with even less formality or public scrutiny. Over seventy major railroads, including all trunk lines, received land through government grants of one form or another. Eventually 9½ percent of the land area in the continental United States was deeded to the railroads.[1]

Land grants generated further advantages for the major railroads. Since the companies agreed to give reduced rates for government merchandise (20 percent for mail, 50 percent for other), they were virtually guaranteed enough government business to cover operating expenses. Nonsubsidized short-line railroads were much less competitive, being forced to set higher rates to cover costs incurred in construction, such as the purchase of land.[2]

Moreover, other benefits from land grants were deliberately intended to promote the railroads' solvency. The land actually granted to the companies was mostly uninhabited, especially in the West, and involved areas much larger than actually necessary to lay track. Enough was allotted on either side of the right-of-way to develop towns, build large farms, or construct operational facilities. In an effort to populate these areas, the government permitted the railroads to sell plots of land to settlers, and in fact some companies became large-scale colonizers, sending recruiters to the East and Europe to extol the virtues of their particular tracts. Some even tried to develop cohesive communities by colonizing certain immigrant or religious groups in a particular area. Occasionally the railroads sold land along their routes to established towns, a source of especially quick profit.[3]

Widespread abuses in the railroad industry such as rebates, drawbacks, and pools became commonplace, enraged the public, and eventually forced the federal government to regulate railroad business practices. In 1887, the Interstate Commerce Commission ostensibly was created to do just this—to assure the consuming public that rates were fair and reasonable and to eliminate the threat of monopoly posed by the railroads. Indeed, most historians concede that the establishment of the ICC was a substantial first step toward effective regulation of the railroad industry.[4] Revisionist historians, however, contend not only that ICC was unable to contain the railroads but that its establishment was actually advantageous to the industry. While limiting railroad actions, federal regulations also cushioned the railroads from severe economic swings and the sometimes costly effects of free competition. Active government regulation thus enabled the railroad industry to stabilize.[5]

Underlying federal railroad regulation was the premise that the railroads were entitled to a "reasonable" profit, one that would guarantee them sufficient revenues and profits to survive difficult times. Many railroads realized that they needed the protection of the federal government from disruptions such as the powerful Granger movement,[6] which represented agribusiness. Moreover, railroad management was aware that many midwestern and western roads were built ahead of demand with the assistance of government subsidies, and that it would take several years of operation for them to break even. Their very survival depended on government support.[7]

World War I

The years immediately preceding U.S. entrance into World War I bore out suspicions that the ICC was not effective in regulating the railroads;[8] neither had it succeeded in controlling the industry, as the critics would have liked, nor did it really help the industry adjust to economic swings, as railroad management would have liked. Deficiencies and shortsightedness in ICC policy became apparent as World War I loomed over the United States. To absorb the dramatic increase in traffic between 1907 and 1917, the railroads made enormous capital investments—but only in construction, not in maintenance. Labor and material costs rose so fast that company reserves could not cover operating expenses. While industry revenue was high and traffic was increasing dramatically, revenue per mile dropped.[9] The ICC was able to protect the industry from some problems, but it could not compensate for poor management or its own neglect in imposing minimum maintenance standards.

U.S. involvement in World War I greatly complicated the railroads' precarious situation; they were not prepared for the pressures of a war-oriented economy. Rising labor costs and deteriorating facilities were exacerbated by traffic congestion; thousands of loaded boxcars awaited workers and space to be unloaded in terminals all over the country.[10] Likewise, the military draft depleted the ranks of railway labor. Maintenance-of-way crews, in particular, were affected by the draft and by emergency wartime promotions to higher job classifications, which occasioned neglect of track and plant maintenance. What remained of railway labor was seriously demoralized, since the war had brought a steep rise in the cost of living, with no raises and no prospect of any. Moreover, only a minority of railroad men, skilled and semiskilled, were organized into unions recognized by management.[11]

At the outbreak of World War I, four independent railroad unions, representing 20 percent of railroad labor, received industry recognition and contracts; they were the national brotherhoods for engineers, firemen, conductors, and trainmen and comprised the highest-paid and most prestigious of the railroad occupations. The shopcraft unions (machinists, boilermakers, blacksmiths, sheet metal workers, and carmen) were affiliated with the American Federation of Labor, but they secured only sporadic recognition and many fewer contracts than the Big Four. The remaining groups of workers (clerks, stationmen, freight-house men, maintenance-of-way workers) had unions, but the unions excluded unskilled workers, so membership was low and contracts were sparse.[12] The great majority of railroad workers, then, were unorganized and quite vulnerable to the policy decisions of corporations.

To no avail, the federal government pleaded with railroad management to voluntarily coordinate industry policy decisions in order to improve their delivery of services. Uncoordinated traffic moving eastward created congestion so severe that one company president publicly admitted that service on his road was on the verge of collapse.[13] New England was threatened with a shortage of coal by December 1917, during an exceptionally cold winter. Railroad efficiency declined about 30 percent with the cold weather, and the ICC finally recommended government intervention to President Woodrow Wilson. On December 26, 1917, Wilson announced that he was appointing William McAdoo as the director general of the Railroad Administration, an office that was to be responsible for all rail transportation for the duration of the war.

The ad hoc nationalization of U.S. rail transportation had no precedent; prior government intervention in the private sector had been extremely limited, respecting the autonomy of private business above all. But in this instance the federal government assumed direct control of a floundering industry considered necessary for national defense and security, putting aside the objections of management. McAdoo assumed the responsibility of overseeing scheduling of passenger and freight service, some daily management decisions, and labor questions. The Railroad Administration turned out to be much more independent of the railroads and even the government than anyone expected. The companies intensely disliked their relationship with McAdoo and the Railroad Administration, and they did not soon forget it.[14]

On the other hand, railroad employees and the unions enjoyed greater recognition and reciprocity with McAdoo and his agency than they ever had with railroad management. McAdoo created a Division of Labor and named W. S. Carter, a former president of the brotherhoods of Locomotive Firemen and Locomotive Engineers, its administrator. The Railroad Administration officially removed all obstacles to unionization, thereby facilitating further organization of railroad employees. The Division of Labor issued mandatory guidelines that raised and standardized wages, developed regulations and grievance procedures for seniority and promotion, abolished piecework, instituted disciplinary codes, and established a wage commission. These reforms addressed problems that had provoked the mayhem leading to nationalization.[15]

The Railroad Administration was dismantled after World War I. But most railroads were in better shape after World War I than before it; increased traffic, settlement of protracted labor difficulties, and more efficient procedures imposed by the Railroad Administration benefited most companies. Although the decade of the 1920s was favorable for the industry, as it was for the U.S. economy in general, serious signs of devitalization did not bode well. While most companies showed a respectable profit of around 4½ percent throughout the decade, growth of freight shipments slowed and passenger service actually diminished before the end of the decade. Competition from automobiles, pipelines, and trucks began to affect the railroads' business, initiating a decline that worsened over the next decade.[16] The stock market crash of 1929 further devastated the railroad industry.

The Great Depression and the New Deal

The Great Depression wrought havoc on the railroads. Revenues dropped a billion dollars a year in 1930, 1931, and 1932, resulting in a 1933 income that was less than half that of 1929. Freight service continued to decline and passenger services almost collapsed. Despite the railroads' efforts to compensate for loss of business by dismissing employees, reducing wages, and modifying maintenance priorities, the industry was not able to regroup.[17]

The already horrendous financial condition of many railroads throughout the country continued to worsen, which inevitably meant bankruptcy for many. By the end of 1935, more railroads were in receivership than at any other time in U.S. history.[18] Worse, investor confidence in the industry eroded throughout the 1930s, and creditors became more vociferous in their criticism of railroad management. For their part, railroad managers could no longer follow their customary strategy of selling low-interest bonds to conservative investors to raise working capital. Lack of buyer confidence forced the railroads into the risky, high-interest speculative bond market, further increasing their operating costs.[19]

In accordance with U.S. laws, bankrupt railroads operating from receivership were reorganized and placed in the hands of a trustee/receiver; the corporations were accorded legal protections that maintained their solvency and prevented certain legal actions such as lawsuits. However, any funds available to the company were to be used to pay debts and finance operations, not to pay dividends to investors. During the decade 1932 to 1942, two thirds of all railroads were unable to pay dividends, and indeed three fourths of railroad stock did not yield dividends until 1950.[20]

The only factor that prevented the wholesale collapse of the railroad industry was firm federal financial backing through grants from the Reconstruction Finance Corporation.[21] Despite attempts to avoid overt government subsidy of rail transport, the RFC granted $98 million to railroads of all classes by mid 1932.[22] Unfortunately, railroad management decided to spend this working capital on optional investment in stocks and bonds rather than on maintenance or debt reduction.[23] Poor management decisions, even on directly subsidized government roads, hastened bankruptcy proceedings.

Toward the end of the 1930s, business stimulated by the war in Europe and precautionary defense preparations in the United States eased the railroad industry's situation. The Illinois Central, for example, experienced a phenomenal 59 percent increase in freight traffic from June to October 1939, the largest such upturn in its history.[24] The Pennsylvania ordered some 2,500 freight cars, 50,000 tons of rail, and 20 electric locomotives in 1939 to handle the business it expected to be generated by the European war.[25] U.S. railways handled more business in 1940 than at any time during the depression ($4.3 billion in 1940 alone).[26]

World War II

With memories of World War I nationalization still fresh in their minds, railroad management, though optimistic about their prospects for renewed prosperity, were also aware that poor performance might provoke another nationalization scheme. Even railroad executives, however, conceded that their contribution to the war effort hinged on coordination. To forestall another labor-oriented nationalization proposal, the railroads gladly cooperated with Ralph Budd, president of the Burlington, who was appointed commissioner to the Council of National Defense in 1940. Budd represented the industry until 1941, when President Franklin Roosevelt established the Office of Defense Transportation with Joseph Eastman as director.[27] Roosevelt's program emphasized the voluntary cooperation of the railroad industry in responding to the evolving needs of the war effort, but *without* the power of enforcement.

World War II offered the railroads the real possibility of a secure and solid recovery. Defense industry and military business increased traffic so much that some companies had to push their already strained facilities. Half of the passenger business and almost three quarters of the freight traffic after 1940 was a product of the war effort,[28] and some railroads accumulated enough profits to develop sinking funds that contributed toward retiring the huge debts remaining from the depression.[29] The Southern System, for example, a strategic carrier that linked practically the whole South and was virtually decimated by the depression, experienced an especially dramatic upsurge in business during the war, since its principal freight was coal. The company paid dividends during the war for the first time in eleven years.[30] The Southern Pacific, of which I will speak later, amassed a sinking fund sufficient to reduce its depression debt by 25 percent, or $190 million. It also initiated much-needed reforms of its unwieldy, debt-ridden financial structure.[31]

Increased traffic brought problems as well. Inflation, caused by rising material and labor costs, and disruptions arising from court battles negated some gains. The critical point came around mid 1943 when mounting inflation started to cancel the benefits of rising revenues. In 1944, gross revenues on Class I roads increased around $11 million, with freight traffic increasing around 2½ percent and fixed operating costs soaring 15 percent.[32] Actual earnings—that is, revenue adjusted for inflation, taxes, etc.—dropped 47 percent in 1944 on the Baltimore and Ohio, 31 percent on the Illinois Central, and 27 percent on the Texas and Pacific.[33]

The domestic war effort obligated railroad management to establish expenditure priorities, but some executives were pressured by trustees and bondholders to apply their accumulating cash reserves to debts instead of improvements or operations, a disastrous strategy considering the already deteriorated condition of the roads. During the summer of 1943, for example, the trustees of the Missouri Pacific sought court permission to override railroad management and use part of their accumulated $10 million for debts.[34]

Many principal railroad corporations were still operating out of receivership imposed during the depression, which meant that trustees—or at times the Interstate Commerce Commission—could impose major policy decisions on the company, regardless of company management. Most reorganizations had been executed through section 77 of the Federal Bankruptcy Act of 1933, intended as a reform measure. Although ambiguous, the act empowered the ICC to administer a company in receivership if it deemed such a course of action appropriate; it was to receive petitions from the railroad or its creditors, to judge the validity of their requests, to ascertain the value of the property involved, to nominate possible trustees, and even to formulate a reorganization if a reasonable plan was not forthcoming.[35] After the act was implemented, many questioned the legitimacy of granting the ICC such powers, and the controversy eventually reached the Supreme Court, which ruled that the ICC was vested with the authority to oversee and even supervise railroads in receivership.[36] Consequently, many proceedings not completed during the depression were closed after the 1943 Supreme Court decision. A landmark case was that of the Western Pacific, whose dispute with the ICC had lasted nine years and was resolved in the ICC's favor in 1943.[37]

Toward a Symbiotic Relationship

Obviously the federal government has influenced, and at times dominated, the U.S. railroad industry from its inception in the nineteenth century through its routine policy and operations in the twentieth. In its early stages, the government, both national and state, subsidized railroad construction to ensure the development of regional and transcontinental rail systems and to control the routes the rails would take. Indeed, public discussions about railroad routes assumed a significant political dimension because of the rails' potential influence on regional economic development.

The federal government's interest in the railroad industry, however, did not stop there. Although ostensibly designed to monitor abuses in the industry, the ICC eventually came to merge the interests of the railroads and their managements (and trustees) with that of the government, in the process blurring its functions and jeopardizing its integrity.

Over time the railroads came to realize that they could promote their own agendas with the government, basically because the government stood to lose a great deal if the rail industry defaulted. Except for the nationalization of the rail industry in World War I, U.S. railroads enjoyed an exceptionally supportive relationship with the federal government, and indeed even expected assistance.

2

Mexican Labor on U.S. Railroads

In its petitions to the government in 1941 and 1942 to legally import Mexican workers for track maintenance, the Southern Pacific explicitly cited its long-standing practice of contracting *mexicanos* as justification for its request. The railroad implied that contracting *mexicanos* had satisfactorily met its unskilled labor requirements in the past, and that they again would most appropriately provide the best source of *peones de vía*. Indeed, upon the arrival of the first railroad braceros in the United States, the Southern Pacific delivered a message to them through B. R. Martínez, the auditor of payroll, to that effect.[1] Such a seemingly simple comment, however, belies the enormous historical significance of Mexican immigrant labor in the construction and maintenance of southwestern and midwestern railroads. Perhaps because the railroads are no longer a dominant part of U.S. life, and in fact, their decline predates the burgeoning research on Mexican immigration of the 1970s and 1980s, railroad employment has not received the attention it deserves.

Immigrant Workers on the Railroads

The U.S. railroad industry discovered quite early that the systematic recruitment of immigrant workers for track construction, and later track maintenance, provided the most cost-effective and controllable source of labor open to them. The first railroads on the East Coast to launch large-scale construction in the 1830s and 1840s—for example, the Baltimore and Ohio and the Pennsylvania—often hired construction workers in established Irish and German immigrant neighborhoods near their facilities in New York, Philadelphia, and Boston. As the tracks stretched westward toward the Old Northwest, these companies tried to retain the immigrant workers and hire more along the way—an impossible task, since they were building in sparsely populated rural areas where, in fact, many of these same immigrant track workers left the railroads to farm. Track construction work, which entailed grading land and laying rail, was among the least prestigious, most dangerous, and most demanding un-skilled work of the nineteenth century. Moreover, the railroads discovered that potential construction laborers became ever more scarce as the railroads pushed beyond settled areas. Temporary contract labor represented the only option open to most rail developers.

Irish and German immigrants were the first wave of immigrant track workers. Irish workers dominated the rolls for the New England roads built during the early nineteenth century. Midwestern roads also hired Irish immigrants, as well as Germans, often recruiting them in eastern cities and transporting them to construction sites. For example, one Roswell Mason, acting for the Illinois Central, launched a recruiting campaign in June 1852 in areas served by the company, but it proved entirely unsuccessful. Mason could not lure local unskilled laborers, some of them immigrants, since they were already employed. Therefore Mason contacted the Irish Emigrant Society of New York and arranged for a large group of Irish immigrants, along with 1,500 Germans, to be transported to the work site in Illinois. A lack of formal contracts or written commitments, compounded by atrocious working conditions and opportunities for better-paying jobs in local agriculture, made it difficult for the Illinois Central to retain construction workers. The Illinois Central management tried to intimidate workers into staying by delaying wages, but, not surprisingly, the workers reacted violently.[2] In the course of the Illinois Central confrontation and other subsequent railroad strikes, many railroad companies came to regard Irish workers as undesirable troublemakers.[3]

In the South before the Civil War, the railroads depended on African American labor for all but the most skilled and prestigious job classifications, at first "renting" slaves owned by local farmers. As southern agriculture became more profitable and farmers became reluctant to "rent" their slaves, southern railroads found it more economical to purchase their own slaves. The Nashville and Chattanooga, the South Carolina, and the Montgomery and West all decided that, in spite of the expense and administrative commitment it implied, their best option was the purchase of their own slaves. After the Civil War, southern rail developers generally hired freed slaves for unskilled jobs but found them unsatisfactory; they seemed unwilling to settle down and work for wages, undoubtedly due in part to insensitive management and absurdly low pay. By 1880, however, African Americans were working side by side with former Confederate soldiers and dominated track maintenance and other unskilled classifications.[4]

The construction of tracks for the Florida East Coast Railway at the turn of the twentieth century illustrates another strategy. Having found that supplies of the usual laborers, African Americans, were insufficient, management solved its problem by recruiting track workers from Italian immigrant neighborhoods in the Northeast. In this instance, rail developers consciously took advantage of the traditional *padrone* system. Acting essentially like brokers, *padrones* located and hired prospective workers, transported them to the work site, and at times provided them with room and board. Frequently, *padrones* acted as bankers and lenders. For his part, the worker was required to work as specified in the contract and pay the *padrone* a *bossatura* or fee for services rendered. Abuses of the *padrone* system were common, since no regulations existed to prevent false advertising, to guarantee minimum living and working conditions, or to curb the power of the supervisors, be they *padrones* or regular railroad foremen. The *padrone* system, adapted to labor recruitment, was advantageous for the rail companies because the burden of hiring and supervising was assumed by the *padrone* and financed by the workers themselves through payment of the *bossatura*.[5]

Railroad construction west of the Mississippi, which accelerated after the Civil War as part of a national effort to built a transcontinental road, was also plagued by a scarcity of unskilled labor. Eventually some companies engaged in large-scale contracting to obtain workers. As an experiment, Charles W. Crocker, a Central Pacific manager, transported fifty Chinese immigrants from California to the Pacific Northwest to work on construction crews. The company was so pleased with them that it decided to institute direct recruitment from China. Shortly thereafter, the Central Pacific began importing immigrants directly from Canton, and up to 6,000 Chinese men were on the payroll at any time.[6] The practice acquired de jure status with the promulgation of the Burlingame Treaty of 1868, which provided for free and reciprocal immigration between the United States and China. Bitterly opposed by everyone except the railroads, the treaty legalized Chinese contract labor and ushered in a tragic chapter in the history of Chinese immigration to the United States.[7] Although their employment as track workers amounted to servitude, it was the Chinese who dynamited their way through the Sierra Nevada so the Central Pacific could meet the Union Pacific at Promontory Point, Utah, in 1869. Working from sunrise to sunset, summer and winter six days a week, the Chinese were the victims of many abuses. Unsafe conditions and harsh weather killed many Chinese track workers.[8] The workers, however, had few options. All told, between 12,000 and 14,000 were hired for the completion of the Central Pacific portion of the transcontinental railroad.

In the 1870s, Chinese immigrant workers were hired to build the Northern Pacific near Portland, Oregon. During this period, they were also employed by Colis Huntington for construction of the Southern Pacific south from San Francisco, then east across the deserts of Arizona and New Mexico, ending at El Paso. Some southern railroads recruited Chinese immigrants on the West Coast and transported them to sites in Tennessee and Alabama. Clearly the railroads were pleased with the work of the Chinese; they were hard-working, docile, and relatively inexpensive.

For a variety of reasons, Chinese immigrants were not assimilated, or even really acculturated, by mainstream U.S. society. Their isolation, exacerbated by factors inherent in the United States, particularly in California, fueled a xenophobic and racist national dialogue that resulted in the passage of the Exclusion Acts of 1882 and 1884. Whatever the basis for the legislation, its effect was to prohibit the immigration of Chinese laborers to the United States. Although some Chinese continued to migrate illegally across the Mexican border, an important source of unskilled labor had been eliminated.

Southwestern railroads turned to other immigrant groups. Japanese immigrants supplanted the Chinese in Southern California.[9] Some railroads in East Texas recruited African Americans from the Deep South to work the tracks up into Texarkana, near Arkansas. Others in New Mexico brought Italian and Greek immigrants from eastern cities, only to find them difficult to manage. Italians, according to railroad management, were prone to fighting unless they were from the same town in Italy; Greeks allegedly were open to graft, which eroded discipline within the crews. Some roadmasters in California considered the solidarity among Japanese an impediment; if one worker was dismissed, the rest would resign in protest.[10]

Moreover, the requirements and conditions of track work evolved as the railroad industry matured and expanded. The first track workers, as we have seen, graded the land, laid the rails, and moved along to the next section of track. Many early roadbeds, in fact, were hastily built and poorly engineered, often with inferior materials. At first, railroad developers did not anticipate that the tracks would require so much regular maintenance; they quickly had to rehire former track construction workers to repair faulty tracks. As the railroad industry and individual companies stabilized, most roads installed maintenance-of-way departments to oversee the tracks.[11]

Track maintenance tapped the same labor supplies as construction, and although a more stable employment than construction, it was still the lowest paid and least desirable of all railroad labor. Moreover, track maintenance was unsafe (in the early days, those injured or killed were not entitled to compensation) and normally offered little job mobility, since track workers often remained assigned to the same section for many years. Some only received seasonal or temporary work. Perhaps worst of all, the job often required employees to live in company boxcar camps near the tracks, which generally were expensive for the workers, poorly equipped, and very isolated. Such unpleasant working conditions attracted men with few other options—the chronically unemployed, immigrants, vagrants. Unfortunately, the isolation of railroad maintenance tended to reinforce the workers' low status rather than ameliorate it. Contacts with area residents were sporadic, not always affable, and often confirmed negative stereotypes of track workers, whoever they were. Unlike other types of railroad workers, maintenance-of-way workers suffered scorn.[12] An interview with a longtime resident of Baja California who began a thirty-year career on a border railroad as a track worker confirms this; he recalls local residents yelling "¡Cholitos!" (Little mestizos!) at track crews in the 1920s.[13]

Mexican Workers

After the transcontinental railroad was completed in 1869, the southwestern roads began in earnest to build tracks across the deserts and mountains. Their construction projects, in high gear by the 1880s, coincided with the increased availability of Mexican workers on the United States–Mexican border. Some construction bosses were already hiring Mexican American workers from New Mexico, California, and Texas, but the demand far exceeded the supply.[14] Although the border at that time was relatively open and offered little impediment to those crossing it to work, Mexican border towns were sparsely populated and could not provide large numbers of unskilled workers. This is not to say that no migration north took place; for example, miners from Sonora had trekked north to California to pan for gold as early as the 1840s and 1850s, perhaps even the famous Joaquín Murieta.[15] Also, some Mexican immigrants from the border area, as well as migrants from the interior, had already been employed along southwestern tracks. But the systematic recruitment of Mexican immigrants for U.S. railroads did not really begin until the 1880s.

Railroad employment profoundly affected the movement of Mexican immigrants within the United States; it influenced settlement patterns, especially outside the Southwest, facilitated employment opportunities in other industries, and introduced large visible groups of Mexican workers to a broader cross section of U.S. society. It may not be obvious today, but many Chicano barrios throughout the Southwest and Midwest trace their origins to settlements of Mexican immigrant railroad workers.[16] Likewise many Chicano corridos of those barrios contain references to work on the *traque* (track).[17] It is commonplace for Mexican Americans to refer to relatives, such as *tíos* or *abuelos,* who worked on the railroad.

Mexican migration north through railroad work occurred in three phases that are related and overlap somewhat but are still discernible. The earliest phase, in the 1870s and 1880s, was the movement north of Mexican workers from the Mexican central plateau to the border region. These workers were employed on construction crews on railways that were being built in northern Mexico.[18] The second phase—most prominent in the 1880s, 1890s, and opening years of the twentieth century—was characterized by extensive recruitment by southwestern regional railroads, such as the Southern Pacific, of Mexican workers who generally had already migrated to the border.[19] The final phase, almost concurrent with the second, was distinguished by Mexican workers reaching the Midwest and, to a lesser extent, eastern states, the result of step-migration.

Railroad development in Mexico lagged behind that of other countries; the first road connecting Mexico City and Veracruz, inaugurated in 1837 by a Mexican consortium and plagued by difficulties, was completed as late as 1882, with British money. Yet Porfirio Díaz recognized the importance of a modern transportation system for Mexican economic progress, and after unsuccessful attempts to foster construction of local and regional lines through subsidies to the states, he arrived at the same strategy that Benito Juárez used to finish the Veracruz line: foreign capital and technical expertise. Díaz's master plan called for a network of railroads to be built east and west that would connect Mexican ports with the hinterland, and others north and south that would tap into the expanding North American economy. The Mexican Central Railroad, financed through capital from New England, completed the road joining Mexico City and El Paso, Texas, in just four years. Shortly thereafter Ferrocarriles Nacionales de México laid tracks from central Mexico to Laredo, and the Sonora Railroad between Guaymas and Nogales. Together these three railroads formed the basis of an efficient and rapid transportation system in northern Mexico.[20]

The establishment of modern transportation systems in the late nineteenth century truly transformed northern Mexican economy and society. Some scholars have hypothesized that this transformation led to increasing discontent in the region, a major cause of the Mexican Revolution. Moreover, mines and other industries now had a ready mode of transport to ship their goods to Mexico City or the United States.

In any event, the effect upon the movement of people was notable. Migration took two forms. Since the roadbeds passed through harsh, unpopulated desert areas, railroad builders had no choice but to recruit and transport construction workers from central Mexico; many of these individuals never returned home.[21] Second, the completed lines offered seasonal maintenance employment to those in the central plateau who could use the work as a strategy to reach the border. Likewise, middle-class migrants with funds at their disposal could simply purchase passage to Ciudad Juárez.

Unfortunately, the historical documents that describe and quantify this migration north remain unidentified.[22] Normally part of the arrangement that unskilled labor made with railroad developers was free return transportation to the point of recruitment at the conclusion of the work contract. Yet Victor Clark observed in 1907 that few workers chose to use the return passage, opting apparently to remain at the border. One official of the National Railways claimed that almost all of a contingent of 1,500 *peones de vía* (track workers) had chosen to stay in the north and leave their employment. The railways were therefore obligated to hire labor agencies in Mexico City whose *enganchadores* (contractors) had little difficulty in locating workers in the countryside willing to go north, and replenish the supply of *traqueros* (track workers).[23]

Railroad demand for unskilled labor coincided with a rapidly deteriorating situation for rural workers generally in Mexico. Porfirio Díaz's scheme for foreign colonization of undeveloped rural areas was accomplished through the disintegration of rural society. Those campesinos working on haciendas suffered falling wages and deteriorating conditions. The average Mexican worker had little to lose by accepting employment on northern tracks, however onerous the work.[24]

The growing difference between the wages of central and northern Mexico likewise spurred migration. In 1900, the majority of workers in the interior earned between US$.20 and $.25 a day, while a common laborer in Ciudad Juárez earned US$.75. Inflation during the *porfiriato* (Díaz regime) doubled prices while wages remained unchanged, so it is small wonder that workers chose the uncertainties of migration north over the certainty of a disintegrating rural standard of living.[25]

The Mexican Central Railroad probably transported the majority of Mexicans north during the *porfiriato;* it was the first to transport construction and track workers and to initiate passenger service. One of many who arrived in El Paso in 1910 recalled that the fare on the Mexican Central from Mexico City was quite accessible, but since the fare was between US$10 and $15, surely only middle-class migrants or well-placed campesinos were able to travel without working.[26] U.S. railroads and other employers viewed the arrival of experienced Mexican railroad workers in El Paso–Ciudad Juárez with favor, since they represented an ideal solution to their labor shortage. Stimulated partly by the arrival of the Southern Pacific from California in 1881, El Paso had been transformed into an important railroad center and supply depot for many southwestern industries.

At this point the second phase of the migration of Mexican railroad workers begins, that of employment in the U.S. Southwest. Even if larger absolute numbers of Mexicans were hired by southwestern agriculture, the largest proportion of Mexican immigrants in 1900 were found among southwestern track crews.[27] McWilliams estimates that from 60 percent to 90 percent of the section and extra gangs on eighteen railroads from 1900 to 1940 were Mexican.[28] More specifically, in 1900 Mexicans constituted 15.1, 35.5, and 14.6 percent of the section crews in New Mexico, Arizona, and Texas. Twenty years later, the percentages had increased to 32, 81, and 48.[29]

Besides restricting the immigration of Chinese workers, the Exclusion Acts of the 1880s prohibited all foreign contract labor, since this had been the arrangement that so easily permitted the employment and migration of Asian labor.[30] Although the arrangement with Chinese workers suited the railroads, they would have found it difficult to pursue with other immigrants on such a massive scale. Other unskilled immigrants (e.g., Italians and Poles) lived afar on the East Coast.[31] Large numbers of unemployed and unskilled Mexican workers at the border with few resources and disposed to work for low wages—albeit higher than they would have earned in Mexico—made it possible for the railroads to continue with a variation of their contract labor strategy. That the *mexicanos* were so close to the hiring offices in El Paso enabled the railroads to circumvent the foreign contract labor law. By the 1890s, it was common practice for recruiters in El Paso to seek out workers in Ciudad Juárez and assign them to distant track sections. The policy persisted into the 1920s.

The Southern Pacific first hired Mexican immigrants in El Paso for their tracks in California in 1893; by 1900, 4,500 Mexican immigrants were normally on the payroll at any time. Carey McWilliams claims that by 1906 the Southern Pacific was importing two or three carloads of Mexicans to California weekly. Indeed, the section of Los Angeles known today as Watts was originally called Tijuata, and was established around 1905 as a *colonia* (settlement) of Mexican railroad workers.[32]

These carloads of *cholos* (mestizos), as they were called, also arrived in Santa Barbara north of Los Angeles for track work in the 1890s. They augmented a *colonia* there that antedated the Mexican American War. Although most lived in makeshift boxcar camps north of the city, many were eventually absorbed into permanent track maintenance crews, and later into shopwork in the city. The first workers living in boxcar camps were paid $1.50 to $1.75 a day, but because they lived in housing provided by the railroads, $5.25 was deducted weekly by Southern Pacific for room and board. Not surprisingly, the *peones de vía* moved to the city when they were able and formed what became the Lower Eastside barrio near the freight yard. The arrival of these workers to Santa Barbara coincided with and contributed to the city's economic boom early in the century; the coastal railroad stimulated tourism. Later they were dispatched to build the coastal railroad connecting Southern California with San Francisco. Thereafter some were hired by the Pacific Electric Interurban System, the Los Angeles metropolitan system.[33]

San Bernardino's *colonia* of the late nineteenth century, about sixty miles east of Los Angeles, also had its origins in unskilled railroad work. Originally founded as a Mormon city in the 1860s, San Bernardino did not prosper until the Atchison, Topeka and Santa Fe arrived in the 1880s and established its yard and maintenance facility. The railroad hired Mexican immigrant workers for maintenance of the yard, and in fact developed the adjacent area as a *colonia*. By 1900, San Bernardino had a recognizable *colonia* known as Cholo Heights.

Obviously such broad dispersal of Mexican workers from the principal point of entry, El Paso, required organization. The network of labor contractors based in El Paso serviced the needs of southwestern industry, primarily the railroads, and to a lesser extent, the mines. Some were independent contractors, responding to requests from several employers; others worked exclusively for one railroad. Normally quotas were filled in the El Paso–Ciudad Juárez area, but *enganchadores* were regularly dispatched to the interior to supplement the labor pool. A contract between recruit and recruiter cemented the arrangement; the *enganchador* collected his money when he sold the work contract to the employer upon delivering the workers.[34]

Immigrant contract labor, it will be recalled, had been prohibited by the 1880s legislation, a measure specifically aimed at the Chinese but applicable to all immigrants. Although a few El Paso contractors were arrested for violating the law by recruiting Mexican workers in Ciudad Juárez, the law was mostly disregarded at the border. Completion of the Southern Pacific in 1881, and subsequently the Mexican Central, further stimulated an expanding mining industry and financial community, thereby laying the foundation for a prosperous local economy that required nearby available unskilled labor to sustain its growth. The stream of immigrants continually arriving in Ciudad Juárez mattered more than the enforcement of the Exclusion Acts.

Mario García's study of the Mexican community in El Paso at the turn of the century imparts a taste of labor recruitment operations then so large a part of city life. To give an example, the firm of Murray and Reedy, located near the border, used newspaper advertising in 1906 to recruit 1,000 workers to perform various jobs associated with railroad construction, and promised a wage of $2.00 a day plus free transportation. However, other agencies such as Zárate and Ávila, the Hanlin Supply Company, and the Homes Supply Company collaborated exclusively with the Southern Pacific and the Santa Fe, and offered a wage of only $1.00 a day. In 1911, the Dillingham Commission reported that between July 1908 and February 1909 five labor agencies in El Paso recruited and delivered 16,471 Mexican immigrants to several railroads.[35]

García also tells of the initial disruptive effect of the Mexican Revolution on labor recruiting in El Paso. In spite of the availability of track work and aggressive campaigns, orders for railroad labor could not be filled. New arrivals were few early in 1911, since revolutionary activity had interrupted rail service in northern Mexico. One recruiter reported that he could find only 509 applicants for an order of 500; when the Mexican Central resumed operations in late spring, the first train carried 1,000 prospective workers. Local El Paso newspapers relate that each subsequent train carried about 300 workers.

Southwestern railroads generally found it difficult to retain their workers; hence recruitment was a constant process. Not only were working and living conditions substandard at best, but the pay was low—and even lower when room and board were deducted. Southwestern mines and growers often hired their unskilled seasonal workers directly from maintenance and construction gangs, offering more stable working conditions and better pay. Although this was bothersome for the railroads since they had to pay labor contractors for replacement workers, these same mines and growers were often the company's most important commercial customers. These industries formed a symbiotic relationship, sharing the labor pool mobilized by the railroad and thereby supporting one another's development. Without the railroads to ship their products, the mines and agriculture of the Southwest would have had no outlet for their products.

Beyond the Southwest

At least for some railroad workers, employment on the railroads provided an opportunity for geographic mobility. Track workers were normally assigned to a gang that cared for a given stretch of track; in unpopulated areas like the Southwest at the turn of century, that could mean a radius of a hundred miles. Once Mexican track workers arrived at the end of their stretch of track and their contracts terminated, it was not difficult for them in times of labor shortage to transfer to the following stretch. For instance, the Atchison, Topeka and Santa Fe Railroad, a major employer of Mexican workers in El Paso, was a regional company whose tracks spread up into Kansas, then a principal distribution center linking the Southwest with the industrial Midwest and East. One of the oldest and most established *colonias* in the Midwest, in fact, is to be found in Argentine, Kansas, near the Santa Fe shops.[36]

Other midwestern railroads also began to hire Mexican immigrants, either contracting them directly at the border (in El Paso) or hiring those who had worked their way north. By the outbreak of World War I, South Chicago already had a sizable Mexican community. Paul Taylor, whose pioneering studies in the 1920s explored midwestern Mexican Americans, describes the experiences of Mexican immigrant railroad workers who arrived in Chicago to find work in industry—principally steel plants and meat packing—that was, if not pleasant, at least more attractive. In fact, adults of Mexican descent living today in South Chicago, until recently employees of the same steel plants as their forebears, trace their origin in Chicago to those same *peones de vía*. Their knowledge of Spanish is at times limited, but their identification with those first immigrants is firm.

Other Mexican railroad workers found Omaha, Nebraska, through Central Pacific tracks and stayed to work in plants owned by Swift, one of the nation's largest meat packers. Others, working on the New York Central, stayed in Detroit, some obtaining employment in automotive plants.

Others traveled as far as Oregon and Washington through railroad employment. In fact, the first Mexican immigrants had arrived in Washington's Yakima Valley by 1907, partly as a result of track work. One estimate puts the percentage of Mexican workers on railroad track maintenance gangs on nine northwestern systems at 60 percent by 1929.[37]

The journeys of workers in this last phase of railroad work were quite different from those of their compatriots in the Southwest; their experiences were more akin to those of European immigrants. First, they were far from their homeland; although Mexican workers continued to migrate and some returned to Mexico to visit and live, they could not return as easily as workers in the Southwest. Moreover, upward mobility was easier for them to achieve, since the range of job possibilities in the diversified labor markets of industrialized cities was much broader than in the Southwest. If one, for example, chose to stay in Chicago and accept an entry-level position in a steel plant, one could hope to learn more specialized and higher-paying skills, which could eventually lead to a better job. This simply could not happen out on the tracks in rural New Mexico or in the Arizona mines. Unfortunately, most Mexican immigration has coincided with a slowing U.S. industrialization, which peaked around World War I, at least in terms of demand for unskilled workers. Mexican immigrants arriving in Kansas City or Chicago in the 1920s could not expect to find as expansive a labor market as previous generations of European immigrants had. Even so, the industrial Midwest offered the potential of high-paying jobs.

The arrival of Mexican immigrant workers in the industrial Midwest and their direct confrontation with an industrial workforce brings us to an important social reaction: the position of organized labor in the United States toward Mexican immigrants. It concerns our general discussion of the World War II bracero program because Mexican workers were recruited at that time to augment or replace unionized maintenance-of-way workers. Before the noticeable arrival of Mexican workers in midwestern industrial centers around World War I, the majority concentrated in work that was physically isolated, essentially far from mainstream society's view and out of organized labor's way, such as track work, mining, or agricultural work. Job actions taken by *mexicanos* before World War II were mostly independent of organized mainstream labor. Moreover, railroad workers of all classifications were in the throes of unionization around World War I, especially track workers and other unskilled workers. The issue of Mexican immigration, then, could not be ignored when they arrived in the big cities, the territory of the powerful unions.

3

The Railroad Brotherhoods

A singular aspect of the railroad bracero program was the existence of railroad unions in the 1940s in both the United States and Mexico. The fact that such a program was instituted within their jurisdiction challenges common notions held about temporary contract labor programs. But what was the condition of the brotherhoods during the war? Did they benefit from war prosperity? What was their attitude toward the railroad bracero program?

The depression had paralyzed the efforts of the railroad brotherhoods to pursue raises or improvements in working conditions, especially for unskilled workers; in fact, some workers suffered salary reductions allegedly to save their jobs. Many railroad employees, including Mexican and Mexican American workers, lost their jobs on the railroads; management emphasized dividends over maintenance. Not surprisingly, railroad management's relations with the unions were strained.

As World War II opened, railroad workers were struggling with long-stagnant wages. Worse, inflation for the period was 21 percent for housing, 47 percent for food, and 32 percent for clothing, according to conservative Department of Labor estimates.[1] Given the scarcity of labor and rising costs, the time was propitious for the railroad brotherhoods to again seek an industry-wide pay hike. Wages for unskilled railroad labor were among the lowest in any U.S. industry at the time. If the railroads viewed the war as their chance to recoup and regroup, so did the unions.

A Wage Increase, Finally

The railroad unions presented a formal request for a wage increase to the carriers toward the end of 1942. Negotiations between the railroads and the unions produced no results, so an emergency board was organized to conduct further talks. The railroads, brotherhoods, and the emergency board agreed to a straight, across-the-board wage increase of 8 cents an hour for all classifications of labor. Necessary government approval was blocked by Fred Vinson, the Economic Stabilization director. An unprecedented second emergency board, summoned to discuss the same increase, approved the same 8-cent increase, but Vinson again refused to okay the increase. Although ad hoc negotiations developed between Vinson and the unions, the railroads and the unions also began meeting together.[2]

The wage dispute between the unions and the railroads, complicated by the federal government's position, remained unresolved and confused throughout much of 1943. But in spite of Vinson's third attempt to veto a raise and his efforts to undermine the legality of an agreement, the railroads and unions signed an agreement on August 7, 1943, for a raise of 8 cents an hour, and the National Railway Labor Panel ruled that the agreement was valid and binding.[3] Even the Senate Finance Committee determined that the August agreement should stand. Railroad workers maintained their pressure for an even higher raise by threatening to strike, but rumors that Roosevelt was wavering on his pro-labor position supported Vinson's vetoes. The government did technically take control of the railroad industry for a short time in January 1944 to scare the workers, which surprised everyone.[4] The wage dispute was eventually resolved in mid 1944.

The Brotherhoods

Like most other unions in the United States, the railroad brotherhoods had historically been reticent—even negligent—in organizing racial and some ethnic minorities and addressing issues pertinent to them. Until well into the twentieth century, U.S. unions were confined to crafts and skilled trades and included basically white semiskilled and skilled men, to the exclusion of everyone else. Class division, prejudice, industrial organization, and the attitudes of union leadership all contributed to this nonrepresentative union membership and to unions' lack of accountability to working-class demands.

The organization of unions in the late nineteenth century in San Francisco to eliminate Chinese immigrant workers is a particularly graphic example of how U.S. labor leadership used racial and ethnic antipathy to define the parameters of their organizations. The decline of California gold mines and an increase in immigration had significantly augmented the presence of Chinese and many other workers in San Francisco, many of whom were unemployed. A demagogue, Denis Kearney, rallied much local working-class support in the 1870s in his public campaign to rid the city of Chinese immigrants. An organization with similar objectives, the

Workingmen's Party, ultimately collapsed (partly because later Kearney, as its leader, was not disposed to incorporate fledgling unions), opening the way for other union leaders to appropriate anti-Chinese nativism as their banner. Because the Chinese were considered more akin to African Americans than to European immigrants in the United States in the 1870s, the unions pitted European-stock individuals against the Chinese, and tethered their frustration to the unions and their affiliation with the Democratic Party. Even the American Federation of Labor, which in its formative years promoted the inclusion of African Americans, eventually allowed the exclusion of Chinese.

Many politicians in California from both parties exploited this nativism to accrue power and position, and their efforts coincided with similar movements in other states. The culmination was the approval of the Exclusion Acts of 1882 and 1884, which ended Chinese immigration, outlawed foreign contract workers, and legalized xenophobia.[5]

More directly related to Mexican immigrant workers were the experiences of copper miners in the U.S. Southwest. Union organization in western copper mines by the Western Federation of Miners early in the twentieth century was at times accomplished by openly excluding Mexican and Mexican American miners or pressuring them not to join. Although some union leaders for political or ethical reasons favored recruiting Spanish-surnamed miners, many locals in the Southwest excluded them and sometimes Eastern European immigrants. The surprising Clifton-Morenci strike (1903) in Arizona against the Phelps Dodge Corporation miners by mostly Spanish-surnamed and a few Italian miners reflects their difficult position wedged between organized labor and company management. Although Mexican miners were employed at the bottom end of a dual-wage structure in their work for the copper mines and many others, the Western Federation of Miners frequently used divisive tactics to bolster the wages and positions of Anglo and Irish immigrant workers at the expense of Spanish-surnamed miners.[6]

Union policy throughout U.S. industries, then, was hostile toward some minorities. The railroad brotherhoods were not much different. In the early days of southern railroads, and even during World War I, for example, African Americans constituted the majority of firemen. Their task was to shovel coal into the engines, or "stoke the engines"—a demanding, poorly paid job until mechanization eliminated most of the physical strain. World War I created more lucrative employment for African Americans outside the railroads, and McAdoo conceded equal pay to African Americans largely to keep them working for the railroads.

Firemen's pay thus was placed on a par with other railroad work, making the position desirable to white workers. Whites slowly eased African Americans out of firemen's jobs into lesser-paid classifications until there were few African American firemen by World War II. In January 1942, African Americans complained to the Fair Employment Practices Committee, a war agency designed to monitor discrimination against African Americans in defense industries, that southern carriers and the brotherhoods of Locomotive Firemen and Locomotive Engineers were conspiring to exclude them from certain better-paying railroad jobs.[7] In 1943, the FEPC issued an order requiring southern carriers to promote African Americans to vacant firemen's positions. Many railroads had African Americans in their employ who had worked as firemen in years past but did not promote them to firemen, despite the fact that a documented need existed for over a thousand firemen.[8]

Much of the blame for racial discrimination on southern railroads must be borne by the white railroad brotherhoods, in particular the Brotherhood of Locomotive Firemen and the Brotherhood of Locomotive Engineers. Most railroad union leaders felt it would be impossible for whites to effectively organize African American workers; therefore no recruitment campaigns were mounted among African Americans. Predominantly white railroad unions had few African American members and apparently felt little responsibility to correct the situation. African American railroad workers were a disenfranchised group among railroad employees, although sometimes affected by union agreement.

The Brotherhood of Sleeping Car Porters was the first railroad union to become predominantly African American and during World War II served as a catalyst for all African American railroad workers. A. Philip Randolph, its president, threatened to stage a march of 100,000 African Americans in Washington, D.C., in 1942 to publicize their demand for equal employment opportunities. To avert such a public display, Roosevelt established the FEPC to monitor employment opportunities for African American workers in defense industries. The committee did not have the power of enforcement but certainly was an important first step in recognizing and rectifying discriminatory practices toward racial minorities in the United States. Subsequently, potential discrimination problems arising from the railroad bracero program were submitted to the FEPC for consideration.

To counter the lack of response to African American workers by the brotherhoods of Locomotive Firemen and Locomotive Engineers, the Sleeping Car Porters established the Provisional Committee to Organize

Colored Locomotive Firemen.[9] Surprisingly, this action elicited support from the general public. Widely read periodicals such as *Time, Christian Century,* and the *Nation* commented on the apparent double standard of the union movement. Railroad unions were loudly advocating the right of railroad workers to a decent living wage while they were facing discrimination charges from the FEPC.

The Brotherhood of Maintenance of Way Employees' record was not much better. Founded in 1887 as a fraternal organization by a group of maintenance-of-way engineers, membership was at first confined to white foremen with at least six months' experience, a stringent requirement in an industry with a very high labor turnover, in which the majority of track workers were unskilled and seasonal. Track workers were originally not included as members, but as the organization became more a mainstream union its president, John T. Wilson, correctly perceived the need to organize white unskilled track workers. However, the railroads were afraid of the potential collective strength of a maintenance-of-way union that joined foremen with track workers. In 1891, the union's convention finally approved equal membership for white track workers, not a moment too soon since many potential members for the union had already elected to join Eugene V. Debs's more democratic American Railway Union, associated with the American Federation of Labor, although the Brotherhood of Maintenance of Way Employees itself affiliated with the AFL in 1900. However, not until 1917, at the height of the World War I crisis, did that union permit African American track workers to join the organization.[10] Since the majority of track workers in the South were African American, its policy was absurd.

Mexican Labor

In many respects, Mexican immigrant workers did not conform to the profile of other minority groups. The particular conditions of Mexican immigration greatly affected unions' attitude toward all Mexican and Mexican American workers, especially undocumented immigrants.

Mexican workers were employed before World War I in industries already covered by union organizing—mining, railroads, steel plants, etc.—but the attitudes of organized labor were at least ambivalent and often openly hostile. In 1919, John Lewis openly advocated before the national AFL convention that Mexican immigration be legally suspended, indicating that the issue was of particular importance for domestic miners and railroad workers; therefore, the AFL policy prohibiting the membership of undocumented Mexican immigrants is not surprising. When this strategy was not effective in slowing Mexican immigration, the AFL approached the Confederación Regional Obrera Mexicana in the mid 1920s with the proposal that it cooperate with President Elías Calles to voluntarily restrict migration from Mexico. Nor was this effective; Mexican workers continued to find jobs in the United States.[11] The next move of U.S. organized labor was to pursue legal restriction of Mexican immigration to control the threat that Mexican workers represented. Local AFL chapters also mounted anti-immigration publicity campaigns. The San Antonio consul reported in the 1930s that union members were "distribuyendo en la jurisdicción de este Consulado General ciertos volantes que atacaban a los mexicanos que presten sus servicios con las compañías ferrocarrileras de este país."[12] Writing in 1947, Carey McWilliams remarked that the policies and actions of the AFL were predicated on its perception of Mexican workers, not as individual workers, but as an anonymous group competing with U.S. workers for a limited number of jobs.[13]

However, this does not mean that Mexican workers did not organize to improve working conditions. Several examples of the collective actions of agricultural workers (Alianza Hispano-Americana in Colorado and Wyoming) attest to the determination of many Mexican workers to improve their prospects. The following references indicate that railroad workers also sought to improve their working conditions.[14]

Mexican immigrants employed on the Pacific Electric Railway in Southern California, which was owned by the tycoon Henry Huntington, formed La Unión Federal Mexicana and in the spring of 1903 demanded a raise from 17½ cents to 20 cents an hour, with extra compensation for evenings and Sundays. At first management agreed, but Huntington overrode their decision and 700 Mexican workers walked off the job. Huntington recruited Mexican strikebreakers in El Paso, brought them to Los Angeles, and paid them 2 cents more an hour than La Unión had requested. Huntington, supported by local organizations, was determined to keep Los Angeles a union-free city. The union gained some recognition in organized labor circles, but a walkout of white members of the Amalgamated Association of Street Car Employees to support the Mexican workers failed to elicit support; subsequent job actions of La Unión also failed.[15]

Two hundred Mexican workers struck the El Paso Electric Street Car Company in 1901 for higher wages, but management retaliated by hiring workers from across the border as scabs. Local police helped the company by protecting the strikebreakers; after negotiations the company promised to refrain from hiring outsiders but refused to give raises. Mexican workers struck the company again in 1905.[16]

Two hundred *mexicanos* working in 1897 on the tracks at Mammoth Tank, west of Yuma, Arizona, struck to protest working conditions. A misunderstanding ensued with the local sheriff that resulted in the action's leaders going to jail in San Diego.[17]

The official history of the Brotherhood of Maintenance of Way Employees, moreover, describes job actions in which *mexicanos* or Mexican Americans must surely have collaborated. In August 1905, the struggling union called a strike against the Denver and Rio Grande for refusing to negotiate, although the company had already granted wage increases to other organized groups. The strike lasted until February of the next year, with the company employing scabs. In February 1910, the Southern Pacific refused to meet with union representatives to discuss improvement in working conditions and issued instructions to its employees to relinquish membership or leave the company.[18]

This brief overview illustrates the historical reluctance of most U.S. unions to effectively incorporate many racial and ethnic minorities. Some labor leaders even displayed overt hostility toward Mexican workers. Unskilled Mexican workers employed throughout the U.S. economy, then, were generally excluded from unions on the eve of World War II, partly as a result of employment conditions, but more often due to the ambivalent and shortsighted vision of the unions themselves. Although war-related labor shortages provided unions with leverage, Mexican and other minority workers were not necessarily affected.

4

World War II and U.S.–Mexico Relations

The wartime bracero program arose from an international context; it was the effect of World War II on U.S.–Mexican relations that made its implementation feasible. Neither before nor after the war, has Mexican migration enjoyed the same degree of diplomatic collaboration as in the bracero program during the war. Indeed, Richard Craig in his seminal work on the agricultural program attests that the bracero program represents the inseparability of domestic and foreign policy.[1]

Latin American and U.S. Diplomacy

The ideological thrust of Roosevelt's Good Neighbor Policy introduced during the Great Depression suited the war effort, inter-American solidarity, and, in particular, wartime U.S.–Mexican relations. This is not to say that the policy was democratic or sensitive to Latin American culture, only that it was flexible.[2] The policy exchanged overt military might for negotiable economic dominance as the keystone of U.S. influence in Latin America, a perspective that easily accommodated the advent of war. It promoted vigorous economic relationships in the Western Hemisphere[3] to assure the continued flow of raw materials to the United States and to foster a market for U.S. manufactured goods and capital in Latin America.[4] Further, the policy was allegedly intended to encourage voluntary cooperation and support among Latin American countries by setting an example of nonaggression and nonintervention, on the assumption that fellow American republics would respond likewise.[5] Roosevelt envisioned a loosely organized Western Hemisphere voluntary common market as the theoretical goal of the Good Neighbor Policy. Such a strategy would have consolidated hemispheric support for U.S. foreign policy. World War II, however, interrupted Roosevelt's plans for the policy.

Accelerated German aggression after 1939 dramatically affected Latin America and intercontinental relations, even before the United States became officially involved. U.S. fears that Germany was executing plans to infiltrate Latin America were seemingly confirmed by prominent German minorities (in Argentina and Mexico, among others) and by eight trade agreements Germany signed with various Latin American countries between 1934 and 1939, granting valuable trade concessions.[6] The Axis' potential presence in the Western Hemisphere worried many in the United States, and emphasized the strategic importance of Latin America (supplies and geographic location) for the emerging opposition to the Axis threat.

Of more immediate concern for the Western Hemisphere, however, was the British blockade of Europe, which cut off several Latin American countries from major suppliers of manufactured goods and from an important market for Latin American raw materials.[7] Some Latin American countries lost up to 30 percent of their export trade because European partners were unavailable; the more industrialized countries, like Argentina and Chile, lost even more.[8] The United States's "economic defense" was to intensify and broaden its economic relationship with Latin America—buying surplus raw materials and selling manufactured goods when possible to forestall economic disaster.[9]

Mexico's Position

The basis for inter-American economic cooperation had already been laid, therefore, before the entrance of the United States into the war, and would remain the foundation for the U.S. hemispheric posture during the course of the conflict. The United States did not consider direct military support from Latin America necessary or desirable. Availability of sites for supportive military installations throughout Latin America was more important and, in fact, indispensable in the opinion of some.[10] For example, active military protection of the Panama Canal was deemed a priority. Subsequently, the United States and various Latin American countries organized Latin American conferences that were intended to solidify hemispheric support; develop lines of financial, economic, and strategic cooperation; and demonstrate inter-American unity.

Brazil and Mexico were pivotal; they were the only Latin American countries that declared war against the Axis. German ships destroyed Mexican naval vessels (*Potrero del Llano* and *Foja de Oro*) in the Caribbean, events that compelled the government to take direct action. The attacks and the declaration of war effectively neutralized opposition on the right within the Mexican government and enabled then president Manuel Ávila Camacho to consolidate his administration and popular support. Assuming the role of a "wartime statesman," Ávila Camacho successfully convinced an indifferent Mexican society that support for the Allies was in their interest.[11]

The preceding presidency of Lázaro Cárdenas had proved particularly difficult for bilateral relations. Cárdenas had pursued an economic nationalist strategy in many arenas that culminated dramatically in the expropriation of petroleum in March 1938. While the Cárdenas administration and subsequent ones made it clear to the United States that the limits of economic nationalism had been reached, the oil expropriation remained a symbol. Nonetheless, Cárdenas understood that to forestall antagonism from the United States, he would have to compensate the Seven Sisters, the principal foreign oil companies. Therefore, Cárdenas immediately opened negotiations with the United States and the oil companies and U.S. private citizens to settle their claims. Indeed, Stephen R. Niblo writes that Mexico was quite disposed to cooperate with the United States during World War II in part because the oil expropriation had put Mexico on the defensive, but also to facilitate access to resources for industrial development.[12] On November 19, 1941, the United States and Mexico signed a general agreement whereby Mexico agreed to pay $40 million to the United States to settle a number of long-standing issues, including some debts dating to the *porfiriato*. The agreement also addressed currency exchange problems, thus opening the way for the United States to again purchase Mexican silver.

War creates unexpected alliances; that Mexico would feel obligated to declare war against a European country surprised many. The United States shipped almost $100 million worth of heavy equipment to Brazil and Mexico through Lend-Lease Agreements, whereby each country would pay reduced prices for the equipment, the payments being deferred until after the war.[13] Mexico, as well as many other nations around the world, purchased U.S. heavy machinery for agriculture, mining, and industry.

Mexico's strategic position and diverse mineral deposits caused many in the United States to take its southern neighbor a little more seriously. However, allegations of Fascist activities in Mexico created apprehension in the United States about Mexico's true sympathies. A book published in 1942, *Covering the Mexican Front: The Battle of Europe versus America,* by Betty Kirk, expressed just these points. In this curious book, Kirk, a journalist, presents a rather subjective, stereotypical view of Mexico and the "Mexican Front." Kirk discusses the Falanga Española, the most prominent Fascist organization in Mexico, which was active throughout the 1930s and blatantly pro-Axis in its weekly, *Hispanidad.* The association promoted the Axis cause and openly collaborated with Spanish Fascism. Other U.S. journalists even implied complicity between the Mexican Catholic Church and Fascists to advance their cause within Mexico and beyond, namely, the United States. Such public Fascist sympathies in a country neighboring the United States made many observers uncomfortable.[14]

Yet U.S. defense industries needed raw materials; supply lines from other producers had been severed. Even before Pearl Harbor, in fact, the Douglas-Weichers Agreement, signed by the two governments on June 15, 1941, stipulated that Mexico would sell all available strategic materials to the United States.[15] This and other agreements were economic in character and were designed to bolster the sagging Mexican economy as much as to secure the necessary supplies for defense industries. Many U.S. political leaders believed that fostering a robust Mexican economy was the most efficient strategy for consolidating Mexican support and neutralizing politically dangerous opposition. A strong and dynamic domestic economy ensuing from U.S. aid would, according to this interpretation, encourage confidence in the United States and the Allied cause.[16] Some sectors in Mexico—notably organized labor (for example, the outgoing Confederación de Trabajadores Mexicanos leader, Vicente Lombardo Toledano), the intellectual community, and the lower middle class—were not necessarily against Mexico's declaring war against the Axis but did not view an alliance with the United States favorably. However, as U.S. Ambassador George Messersmith observed in 1942, the upper middle class and others "enjoying the greatest measure of economic reward" from war-related business supported Mexican collaboration with the Allies.[17] President Manuel Ávila Camacho, Secretario del Estado (Secretary of State) Ezequiel Padilla, and several former presidents, including Lázaro Cárdenas, publicly declared their allegiance to the Allies, their support for the United States, and their recommendations for finalization of bilateral agreements with the United States.[18]

The purpose of these bilateral agreements was to channel Mexican raw materials into the U.S. war effort. In the 1940s, Mexico had impressive sources of tungsten, magnesium, mercury, mica, lead, and many other metals indispensable to defense industries. Still basically undeveloped, some were extracted by self-employed indigenous miners and bartered locally for rice and beans, although some reached the metal markets of Mexico City, San Luis Potosí, and Iguala. Sudden Japanese demand for Mexican metals in 1940 made the situation more urgent for the United States, since Japan was willing to pay higher prices than the United States. As late as 1941, the Japanese government and private business representatives were trying to ship these essential minerals to Japan, loading the goods onto Japanese ships waiting in Mazatlán and Manzanillo. One observer estimated that between April 1940 and July 1941 Japan purchased a two-year supply of mercury.[19] In addition, the American Refining and Smelting Company, a U.S. company, in the spring of 1941 contracted to ship 3,000 tons of zinc to Japan from its plant in Rosita, Baja California. Subsequently Mexico agreed to reformulate its export policy for Allied needs but wanted to sell to the United States on a more favorable basis.[20] As early as 1939, the United States formally agreed to absorb excess supplies of certain products, such as hemp, through the Federal Loan Agency.[21] Mexico acquired significant price increases for certain metals through agreements such as the Suárez-Bateman Agreement of 1942, doubling their revenues in some cases.[22]

Officials from the Mexican Embassy in Washington directed the attention of the U.S. government to priorities for the development of the Mexican economy, areas that coincidentally could contribute substantially to the war effort. In exchange for providing the United States with raw materials, the Mexican Embassy suggested, the United States might focus its economic activity in several target areas: (1) increased yields of oilseed and bananas, (2) higher production of manufactured and semi-manufactured goods, (3) development of high-grade ore to be sold to the United States, (4) increased production of fertilizers and heavy chemicals, (5) additional capacity to generate electricity, (6) improvement of Mexican railroads, (7) development of dry docks to repair U.S. ships, and (8) completion of dams, highways, and irrigation systems.[23]

The Mexican-American Commission for Economic Cooperation, an outgrowth of the Inter-American Development Commission, was established in 1943 and was designed to promote "development enterprise" in Mexico,[24] in other words, the business sector. Its activities were coordinated through Nelson Rockefeller at the office of the Coordinator of Inter-American Affairs in the State Department. Functions of the commission soon expanded to include promoting agriculture, transportation, public works, fisheries, and tourism. The commission approved and funded fifty-eight projects with its own moneys, although it was supervised by other agencies.

The refurbishing of Mexican railways is of particular interest; indeed, the railways received more and longer support than most other projects. Mexican railroads were crucial to the movement of strategic raw materials from Mexico and other Latin American countries, since German submarine activities made Caribbean waters dangerous.[25] On November 18,

1942, an exchange of diplomatic notes in Mexico City initiated the U.S. Railway Mission, headed by Oliver Stevens, to refurbish Mexican railroads through financial and technical assistance. Rehabilitation assumed two phases: first, actual maintenance and rehabilitation, some done by U.S. contractors, the rest by Mexican companies, under the supervision of Stevens and his staff; and second, Stevens' technical mission in Mexico City, which provided consultants, information, and recommendations to the Mexican railroads. Funds for rehabilitation were substantial, amounting to $7 million from 1942 to mid 1944, with $2 million coming from Nelson Rockefeller's office and the rest from the President's Emergency Fund. Stevens maintained a large office; at one point up to fifty U.S. technical experts were assigned to his Mexico City office.[26]

The U.S. Railway Mission also organized a special program to send skilled workers employed by the national railroad of Mexico, Ferrocarriles Nacionales de México, to the United States to train in the use of certain equipment the mission was installing in Mexico. Although the program was not extensive, U.S. government officials raised many questions about the activities of the skilled Mexican workers that went to the United States. They wanted to know if they were participating in a training program or if they were actually working for the railroads.[27]

The success of the mission may have been illusory. Through diplomatic correspondence, Ambassador Messersmith alerted the State Department in 1943–1944 that the U.S. Railway Mission was selling defective, second-hand railroad equipment to Ferrocarriles Nacionales in excessive quantities and at times at exorbitant prices. Messersmith then alluded to a conspiracy among railroad employees in the two countries to split the profits.[28]

One must also question the tact of Stevens himself. After his return to the United States at the end of the war, Stevens published an article in a widely circulated industrial journal, *Railway Age*, severely criticizing what he considered to be gross mismanagement of Mexican railways. Although some comments may have been valid, to publish such a scathing article in the United States after the fact was not prudent.[29]

Finally, the United States ceased dispatching additional freight cars to Mexico with U.S. manufactured goods. These freight cars were supposed to be returned from Mexico filled with raw materials, but a disproportionate number were to be found in Mexico, unable to proceed north because of labor shortages and scheduling problems (goods shipped to Mexico did not always arrive when return shipments were ready). Although it does not bear directly upon the railroad bracero program, the railroad car "embargo" constituted a difficult secondary issue that affected discussions between the two countries about Mexico's contribution to the war.[30]

The development of the bracero programs during the war as a binational effort to secure Mexican labor for U.S. agriculture and railroads was entirely consistent with the thrust of U.S.–Mexican relations at the time. While many moderates and liberals in Mexico vehemently objected to the programs, others in the Mexican government justified sending their compatriots to the United States to perform the most menial of work—labor done at painfully low wages and at times in woeful conditions[31]—by reminding themselves that they were contributing to an international war effort to defeat the country that had destroyed Mexican ships in the Caribbean. Although a detailed study of wartime diplomacy obviously is not possible here, the intrinsically international character of the project affected relations between the two countries. In fact, some problems internal to the bracero programs became diplomatic concerns.

5

Prior Mexican Migration to the United States

Mexico and the United States reached agreement in several arenas of wartime collaboration within a broad economic and political framework. Perhaps the most sensitive issue between the two countries during the war was the prospect of recruiting Mexican workers to go to the United States as temporary contract labor. Events of the recent past gave Mexico every reason to hesitate to accede to the U.S. government's request that Mexico make its workers available. The painful repatriation of the early 1930s as well as the abuses of the informal temporary contract labor program of World War I justified Mexican reluctance to extend its war effort to include workers.

The Bracero Program of World War I

A brief summary of the little-known "first bracero program" is in order, since its memory haunted the Mexican government and served as a dress rehearsal for the bracero programs of World War II.[1] The period of World War I coincided with significant migration north from Mexico, for during the 1910s many Mexicans moved to the border region in response to the Mexican Revolution. Those arriving at the border easily found work in the United States, since domestic mobilization for the war, which stepped up around 1915, together with the subsequent U.S. entrance into the war greatly stimulated business. In addition, many steel mills, meat-packers, and other food-processing facilities and industries, which traditionally had depended on European immigrants, experienced dramatic labor shortages after the passage of the Immigration Act of 1917.

The Immigration Act of 1917 was the legislation for which nativists and xenophobics had been struggling for a long time. Based originally on the recommendations of the Dillingham Commission, the law restricted European immigration, raised the entry fee (head tax) to $6.00, reiterated the exclusion of temporary contract labor contained in the Exclusion Acts of the 1880s, and for the first time introduced a literacy test for prospective immigrants. The bill's authors instituted the literacy test to screen new immigrants because they feared heavy immigration after the war; however, they did not anticipate either the economic repercussions of World War I or the Southwest's desperate and chronic need for unskilled labor.

At first the 1917 act was enforced along the border rather strictly. Since Mexican immigrants could not afford the head tax or, for the most part, read, legal immigration dropped from 56,000 in 1916 to 3,100 in 1917. Although illegal immigration at least partially averted labor shortages in industries unaffected by the law, southwestern agriculture suffered. Sugar beets in Colorado could no longer be harvested by Germans and Russians, and Southern Europeans could not supply California agribusiness with unskilled labor. Agribusiness was quick to remind the federal government that it needed farmworkers to provide the food that would fuel the war effort.

The Immigration Act of 1917, however, had a loophole: under the ninth proviso of section 3, the secretary of labor (then in charge of immigration) could set aside any provision of the law if economic conditions warranted it. Therefore on August 23, 1917, Secretary of Labor William Wilson specifically exempted Mexican agricultural workers from any and all requirements of the act; the measure was to be effective until 1921. Mexican workers were now free to immigrate to the United States. Prospective workers only had to indicate their intention to work in the fields as they crossed the borders; all told, 72,000 workers registered as unskilled agricultural workers under the procedure. No government supervision from either side of the border was included.

Nonagricultural concerns were not excluded. Railroads, mining operations, and other industries informed the government that they too were unable to discharge their wartime obligations for want of unskilled labor. Their petition was reinforced by an official request for Mexican immigrant workers from McAdoo's Railroad Administration. Thereupon Secretary Wilson issued a waiver to the Immigration Act of 1917 in July 1918 to permit the unrestricted entrance of Mexican railroad, mining, and construction workers. This waiver was also valid until 1921.

This simple unilateral procedure by the secretary of labor, then, constituted the legal and operational basis for the so-called first bracero program. No program administration, government or otherwise, was anticipated, since no one in the United States felt it necessary or appropriate. In part, this is why there is so little documentation about the first bracero program; no office monitored it. The bracero program of World War I resulted from revoking part of an Immigration Act, not from implementing a planned project.

Although prospective employers were technically required by Secretary Wilson to abide by certain bureaucratic procedures, in reality little actual control was built into the World War I bracero program. Employers were required to formally request laborers from either the Bureau of Immigration or the Department of Labor, indicating the number of workers desired, place of employment, wages, and job description. With the permission of the Department of Labor, employers could proceed to the border to identify Mexican immigrants who theoretically had already legally crossed to the United States and registered with the Department of Labor. In practice, it was not difficult for them to contract workers who had migrated illegally to avoid registering with the government or paying the head tax, or to identify workers who had not yet crossed the border. The Department of Labor also distributed guidelines to employers to cover housing and sanitary conditions and length of employment, along with the request that they notify the department if the worker should leave the place of employment. Since neither the department nor the employers had the authority to control the movement of Mexican workers, they were free to move as they pleased. *Excélsior* published several articles in 1917 and 1918, showing that braceros were to be found working in factories as far north as New England and New York, and in packing houses in Omaha and Chicago.[2] The Mexican consul in El Paso even advertised in the newspaper for Mexican miners to return to their jobs in northern Mexico.

A mass voluntary repatriation of braceros in 1917 demonstrated how important Mexican workers had become to the southwestern economy. The Selective Service Act of 1917 required that all males between the ages of twenty-one and thirty-five be registered for the draft; foreign nationals such as braceros were exempted from the draft but were obligated to register. Many braceros misunderstood the law, thinking they would have to enter the military, and consequently fled to Mexico. Others could not prove their Mexican citizenship even with the assistance of Mexican consuls. The federal government, fearing that a lack of Mexican labor would seriously hinder the war effort, embarked upon an extensive campaign to inform the workers that they would not be drafted, even enlisting the assistance of the Catholic Church and Mexican consuls. Once the question of the military draft was clarified, many braceros returned to their jobs.

Mario García reports that although in El Paso migration recovered in 1918, the demand for workers still outstripped the supply. Indeed, El Paso had become an important labor contracting point, where prospective U.S. employers and Mexican workers sought one another. The bracero program of World War I can be considered a product of border recruitment. Even companies from the East, such as the Pennsylvania Railroad, sent agents to El Paso. But U.S. immigration officials were more concerned with law than labor contracting in El Paso and caused many delays by implementing bureaucratic requirements. The effects of these delays and bureaucratic requirements were noticed immediately by the Mexican consul Soriano Bravo, who, worried about the immigrants, proposed that they seek written contracts from their employers. Bravo even sent a sample contract with an English translation to labor contractors, to little effect.[3]

Unfortunately, Mexico was ill prepared in the decade 1910–1920 to assume a viable role in controlling emigration north. The Francisco Madero administration, as well as subsequent ones, drew up plans for rural development that would attract braceros, bring them back to Mexico, and reintegrate them into Mexican society. However, political instability and a lack of financial resources prevented the central government from stopping, or even diminishing, emigration. Likewise, some state governments tried to control migration; Sonora Governor Plutarco Calles, for example, tried to require Arizona labor contractors who were recruiting braceros in his state for the Arizona cotton fields to post a $1,000 bond for each worker. The U.S. secretary of state, Robert Lansing, did not even deem Calles's request worthy of diplomatic recognition, since the cotton companies could procure all the workers they wanted in Sonora without posting any bond.

In 1917, the Carranza administration attempted to gain a measure of control by requiring that the Departamento de Migración inspect emigrating workers and prevent the migration of individuals who did not have a signed, valid contract consistent with Article 123 of the newly written Constitution of 1917. This article contained guarantees of wages, working conditions, and so on. Very few if any Mexican workers had contracts; either the Migración inspectors did not choose to enforce the policy or the workers themselves were collaborating with *enganchadores*. Yet the constitutional clause and the efforts to enforce it are important precedents; they portend subsequent Mexican government attitudes.

In 1920, the Mexican government even published a model contract in the *Diario Oficial* outlining the basic requirements of a formal contract between a Mexican worker and his U.S. employer. No worker was to leave Mexico without this document. For a worker accompanied by his family, the transportation costs of all members were to be borne by the employer. Working conditions and daily minimum wages were specified, as well as free medical care in the case of work-related accidents. Employers were to post a bond as their guarantee of compliance with the contract, and to sign the agreement in the presence of Mexican migration and state government officials. Oddly, supervision for a part of this plan was assigned to the Mexican railroads, presumably on the assumption that since the railroads would move workers north they would be in a position to identify the workers.[4]

Interestingly, the renowned Mexican anthropologist Manuel Gamio, researching and writing about Mexican immigration to the United States in the 1920s, proposed a model for a temporary contract labor program with similar features in *Mexican Immigration to the United States.* Gamio included requirements such as employer-funded transportation, extensive documentation for workers, monitor contracts, the involvement of social groups such as churches and unions, and the colonization in Mexico of undocumented workers.[5]

The Boom of the 1920s

Upon the conclusion of World War I, the demand for unskilled Mexican labor did not abate, to the surprise of many in the U.S. government; on the contrary, employers were eager to maintain their supply of workers. Many returning soldiers and other native workers were not disposed to perform maintenance-of-way work or harvest crops. Nor were economic conditions stable enough in Mexico to keep workers at home, as the Mexican Revolution was winding down. Although Mexican emigrants did not consider the United States a perfect destination, the economic boom of the 1920s at least presented the possibility of steady employment. The potential of life in the United States, even with problems, outweighed the realities of Mexico.

Immigration legislation passed in 1921 and 1924, however, made legal immigration on the part of Mexicans increasingly difficult. The new laws retained the $6.00 head tax but additionally required a $10.00 fee to acquire a visa from a U.S. consul. The 1924 law further established the Border Patrol to monitor the U.S.–Mexico border; although it was not really effective in controlling immigrant crossings, the Border Patrol contributed the constant presence of a law enforcement agency. In response to these measures, informal extra-legal systems of recruitment of Mexican immigrants became more elaborate and sophisticated. *Coyotes* sold their services as guides to prospective Mexican emigrants for $10.00 or $15.00, crossing the border with their clients surreptitiously or using "rented entry permits" to enter the United States.[6]

The U.S. railroad industry continued to be an aggressive employer of these undocumented workers throughout the 1920s. The industry's dependence, at least at a regional level, on Mexican railroad labor was openly acknowledged by railroadmen at various Senate hearings that were conducted toward the end of the decade. In some instances, up to 90 percent of track workers in the Southwest and Midwest were Mexican; Mexican immigrant workers may have been relatively more important for the railroads, in fact, than for agriculture.

Repatriation of Mexican Workers during the Depression

However, consequences of the depression in 1929 and 1930 were immediate and unfortunate for the Mexican community living in the United States. Many companies and industries throughout the United States were forced to discharge large groups of employees, and because Mexican immigrants were usually unskilled and the last to be hired, they were the most vulnerable. Worse, some sectors in some regions of the United States came to blame Mexican immigrants for taking jobs from native workers. Not only were Mexicans discharged, but they became the object of a vicious xenophobic campaign that resulted in forced repatriations in many parts of the country, including California, Texas, even Detroit. Although the repatriations seem to have varied widely in causes, effects, and methods of return to Mexico, the subject raises thorny legal and ethical questions. Some Mexican consuls were able to help their compatriots return to Mexico, but their funds were limited. The Mexican government tried to open *ejidos* (government-sponsored communal farms) and *colonias* (settlements) in rural areas such as Durango, Aguascalientes, Chihuahua, and Hidalgo for the returning workers to settle; largely unsuccessful, the effort at least demonstrated the Cárdenas administration's awareness of the workers' predicament.[7]

During the first year of the depression, many Mexican immigrants, perceiving that their fortunes were declining, returned to Mexico on their own. These were not the poorest of immigrants—they returned to Mexico with cars and furniture. Their return trip was facilitated by free rail transport from the border to the interior, provided by the Mexican government. By 1931, however, more and more Mexican immigrants were becoming destitute and fleeing the United States. A U.S. consul in Nuevo Laredo noted that many had been living in the United States for years, and that the decision to return to Mexico had not been made lightly.[8]

The prospects for Mexican immigrants still living in the United States in 1931 became dimmer. Not only were they subject to the pressures of an economy in depression, but some government offices identified aliens as one cause of the massive unemployment. Newly appointed Secretary of Labor William N. Doak took it upon himself to use the Bureau of Immigration, then part of the Department of Labor, to deport as many undocumented foreigners as possible, in the process theoretically making more opportunities available for native workers. Federal immigration agents conducted raids all over the country and, although members of many national groups were arrested, Mexicans were disproportionately represented among the arrested.[9] The repatriation of Mexican immigrants also became an issue at the local level; politicians with agendas such as lowering unemployment relief costs often promoted the repatriation of Mexican immigrants.

The most infamous instance of repatriation took place in Los Angeles, where the Board of Charities organized and financed the repatriation of 13,000 Mexican immigrants between 1931 and 1934.[10] Other estimates indicate that between 50,000 and 75,000 Mexicans were repatriated from California in 1932 alone, of which 35,000 were from Los Angeles County. The zeal of local Immigration Bureau officials was reinforced by the desire of community organizations such as the Lions Club to return Mexican immigrants. The Los Angeles County Welfare Department even attempted to reach an independent agreement with Mexico whereby it would transport immigrants to the border and Mexico would return them to their hometowns in Mexico. Carey McWilliams reports that the Southern Pacific received $14.70 per passenger from Los Angeles County to transport workers to the border.[11] In general, repatriation from California was not closely monitored.

Reaction in Michigan was quite different. As in California, many of the Mexican immigrants there were undocumented. The Mexican consul in Detroit, with the collaboration of Diego Rivera and a local organization called the League of Mexican Workers and Peasants, urged local immigrants to return to Mexico voluntarily. Transportation to the border was subsidized and coordinated with transportation within Mexico to their homes; the Mexican government promised to facilitate their return by providing land, tools, and other help. Although many did return of their own volition, others did not. Another organization, International Labor Defense, vehemently criticized both repatriation and the Mexican government. Although some Mexican immigrants were returned to Mexico against their will, some researchers have concluded that the movement from Michigan was less onerous than that from California due to closer government supervision.[12]

According to figures developed by the Departamento de Migración, over 400,000 Mexican immigrants returned to Mexico from the United States between 1929 and 1937,[13] most of them under extremely difficult circumstances.

The unfortunate consequences of unregulated and unadministered Mexican immigration to the United States for immigrants and for Mexico were not lost on the Mexican government. Unilateral recruitment at the border for temporary contract workers during World War I demonstrated the disagreeable results of such procedures on unprotected workers, the attendant labor shortages in northern Mexican industry and agriculture, and the vulnerability of the Mexican government. The massive unemployment and forced repatriations of the Great Depression, very close in time to World War II, painfully showed the Mexican government the truly precarious position of Mexican workers, legal and undocumented alike, in the U.S. economy, as well as the devastating social, economic, and political consequences of large-scale repatriations for the Mexican community in the United States and for Mexico.[14] Many Mexican experts and government officials resolved that a repeat of these unfortunate occurrences would not occur and that they would use their leverage to prevent them. Surely, when the U.S. Embassy first approached the Secretaría de Relaciones Exteriores in 1942 about the possibility of hiring temporary contract workers for U.S. agriculture, many Mexican government officials were, at the least, reluctant to make possible a recurrence of the repatriations of the 1930s.

Part Two

CREATING THE PROGRAM

*Al llegar a West Kentockle
cambiamos locomotora,
de allí salimos corriendo
ochenta millas por hora.*

6

The Agricultural Program

Over 118,000 Mexican farmworkers were contracted through the agricultural bracero program from 1942 to 1944.[1] Although concentrated in California[2] and other agricultural states (Michigan, for example), the workers were assigned to farms and other agricultural activities throughout the United States. Texas was the exception; extreme and persistent discrimination against Mexicans in Texas forced the Mexican government to exclude Texas from the program. Although the agricultural bracero program was renewed willy-nilly until 1964, the phase during the war provides the most appropriate means to compare the employment of agricultural and railroad braceros.

U.S. agriculture did not stabilize its seasonal unskilled labor supply much before the nation's direct involvement in World War II. During the 1930s, the seasonal farm labor force became inadvertently comprised of groups hitherto uninvolved in such low-paying work. One such group was the Okies, dislocated farmers from Oklahoma and Arkansas who had migrated to California—workers who obviously would have preferred higher-paying industrial jobs had they been available.[3] Such opportunities, however, were virtually nonexistent during the Great Depression, when the national unemployment rate hovered around 25 percent. Under those conditions the supply of unskilled workers available to growers throughout the United States was plentiful; employers had no problems finding people to harvest crops. Indeed, during the depression U.S. agriculture maximized its profits at the expense of extremely vulnerable unskilled workers.[4]

However, sudden industrial growth in the late 1930s springing from nascent war mobilization opened job markets for unemployed and marginally employed individuals such as farmworkers. In Southern California, for example, defense industries attracted, and indeed sought, displaced white tenant farmers who had been performing unskilled labor in California fields. By the fall of 1941, they constituted almost 15 percent of Southern California's industrial workforce.[5] Japanese immigrants and

Japanese Americans who had also worked as agricultural workers, principally in California but in other states as well, were being held by the federal government in detention camps, further reducing the potential pool of farmworkers.[6] Moreover, the demand for industrial workers provoked a massive rural-to-urban migration of southern African Americans to northern cities like Chicago and Detroit, eliminating them as well from farm work. Passage of the Selective Service Act and the National Defense Act in 1941 affected the availability of other potential harvesters, such as recent high school graduates.[7] State employment bureaus, especially in Texas, California, and other predominantly agricultural states, utilized extensive networks to locate prospective farmworkers; they even recruited individuals normally outside the labor market such as housewives, students, and scout troops. Municipal employees and government workers were induced to harvest on weekends. At times, whole communities stopped their usual activities so everyone could work in the fields.[8] At best, however, these measures were ad hoc strategies, not real solutions, for large growers.

In his study of the agricultural bracero program in the Pacific Northwest during World War II, Erasmo Gamboa reports that conditions were somewhat different for unskilled labor on farms of that region but that consequences were similar for Mexican labor. During the depression, local growers either hired Mexican farmworkers who had already immigrated to the area or used recruitment networks based in northern California. After the war began, however, northwestern farmers, like their southwestern counterparts, sought additional Mexican farmworkers through the bracero program to meet the dramatically increasing war-related demand for their fruits and vegetables. They did so because contingency plans to augment the supply of harvest laborers—for example, shortening the school year, recruiting the mentally ill, granting military deferments for farmworkers, and closing certain businesses—were inadequate for their needs.[9]

The Department of Agriculture had implemented an interstate farmworker transportation program in 1941 in an attempt to provide workers where they were needed. By 1943, it became patently clear that even these extraordinary measures were not functioning. For some time the War Manpower Commission maintained that low wages explained the lack of farmworkers. After 1941, agribusiness appealed to the USDA to permit the importation of Mexican agricultural workers. But the War Manpower Commission and the USDA feared that the status of domestic farmworkers would be compromised by the introduction of temporary contract labor, thus neutralizing the efforts of the Farm Security Administration during the depression to improve their prospects.[10]

The federal government, particularly the USDA, was ambivalent about the importation of Mexican workers. Memories of the deplorable bracero program of World War I and the more recent repatriations of the 1930s were uncomfortably fresh.

Farmworkers—South of the Border

However, southwestern growers never forgot that a solution for their labor shortage lay in Mexico. Employment of Mexicans was as important for southwestern and midwestern agriculture as it was for the railroads. Many agricultural concerns had actively sought Mexican workers at the border before the depression and in some instances depended almost wholly on Mexican immigrant labor for some phases of production.[11] The citrus industry in Southern California, for instance, employed Mexican labor in the fields and also in the packinghouses.[12] By early 1940, many growers were aggressively seeking options for acquiring farmworkers, and so the call for Mexican labor became more acute.[13] By and large, like their counterparts in World War I, the growers felt the federal government should assume a prominent role in furnishing workers, especially from Mexico, since their dire need for labor stemmed mostly from government policy and the war effort. The government was simultaneously increasing agricultural business and depleting the labor supply.[14] Not until the United States entered the war, however, did the federal government consider agriculture's request for Mexican workers seriously.[15]

Early in 1942, the Immigration Service formed an interagency committee with representatives from the departments of State, Agriculture, and Justice, along with the War Manpower Commission, to negotiate a plan for the importation of Mexican farmworkers. Otey Scruggs and Richard Craig both consider the dynamics of this committee to be crucial to understanding the interest-group politics that initiated and sustained the agricultural bracero program until 1964. The committee completed its report in May 1942, and the report became the basis for the international bracero program negotiated later in the year.[16]

A final impetus for the establishment of a bracero program came from the California sugar beet industry, which was particularly affected by the labor shortage. Sugar beets are an especially labor-intensive crop whose demand soared during World War II, since the war rendered traditional sources of cane sugar unavailable. By 1942 many sugar beet workers, both Mexican Americans and legal Mexican immigrants, had accepted more desirable work in defense industry.[17] To make matters worse, the 1942 crop was an unusually large one; the growers were afraid. The sugar beet growers' public campaign for Mexican workers became so widespread that groups of workers gathered in search of work at points along the border, for example, at Mexicali, but they could not fill the need.[18] Consequently, in March 1942 the California sugar beet industry filed formal requests for 3,000 temporary Mexican workers with several government agencies. On May 15, 1942, the U.S. Employment Service[19] certified that a labor shortage was jeopardizing the California sugar beet crop and that the industry needed 3,000 Mexican workers to complete a successful harvest.[20] The departments of Agriculture, State, Justice, and Labor had already discussed importing farmworkers, so in June 1942 the War Manpower Commission directed the USDA to take whatever action was necessary to supply workers for the nation's farms; the prospect of recruiting Mexican workers was included in the directive.

In May 1942 the Mexican Embassy in Washington, D.C., and the U.S. government initiated preliminary discussions about a temporary contract labor program. The U.S. government assumed that the Mexican government would establish minimal guidelines, given the unfortunate consequences of repatriation, and include the Mexican Constitution's Article 123. In fact, Ávila Camacho instructed his cabinet to consider the proposal within the context of a government-administered migration program. Negotiations for the bracero program were conducted during the summer of 1942, and the final exchange of diplomatic notes took place in Mexico City on August 4, 1942.[21] And in fact, the California sugar beet growers received 3,000 workers in time to harvest a record crop that covered over a million acres.

The principles that the Mexican negotiators established, and that for the most part were respected, reflected what they perceived to be the most immediate perils. Article 29 of the Mexican Constitution was mentioned in the agreement. Braceros were not to be used to displace domestic workers but only to fill temporary needs. Recruitment and transportation costs for the workers' trip to the United States were to be provided. A formal contract between each worker and his employer was to be completed, clearly stating work conditions. A minimal level of housing and sanitation was to be guaranteed, and 10 percent of the workers' gross pay was to be deducted and placed in a savings account, to be reimbursed upon the workers' return to Mexico.[22] Braceros were to receive the "prevailing wage," which was to be determined by gauging their wages against domestic wages for the same work, but such determination was almost impossible in the context of unskilled seasonal agricultural work.

A Binational Approach

To protect the workers, Mexico also insisted that both governments administer the bracero program. An ad hoc binational administrative team emerged promptly, whose functions and duties were not really clear at the program's inception but evolved over time. The United States immediately dispatched personnel from the War Manpower Commission and the Farm Security Administration, as well as physicians from the U.S. Public Health Service, to oversee the contracting of workers in Mexico and to collaborate with the Mexican team representing the Secretaría de Trabajo y Previsión Social and the Secretaría de Relaciones Exteriores. Recruitment was conducted at the National Stadium and became a lengthy process; prospective braceros often waited several days to gain admission to the stadium. Once inside, the recruits had to procure approval from Mexican migration and labor officials before proceeding to the physical examination administered by the public health doctors and signing the contract with the War Manpower Commission. The Mexican government was pleased with the fact that the Farm Security Administration had been assigned to participate; the agency had been established in 1937 as a New Deal response to rural social problems, and had earned itself a solid reputation. That the FSA was involved at the very beginning of the program must surely have assuaged some doubts of Mexican decision makers, and in fact may have tempered the influence of the USDA, a reactionary conduit for U.S. agribusiness.[23]

Contracted agricultural braceros were transported north to the border on the Ferrocarriles Nacionales, following elaborate schedules arranged by the binational team. Braceros left from Buena Vista Station in Mexico City and arrived in either Nogales or Ciudad Juárez, where they were transferred to the custody of U.S. government officials who distributed the workers.

Agricultural braceros were contracted not by individual farmers but by local or county farm labor associations[24] established by growers and farmers to supervise the braceros, to oversee their scheduling and living arrangements, and even to construct their work camps. Most braceros were engaged in harvesting, normally completed at any farm in a short time. Sometimes the braceros worked on a different farm every day. The growers organized themselves into these associations allegedly to disperse expenses and utilize the braceros' labor as efficiently as possible. These associations, unfortunately, were reluctant to actually accept responsibility for the braceros' welfare; in the event of an accident or illness, the groups sometimes accepted their responsibility but oftentimes did not. In fact, when the Mexican government insisted that each agricultural bracero sign a contract with his employer, it was probably not thinking of these county grower associations but of responsible individuals who would be liable for the well-being of the workers.[25]

When the first contingent of 3,000 braceros returned to Mexico in the fall and winter of 1942, they reported discrimination, substandard working conditions, and inadequate housing—accounts that reinforced criticism of the program in Mexico and provoked calls to discontinue it. *Excélsior,* for instance, published in late 1942 a series of stories, some sensational, about the experiences of agricultural braceros in the United States. The worst consistently concerned Texas, never known for an unbiased attitude toward Mexican workers; the braceros' most disagreeable experiences were there. In spite of the Mexican government's insistence that braceros not be sent to Texas, some were dispatched there anyway. Later, discrimination against Mexicans became so pronounced in Idaho that the Mexican government also banned that state from receiving agricultural braceros, in 1946.[26]

The protection for workers that Mexican negotiators had sought obviously was not being provided. Motivated by intense criticism in Mexico, the Mexican government had to respond. In February 1943, the Mexican government suspended all recruitment of agricultural braceros in Mexico City—purely a symbolic act, since agricultural braceros would not be contracted until March or April anyway. The agricultural program proved completely unacceptable to the Mexican government. Although some U.S. government officials would have preferred to circumvent the constraints of the bracero program and authorize unilateral recruitment at the border, the U.S. government proposed bilateral talks to modify the international agreement.

In addressing the universal complaint of low wages and wage differentials between braceros and domestic workers, the U.S. government reinforced the stipulation that the prevailing wage be paid by adding working conditions to the criteria. In response to justified Mexican criticism of inadequate employment guarantees, which originally had covered only 75 percent of the contract period, creating the possibility that workers could be stranded in the United States, the U.S. government conceded that providing subsistence at no cost to workers during idle periods would greatly improve working conditions and would not provoke hostility from the farmers. Moreover, the standards for living conditions were simplified and improved; because the original contract had stated that Mexican farmworkers were to be furnished the same housing as domestic farmworkers, the conditions under which they lived varied enormously and in many places were atrocious. The new agreement stated that Mexican farmworkers were to be supplied "hygienic lodging without cost to them." Finally, Mexican consuls were authorized to enter farm property to observe the working conditions and to speak with the braceros. Unfortunately, on occasion farmers denied free entry to consuls.

Original funding for the agricultural program in 1942 was channeled through the President's Emergency Fund, moneys appropriated by Congress for the president to use at his or her discretion. Since the international legal basis for the project had been only an exchange of diplomatic notes, this financing strategy was possible. President Roosevelt was not required to justify his actions to Congress; however, the amounts of capital were limited and, to be sure, many other expenses were paid from this fund.[27] The Department of Agriculture was not satisfied with the financial limitations of this arrangement and so in January 1943 submitted a multimillion dollar funding proposal to Congress to obtain independent, line-item moneys for the agricultural program. Although congressional discussion, debates, and amendments modified the USDA's proposal substantially, it was enacted as Public Law 45. On April 29, 1943, $26 million was appropriated for the farm labor program.

Passage of Public Law 45 represented a defeat for the policies that the Farm Security Administration had tried to institute at the beginning of the program; these were policies that were consistent with the position of the Mexican government. The law appropriated $26 million to continue the bracero program under the War Food Administration and the USDA. Mexico had found the FSA an acceptable participant, since the agency was concerned not just with quantifiable agricultural production but with the quality of rural life. The agency, moreover, had been responsible for recruitment and transportation in Mexico as well as the administration of braceros in the United States. The agricultural employers, for their part, wanted less government "intrusion" and, in fact, resented government supervision. They objected to the FSA using the bracero program as a platform to obtain better working conditions for all farmworkers, Mexican and domestic alike. Thus, when the Mexican government suspended recruitment in February 1943, the farm lobbies increased their criticism of the FSA. In March 1943, the War Food

Administration assumed control of the agricultural program. As the agency's title indicates, it was the wartime office in charge of food supplies. The agency's view of agriculture and the function of the bracero program coincided more with the growers'; the War Food Administration was less concerned with humanity than with food production. Chester Davis, its director, was interested in increasing U.S. agricultural production. The office's notion of government administration of the bracero program was also more compatible with the growers and the USDA, and thus conformed better to stipulations of Public Law 45. The law contained a loophole through which the War Manpower Commission could justify very lax administration. Section 5(g) of the law empowered the Immigration Service with the approval of the attorney general to regulate alien worker traffic and permit the entry of aliens, as long as they had in their possession an identification card with a photo and fingerprints; the section did not require a visa, passport, or contract. Private recruitment started in El Paso, with 1,500 Mexicans entering the United States on one day in May 1943 under the new law.[28]

Agreements with Other Countries

During World War II, the United States also sought and obtained workers from countries other than Mexico through temporary contract labor programs, albeit with important differences. The August 4, 1942, agreement served as the model for subsequent agreements with Jamaica, the Bahamas, British Honduras, Costa Rica, Barbados, and Newfoundland, Canada, to contract agricultural and industrial workers, although in smaller numbers than in the Mexican agreement. These workers were also under the supervision of the Foreign Labor Section of the War Manpower Commission. In June 1945, 16,000 workers from Jamaica, Barbados, and British Honduras were employed in forges, foundries, and food processing, chemical, lumber, and ordnance plants. Three thousand Jamaicans were harvesting fruits and vegetables and 300 Newfoundlanders were maintaining dairy farms in New York.[29]

While the Mexican agreement was formal, those for the other countries ranged from informal for Canada to memoranda of understanding with British West Indian governments. Although the Mexican agreements specified solely agricultural and railroad workers, industrial workers for forges in Michigan were imported from the Caribbean, which the United Auto Workers firmly opposed. Non-Mexican braceros were not as well protected by their governments. Unfortunately, this lack of protection at times translated into lower paychecks. While the average daily pay for a Mexican agricultural bracero in California was $4.55, that for a Jamaican working in Arizona cotton was $1.15. Industrial workers fared slightly better.[30] In any event, attempts to expand the concept of the bracero program beyond Mexico to other parts of the Western Hemisphere had mixed results. Although the number of workers was quite small, these labor agreements do show the eagerness of the U.S. government to find additional labor.

7

The Railroads' Campaign

Like their agricultural counterparts, railroad companies requested the importation of Mexican workers before Pearl Harbor. In September 1941, the Southern Pacific Railroad formally sought permission from the Immigration Service to recruit 600 track workers in Mexico and to transport them to the United States,[1] although lobbying and informal communications on behalf of the railroad industry probably had begun some time before. The company stated that a chronic labor shortage throughout the Southwest was severely impeding efficiency in rail transportation and threatening Southern Pacific's ability to contribute to the war effort; government assistance in procuring workers would be appropriate. Railroad unions protested the Southern Pacific's application, claiming that no existing shortage would justify an international temporary contract labor program. In any event, the Immigration Service denied the request, since there was insufficient evidence to support it.[2]

The burden lay with the Southern Pacific, and eventually other railroads, to establish that a real labor shortage existed, that such a shortage affected the industry's ability to collaborate in the war efforts, and that Mexico represented the best solution. The responsibility for showing that a dire need for track labor existed rested entirely with the railroads. This was a daunting task; it was far more difficult for the railroad industry than for the California sugar beet growers to prove they needed workers. The railroads had to demonstrate to the War Manpower Commission with irrefutable evidence that employment of Mexican citizens was the railroads' most viable option. However, while some agencies such as the WMC and the Immigration Service were skeptical or even hostile to the prospect of a nonagricultural temporary contract labor program, the Office of Defense Transportation was eager to locate track workers, regardless of political boundaries.

By early 1942, the military draft had depleted the ranks of railroad labor;[3] deferments for railroad employees had helped for a while but offered only a temporary reprieve. Railroad industry observers noted that the labor shortage was apparently spreading throughout the country and affected all job classifications, especially unskilled ones.[4] The Association of American Railroads,[5] in conjunction with the Office of Defense Transportation, conducted a survey of the railroads to determine the nature and severity of the labor shortage and to evaluate how it was affecting the industry's contributions to the war effort. They learned that although some measures had been taken to actively recruit employees, the Union Pacific and many other railroads were already being forced to advertise outside their territories.[6] By April 1942, the New York Central was considering retaining employees after the usual retirement age of sixty-five. Joseph Eastman, director of the Office of Defense Transportation, encouraged the railroads to aggressively explore options to increase their workforce.[7] Further, the ODT recommended in the spring of 1942 that age limits should be revised, that retired employees should be rehired, that women should be recruited (as they had been in large numbers in World War I), and that superfluous federal employees should be transferred to the railroads.[8]

The Southern Pacific claimed it took extraordinary measures to replace the 14,718 employees who left to enter the military services and to meet the unusual demands that arose through its contiguity to the Pacific theater of operations; to shipyards, aircraft factories, and war plants; and to the Panama Canal. The company opened many recruitment offices, provided transportation for recruited workers, broadened age limits, upgraded apprentice workers, hired women workers to replace men—it established a special school to teach women telegraphy—and even dispatched trucks through some cities every morning to pick up whatever laborers they could find.[9]

In May 1942, Eastman appealed to the large southwestern railroads to coordinate their track maintenance schedules with the demands for seasonal farm labor, so that both agribusiness and the railroads could utilize the same unskilled workers, in reality an impossible strategy to follow.[10] At the urging of the War Manpower Commission, the Southern Pacific recruited about 2,500 African American workers in the South and transported them to southwestern tracks, just as they had forty years before. High attrition, the result of desertions and resignations, made the venture unmanageable and left the company dissatisfied with African American workers as a solution to their labor needs.[11] In July 1942, the Southern Pacific again requested the importation of unskilled Mexican workers, and again the Immigration Service denied the application.[12] Toward the end of 1942, the company tried once more to recruit track workers in the East for their southwestern tracks, with equally unsuccessful results.[13] Although the size and importance of the Southern Pacific made its experience in mobilizing track labor prominent, there were many parallel efforts throughout the railroad industry by small and large companies alike.

In a final attempt to attract workers to the railroads, the Federal Wage-Hour Administration of the Department of Labor announced an across-the-board raise in August 1942 for all railroad workers; it raised their minimum wage to 40 cents an hour. The action immediately affected 35,000 to 50,000 workers, mostly maintenance-of-way workers.[14] Although the raise was independent of the railroad brotherhoods' campaign for better wages—the pay of other industries was generally higher, sometimes double the new wage—the railroad brotherhoods responded by forming a committee in the fall of 1942 to assist the Office of Defense Transportation in labor recruitment.[15] The Railway Labor Executives Association, a body composed of railroad union leaders, publicly supported domestic recruitment drives. More important, it adamantly opposed importing track workers from Mexico.[16] By the end of 1942, both the railroad industry and the unions felt pressured by the apparent scarcity of labor in an ever-escalating war effort. Both were keenly aware that certain prominent growers were already acquiring workers from Mexico through the bracero program.

By the end of 1942, other railroads made public efforts to hire unskilled workers. Like the Southern Pacific, many railroads were desperate to acquire labor to keep up with the war. Some railroads also contacted the Office of Defense Transportation to request assistance in locating workers. Although most of this agency's files were discarded at the end of the war, the surviving Office of Defense Transportation archives do contain requests from the Northern Pacific and the Great Northern Pacific to find workers.[17] The Northern Pacific also contacted the Immigration Service to inquire about hiring foreign workers.[18] Severe unskilled-labor shortages were spreading throughout the railroad industry and causing concern that they would not be able to meet the new higher demand.

Establishing the Need

While the Office of Defense Transportation supported any effort to find track labor, since it believed railroad tracks had reached the point of dangerous deterioration, the Railroad Retirement Board,[19] as the government agency responsible for railroad labor, was much more circumspect about a labor shortage, and even more reticent about recruiting workers in Mexico. The railroads could not find enough workers, according to Murray Latimer of the RRB, simply because the wages were too low. The RRB had been doing some informal recruitment for the Southern Pacific through its regional offices but was unable to supply the company with more than a few hundred laborers at 46 cents an hour. At the Dallas regional office, for example, in November 1942 only fifteen out of 750 applicants accepted this low hourly wage. Throughout the Southern Pacific's territory, the entrance wage for common labor in industry was 4 to 40 cents an hour more than for track labor. On the West Coast, even migrant farm work paid more.[20]

The RRB also conducted a recruitment drive for the Union Pacific, which corroborated its claim about the relationship between wages and the availability of labor and placed the issue in a more realistic perspective. Until early summer of 1942, Union Pacific wages for track workers were about the same as the Southern Pacific's. The RRB tried to recruit workers for the Union Pacific at this pay but was unsuccessful. The Union Pacific, however, was a little more flexible; it raised wages by 10 cents a day and reduced its commissary charges by 50 cents a day. Moreover, industrial employment was not as appealing for potential Union Pacific employees, since common laborers who worked in industry made less in Union Pacific territory than in Southern Pacific territory. After the Union Pacific raised wages, the RRB was able to place three times as many track workers on the Union Pacific as on the Southern Pacific. The RRB could not, however, attribute the Southern Pacific's inability to recruit workers entirely to low wages. The office stated only that insufficient data had been found to justify bringing Mexican workers to the United States.[21] This declaration was the strongest official statement emanating from the government about the relationship between the railroad worker shortage and the level of wages. When considered in the context of the railroad brotherhood's long-time campaign to bring the wages of unskilled railroad workers into line with those of other industries, the issue of wages in relation to supplies of labor becomes crucial.

Toward the end of 1942, certain labor leaders met with railroad management and worked out a mutually acceptable proposal for the importation of Mexican railroad labor. They submitted a recommendation in November 1942 to the Management-Labor Policy Committee, an advisory body to the War Manpower Commission, that all necessary steps be taken to procure needed workers; their proposal was soon forwarded to the State Department.[22] As the committee that regularly and formally submitted labor's position to the WMC, the Management-Labor Policy Committee consistently objected to the use of foreign labor as part of the war manpower mobilization plans; such labor would pose a threat to the domestic wage structure.[23]

This contrasts with the original agricultural bracero program. No corresponding government agency made similar representations on behalf of domestic farmworkers when the possibility of a bracero program became real. Indeed, no organization even outside the federal government ever addressed the welfare of the agricultural braceros. The little that the Farm Security Administration had accomplished for farmworkers that included Mexican immigrants and Mexican Americans during the New Deal justified their involvement in the bracero program, but the designation of the grower-oriented War Food Administration as the responsible agency for the bracero program compromised whatever concern the federal government had demonstrated for farmworkers. The Department of Agriculture had been reluctant to import workers, motivated not by concern for farmworkers' welfare but by concern for the political costs of such a program.

The War Manpower Commission, based on statistical reports routinely submitted to it by the Railroad Retirement Board during the war, determined that there were few track workers available for employment anywhere in the United States, certainly not enough to adequately maintain the tracks. Therefore, Paul McNutt, chairman of the WMC, notified Cordell Hull, the secretary of state, on December 26, 1942, that his commission was authorizing the importation of 3,000 railroad workers from Mexico; he speculated that eventually 10,000 workers would be required.[24] On January 1, 1943, McNutt reiterated the WMC's position to Earl Harrison, commissioner of the Immigration Service, and informed him he was requesting the State Department to initiate a dialogue with Mexico that would lead to an agreement about recruiting Mexican track workers.[25] These communications marked the beginning of the WMC's involvement in a nonagricultural bracero program.

The railroad brotherhoods, especially the Brotherhood of Maintenance of Way Employees, vehemently protested the WMC's authorization of a nonagricultural bracero program. While the railroad unions had periodically expressed their dissatisfaction publicly and privately, the WMC's action elicited particularly strong reactions from the track workers union's administration. The brotherhood's president and treasurer, Elmer E. Milliman and T. B. Shoemake, met with State Department representatives to formally register their objections to the program; they publicly accused the railroads of intentionally maintaining low wages to maximize profits[26] and also indicated that domestic workers were available at decent wages. As late as February 1943, the Management-Labor Policy Committee of the WMC, whose membership included unions, corroborated the Maintenance of Way Brotherhood's position; its own research, in fact, showed that the railroad wage structure was the principal obstacle to labor recruitment.[27] The State Department sidestepped the issue by claiming that it was only an intermediary between Mexico and the United States and was acting on behalf of the WMC.[28] However, Ernesto Galarza in *Merchants of Labor* reports that the WMC obtained at least verbal consent from the Maintenance of Way Brotherhood for the bracero program; if that is true, it would have to have been given in the first few months of 1943.[29]

In the meantime, railroad management received valuable support that reinforced the desirability of a railroad bracero program. Joseph Eastman of the Office of Defense Transportation strongly advocated a bracero program in testimony before the Management-Labor Policy Committee.[30] In March 1943, Eastman, in collaboration with the Department of the Army, officially declared that deteriorating track conditions occasioned by the labor shortage were contributing to a national transportation crisis that would jeopardize the delivery of troops and war materiel.[31] Eastman even acted upon his own initiative, contacting the U.S. Embassy in Mexico City to urge the implementation of such a program.[32]

The pieces fell into place in the first few months of 1943 for a non-agricultural program. The railroads and the Office of Defense Transportation established, at least formally, that a chronic track labor shortage was hurting the war effort and that Mexico was the most accessible source of labor. The War Manpower Commission certified that the railroads' predicament was legitimate. The unions were neutralized. Now the State Department could act.

8

Negotiations

Early in January 1943, Ambassador George Messersmith in Mexico City received instructions from the State Department to approach the Secretaría de Relaciones Exteriores about expanding the bracero program to nonagricultural industries. U.S. Embassy staff conducted preliminary talks with the SRE while Messersmith returned to Washington to confer with Governor Paul McNutt of the War Manpower Commission about terms of the program.[1]

The Mexican government was not responsive to these first discussions of a nonagricultural bracero program. Unfortunately, no Mexican documents have come to light about this phase of the program, but the Mexican government was obviously not pleased with the course of the agricultural program. Recently returned agricultural workers were complaining about mistreatment, and newspapers like *Excélsior* were publicizing their complaints.[2] Moreover, as Arthur Motley, the War Manpower Commission representative already in Mexico City for the agricultural program, observed, expanding the program might well exacerbate internal Mexican labor problems.[3] The upshot was that many in Mexico, including some in the government, opposed any organized labor recruitment by the United States.[4] The Railroad Retirement Board and the Office of Defense Transportation were powerless to proceed in Mexico until the government changed its mind and agreed to negotiate.[5] Only intervention by the Mexican presidency at the end of January 1943 persuaded the Secretaría de Relaciones Exteriores to begin serious negotiations for a nonagricultural program.[6]

Preliminary informal talks continued; by February, Ambassador Messersmith was more optimistic about the Mexican government's position. Although the SRE had already agreed in principle to a railroad program,[7] its negotiators wanted to delay discussing final details until the War Manpower Commission was ready to actually hire Mexican workers. But the Secretaría de Trabajo y Previsión Social team was anxious to continue the negotiations, as the *secretaría* had already internally established acceptable parameters for a railroad bracero program.[8]

Within a month, however, the Departamento de Agricultura suspended agricultural recruitment, which caused the SRE to shelve talks about a railroad program.[9] Ambassador Messersmith then turned his attention to rescuing the agricultural program; he was correct in his assumption that without a smoothly operating agricultural program there would be no railroad program. Because both governments considered the agricultural program the prototype for other programs,[10] they realized that any problems with it presaged difficulties for projects such as a railroad program. In addition, the Mexican government was less than convinced that a railroad program would be justified under any circumstances; some Mexican officials were understandably worried about how Mexican railroad workers would be treated in the United States.[11]

Especially critical of the bracero program was Secretario de Agricultura (secretary of agriculture) Marte Rodolfo Gómez, who figured in a major personnel shake-up that occurred while Messersmith was in Washington. Officials in other government offices allied with Gómez to criticize the bracero program and other forms of Mexican collaboration in the war effort. Gómez expressed the fear that the agricultural bracero program would drain Mexico of a dangerously large number of farmworkers needed there. Gómez's veto was enough to suspend the agricultural program and forestall the railroad program for a while. Eventually, Ávila Camacho intervened and, with Ezequiel Padilla of the SRE, persuaded Gómez to withdraw his objections, insisting that cooperation with the United States was in Mexico's best interest.[12]

In any event, negotiation of a railroad program was contingent on resolving problems in the agricultural program. Representatives of the Farm Security Administration, which was still responsible for overseeing Mexican agricultural workers in the United States, convened with the Mexican government on March 23, 1943, to work through difficulties, centering mostly on treatment of workers. An amended agreement was reached, and recruitment resumed at the end of March.[13]

Meanwhile, the Agriculture Department further jeopardized the program in March 1943 by proposing, without the support of either the State Department or the War Manpower Commission, House Joint Resolution 96, which proposed transferring domestic administration from the federal government to state agencies. Implementation of the measure would have violated the spirit of a centralized national administration—the basis of the original agreement with Mexico. Ambassador Messersmith stated bluntly that if House Joint Resolution 96 was passed, the agricultural bracero program would be terminated. Appalled that such a measure would be seriously considered, Messersmith wrote:

> I have read some of the memoranda of conversations which the Department has sent me with consternation for they show that some of the members of Congress and some of the farm people at home think that Mexico is a sort of subject state and that we can come down here and herd labor and bring it into our country, do with it as we please. . . . This is putting it baldly, but it is exactly the situation.[14]

During the time that agricultural recruitment was suspended, representatives of farm groups and associations appeared in Mexico to press for resumption for recruitment.

Discussions toward a Railroad Program

Shortly thereafter, three bilateral discussions cemented an agreement for a railroad program. The U.S. Embassy in Mexico designated its second secretary, Robert McGregor, and the War Manpower Commission assigned its envoy to Mexico, Arthur Motley, as representatives. Harry F. Brown of the Farm Security Administration also attended the meetings, since the agricultural program was the model.[15] Oliver Stevens of the U.S. Railway Mission was named advisor-consultant to the program, although he did not attend the preliminary talks.[16] The Mexican government designated the *oficial mayor*[17] from three *secretarías* (secretariats): Manuel Tello of the Secretaría de Relaciones Exteriores, Luis Padilla Nervo of the Secretaría de Trabajo y Previsión Social, and Luis Cortines of the Secretaría de Gobernación. Each side had its agenda.

At the first session, the U.S. negotiators submitted a draft of an agreement for the purpose of discussion; however, the Mexican team maintained that certain provisions would have to be clarified before proceeding to an agreement. The STPS was concerned that in its request for railroad workers the United States was including experienced, skilled railroad workers, that is, employees of Mexican railroads.[18] The concern of the Mexican government was well founded, for the railroads later requested that braceros be allowed to fill jobs that required greater skills than track work; however, at the time of the negotiations, embassy personnel assured the Mexican negotiators that only unskilled railroad workers were being sought. Moreover, the two sides had different notions of the program's scope. The Mexican government was anticipating a request for a group of only 500 workers or so, while the War Manpower

Commission wanted 6,000 workers, 3,000 each for the railroads and the mines. Apparently the Mexican team was caught unprepared; it could not respond.[19]

The second session, held April 3, 1943, also at the SRE, continued to concentrate on terms of the agreement. Differences in working conditions between agriculture and the railroads caused the Mexican team to raise certain valid questions, mostly regarding payroll deductions.[20] Railroad work was notorious for the large deductions taken from employees' pay, especially in the case of track work; track workers were forced to live in camps outside of towns, often run by the company and subsidized by compulsory payroll deductions. The State Department investigated and decided that, like all workers, the braceros would be subject to the Victory tax—a small universal payroll deduction instituted for the duration of the war—but would be exempted from withholding tax. A difficulty arose, however, with requiring that deductions be taken from bracero wages for the Railroad Retirement Board. Although all nonmanagement railroad employees were subject to this deduction and were entitled to RRB benefits upon retirement, administration of the benefits would have been impractical in the case of the braceros, since they would have long since returned to Mexico.[21] To an extent, integrating the braceros into the RRB system would have violated the spirit of the program, since it was a temporary contract labor system outside of normal labor supply and demand. The issue of RRB deductions was left pending, although War Manpower Commission negotiator Motley promised that he would try to arrange an exemption upon his return to Washington, D.C.[22]

The final discussion, which was conducted at the Secretaría de Trabajo y Previsión Social on April 8, 1943, was not a full committee meeting. Only a few Mexican objections remained to be discussed. The Mexican government was still adamant about the infeasibility of RRB deductions, but the issue had not yet been resolved in Washington. Mexican negotiators indicated they would approve the agreement if the RRB deductions could be converted into a group insurance plan. Nonetheless, the wording of the clause on RRB deductions was not changed to meet the Mexican government's position. It is not clear why the Mexican government ceased objecting to the deductions, which remained a part of the agreement.

The Mexican government also requested the U.S. team to clarify the rights and obligations of Mexican consuls and field inspectors. Since some had been denied entry into agricultural camps, the Mexican government was concerned that the same might occur in the railroad program. The U.S. team reworded the agreement to accommodate the concerns of the Mexican government and clearly incorporate the Mexican consuls.[23]

The major remaining reservation of the Mexican government concerned wage guarantees. The original agreement guaranteed each bracero 75 percent of full-time wages for the term of the contract, regardless of the time the bracero actually worked. However, this meant that for pay periods when they worked less than 75 percent of the time, workers might not receive enough to pay room and board. In response to a Mexican request, the agreement was reworded to read that each bracero was guaranteed 75 percent of full-time wages for each thirty-day period, to make sure the braceros had enough money to survive.[24]

In mid April, a tentative agreement was reached when Mexico agreed to a quota of 6,000 nonagricultural workers to be recruited for U.S. railroads. The War Manpower Commission notified the State Department that the agreement had been concluded[25] and that the Secretaría de Relaciones Exteriores was translating the agreement into Spanish.[26]

At this time, in mid April, the Mexican government renewed its demands for guarantees that agricultural braceros would be protected. However, only three days before the nonagricultural agreement was to be formally concluded, the Mexican delegates to the railroad negotiations became aware that agricultural braceros were not to be provided with any kind of support or subsidy when they were not assigned work. This, aggravated by the likelihood that the Farm Security Administration would be replaced after June 30 by the War Food Administration, put the Mexican government on its guard.[27] Finally, the U.S. government agreed to make provisions to subsidize agricultural workers when they were not employed.

More difficult, and in the long run more troublesome, was the U.S. government's ambivalent policy toward bonds to guarantee the workers' safe return to Mexico. Mexican labor law clearly stated that a bond must be posted by prospective employers of all Mexican citizens who left the country for temporary employment. Agricultural braceros had been exempted from bonds because the U.S. government through the War Manpower Commission and the Farm Security Administration, and later the War Food Administration, was named as the employer in the agreement and in each contract; Mexico considered the U.S. government sufficiently responsible as an employer to exempt it from bonds. The language of the nonagricultural agreement could also easily have been construed to mean that technically at least the employer of the railroad braceros was the U.S. government. Had this been done, the railroad companies would have been exempted from posting bonds, thereby saving them a substantial amount of money. In fact, not until mid April did McNutt of the War Manpower Commission even bother to contact either the State Department or the Immigration Service about the bonds,[28] since apparently the Embassy and the Mexican government had informally agreed that the railroad program would be exempted from posting bonds; this information was contained in a memo signed by McNutt before the agreements were finished and was accompanied by handwritten notes. By the end of April the situation had evidently changed, since the railroads were required to post bonds.

An exchange of diplomatic notes in Mexico City between Ambassador Messersmith and Secretario de Relaciones Exteriores Ezequiel Padilla on April 29, 1943, officially concluded the negotiations and constituted the binding agreement that inaugurated the railroad program. The diplomatic notes acknowledged the established and functioning agricultural program as the point of departure and considered the agreement of August 1942 and its amended version of April 1943 as its legal precedents. In fact, Messersmith directly quoted a paragraph from the August 1942 agreement that left no doubt that the original planners of the agricultural program envisioned the utilization of the program in other industries.[29]

The Agreement and Contract

Although brief (five pages), the nonagricultural agreement broadly outlined the program and laid out its legal constraints, prescribed administrative procedures to govern the program, and set down the conditions under which Mexican citizens could work while employed in the United States as railroad workers. Although it was later modified on two occasions in response to specific difficulties, this agreement remained the basis for the railroad bracero program.

The agreement had three parts; the first, entitled "General Principles," comprised its legal regulations. Mexican citizens working in the United States as braceros were exempt from the military draft and were protected from discrimination by Executive Order no. 8802, issued June 25, 1941. At a Mexican request, the text of Article 29 of the Mexican Constitution was included verbatim, to emphasize that the braceros would be accorded the same rights guaranteed them in Mexico. Undoubtedly growing out of the unfortunate bracero program of World War I, the law stipulated that Mexicans contracting to work in other countries were required to have written contracts that guaranteed compliance with the law, that the employers would provide transportation (roundtrip) at no cost to the worker, and that employers would post bond on all contracted employees to guarantee their return to Mexico. Finally, the agreement stipulated that no domestic worker or wage structure would be disrupted by the recruitment of braceros. The War Manpower Commission, the Railroad Retirement Board, and the unions were all aware of the potential effect that an international temporary contract labor program could have on regional domestic labor markets. The international agreement addressed those concerns.[30]

The second part of the agreement, "Procedures," laid out the program's administration, although its writers could not have anticipated many subsequent administrative requirements. With guidelines regulating quotas of workers to be recruited at a given time, and a triangle of contracts among the workers, the railroads, and the U.S. government, the section established legal boundaries for participants. Management lay primarily with the U.S. government, mostly through the aegis of the War Manpower Commission, which executed contracts with each bracero and with contracting railroads. Significantly, the agreement did not require a contract to be completed between railroad employers and the workers; it indeed clearly implied that the U.S. government was the employer. Yet later in this section, the agreement states that "employer" refers to the "owner or operator" of a nonagricultural business in the United States.[31] Moreover, a physical exam, which was to be conducted by both Mexican and U.S. public health doctors following guidelines set by U.S. immigration authorities and the railroad industry, was compulsory. The final administrative requirement represented a bilateral attempt to officially monitor the need for labor in the U.S. railroad industry; the two governments agreed to update and study the railroads' requests for workers.[32]

The final and most detailed part of the agreement describes minimum standards for wages, as well as working and living conditions, and most clearly reflects the Mexican government's position. First, braceros were to be transported from the place of contract to the place of employment and back to Mexico at the expense of the employer. Second, the railroad braceros were to be paid a fair wage, with no unauthorized deductions. For their part, the workers were to remain at the work site for the duration of the contract and to occupy appropriate lodgings if provided by the companies. The braceros could elect one of their number as spokesman to deal with management, unions, or other interested parties. Local Mexican consuls could inspect the workplace and could act as intermediaries in certain circumstances. The braceros were guaranteed 75 percent

of a full-time wage each pay period, and 90 percent for the entire contract. The arrangement could be renewed with certain limitations and
with the approval of the Mexican government. The War Manpower
Commission assumed responsibility for the savings deducted from the
workers' paychecks; these were to be deposited in Mexican banks and distributed to the workers on their repatriation.[33] Even though the railroads
were to oversee much of the administration, the U.S. government's obligation remained.[34]

Further, the arrangement obligated the WMC to cooperate with other
agencies in the course of executing the agreement. Lastly, either government had the right to unilaterally renounce the program and cancel the
agreement.

A triangle of contracts arising from the agreement governed the roles
appropriate to the worker, the railroad employers, and the government
agencies that were involved. The worker signed a contract with the WMC,
the WMC with the railroad employer, and the WMC with the Mexican
government. No contract was completed between the worker and the
employer.[35]

Management of the railroad program as described in the agreement
presupposed the support of a binational bureaucratic apparatus to im-
plement its clauses. Since the scope of the program did not clearly fall
within the aegis of an existing agency, the WMC quickly involved offices
whose functions overlapped the railroad project in some way (in some
instances ad hoc wartime agencies). Collaboration brought together in-
congruous co-workers and meant international responsibilities for normally domestic offices. For example, the WMC and the Railroad Retirement Board both promptly opened offices in Mexico City. Moreover, the
Secretaría de Trabajo y Previsión Social dispatched inspectors to the United
States. By mid May 1943, a complex and sometimes confusing impro-
vised bureaucracy had emerged.

Part Three

IMPLEMENTING THE PROGRAM

El día veintiocho de abril,
a las seis de la mañana,
salimos en un enganche
para el estado de Pensilvania.

9

Operations in Mexico

Excélsior announced on May 14, 1943, that 760 Mexican workers were leaving Buena Vista Station to work for the Southern Pacific Railroad. These workers were among the first of the railroad bracero program. Francisco Trujillo Gurria, secretary of the Secretaría de Trabajo y Previsión Social, made a speech to them, telling them that they were "soldados de la democracia" (soldiers of democracy) in Mexico's collaboration to defeat the forces of barbarity.[1]

The railroad bracero program in Mexico was officially administered in two phases: recruitment of prospective workers in Mexico City (or later Querétaro), and transportation of contracted braceros to the border. These procedures fulfilled the bureaucratic requirements stipulated by the agreement and the contracts; although intended as simple measures to supervise and monitor the execution of the program as it was conceived, they became complicated and intertwined. Active collaboration of Mexican personnel was essential, although U.S. agencies were accountable for most tasks.

The U.S. government had designated the War Manpower Commission as the contracting agency in the railroad agreement, and the WMC was therefore officially responsible for the administration of the project. Indeed, the administrative core of the program in Mexico revolved around the functions of the WMC and its relationship with the Railroad Retirement Board, which was contracted to perform certain tasks; both had representatives and offices in Mexico City. Their collaboration, together with the participation of various Mexican and other U.S. offices, produced the ad hoc bureaucracy that operated the railroad bracero program.

The bracero program was designed partially to meet the Mexican government's insistence on guaranteeing braceros' rights through written contracts and preventing undocumented migration to the United States. All Mexican government officials concurred that the most promising strategy for protecting Mexican workers was to force the U.S. government to take responsibility by stipulating everything in writing. That the U.S.

government made a commitment to assure braceros' housing and working conditions is logical. But the pains the Mexican government took during World War II to control the movement north of undocumented unskilled workers in search of jobs is a surprise.

Recruitment

Actual recruitment was begun when the Immigration Service formally authorized the importation of workers, which was contingent on certification from the WMC that a need existed for unskilled nonagricultural workers that could not be satisfied by domestic workers. The WMC application specified that it was seeking permission to recruit 6,000 workers for the railroads, and cited its year-long unsuccessful recruitment campaign for track workers in the United States as well as the worsening condition of the tracks as reasons for the application. Attorney General Francis Biddle signed an order on May 6, 1943, to legally justify the bracero program under the ninth proviso to section 3 of the Immigration Act of 1917. Although that act made temporary foreign contract labor illegal, another section allowed the hiring of temporary foreign unskilled workers under certain circumstances certified by the Department of Labor. The War Manpower Commission was careful to follow all the procedures required by the Immigration Act of 1917 so that recruitment could begin as soon as possible.[2] Obviously, the War Manpower Commission had everything in place before the final signatures were affixed in Mexico City.

By this time the WMC had already opened an office in Mexico City for the railroad program and had assigned an official, Sam Hough, to oversee operations.[3] The May order enabled Hough to initiate recruitment of braceros in the National Stadium in Mexico City, where the agricultural braceros were already being recruited, through collaboration with the Farm Security Administration. At that time, the Southern Pacific Railroad sent W. H. Kirkbride, chief engineer, to Mexico City to supervise recruitment for that railroad, the Western Pacific, and the Pacific Fruit Express. Other railroads also sent recruiters.[4] However, by May 1943, there was a shortage of eligible workers in Mexico City. Increased quotas for agricultural braceros had seriously drained the pool of potential braceros around Mexico City that was the labor source for both programs. Since the agricultural program had priority, its labor needs were being met first and it was hiring the few eligible workers available.[5] Thus recruitment for railroad workers was temporarily stalled. Hough reacted by proposing a separate, independent recruitment center in Guadalajara—a proposal that the Mexican government dismissed summarily,[6] although, as will be seen, it did not leave the government's mind as a possibility.

The labor shortage ended quickly, and by the end of May many workers were already on the job, mostly in the Southwest in the employ of the Southern Pacific and the Santa Fe railroads. By mid June 1943, enough workers had been contracted to fill the original quota of 6,000.[7] However, news of the railroad bracero program spread quickly, and additional companies throughout the United States requested braceros as a solution to their track labor needs. The WMC therefore processed quotas on June 22 for an additional 9,000 workers, on July 6 for 12,500 workers, and on August 23 for 4,300 additional track workers.[8] Clearly the railroad industry perceived advantages in the program. The Mexican government approved the quota increases.

By August or so, the program had achieved a level of stability, in the sense that an administrative routine had been developed. Workers were recruited and transported to their assigned work sites in the United States through the collaboration of a binational administrative team. However, in September a serious crisis emerged that forced the Mexican government to suspend recruitment for two months.

Many complaints about the quality of working and living conditions had reached the Mexican government already, but a specific incident in California regarding a wage differential provided the immediate reason for the suspension. Many railroads customarily hired contractors to perform certain short-term tasks; it was more convenient and often less expensive, for example, for them to contract a track maintenance company to perform seasonal track section maintenance than to hire an extra track maintenance gang. The contractor would not only do the hiring but would also supervise and manage the workers. Normally, employees working for these contractors were not subject to the same regulations or wage structures as individuals directly employed by the railroads—and workers hired by a track maintenance company contracted by the Southern Pacific were receiving wages twice as high as the braceros. Some braceros hired by the Santa Fe Railroad and assigned to track near Los Angeles found out about this and lodged a complaint with the Mexican consul in Los Angeles.

Mexican and U.S. officials alike became nervous over the incident. Joseph Eastman of the Office of Defense Transportation, in fact, claimed that the capability of the western railroads to discharge their war-related obligations was "at stake in this matter." Manuel Tello of the Secretaría de

Relaciones Exteriores informed the U.S. Embassy that his agency had received so many complaints about the railroad program that it was considering transferring the workers to agriculture or industry.

Recruitment was again disrupted in December when friction developed between the Railroad Retirement Board and the Secretaría de Trabajo y Previsión Social. The RRB had been keeping records on the program since May 1943, maintaining individual folders for contracted workers and aggregate statistical reports. The RRB was following its normal policy of not releasing internal data to other agencies. But to authorize additional recruitment, the STPS needed statistical data that only the RRB had regarding the number, location, and scheduled repatriation of braceros from the United States.[9] The STPS made its position clear, but the RRB refused to release the data. The STPS repeated its position in January 1944.[10] An agreement apparently was reached at that time, since thereafter the RRB routinely forwarded the necessary data to the STPS. Ambassador George Messersmith attributed the impasse to friction between personnel of the two offices.[11]

The recruitment headquarters at the National Stadium also brought unanticipated consequences. Supplies of local unemployed men in the Mexico City vicinity were significantly reduced by bracero recruitment. However, publicity about the program in *Excélsior* as well as other national and local newspapers inadvertently promoted the program. In response, Mexican workers from the provinces migrated to the city to apply. At least 20,000 men, most without resources, traveled to Mexico City in 1943 and 1944 to apply for the bracero program.[12] Certainly for unemployed and underemployed workers the bracero program represented an extremely desirable option. Unfortunately, neither the city nor the bracero program was able to respond adequately to the problems caused by these workers. As a solution, the Mexican government formally proposed that railroad recruitment be removed from the city later in 1944 and be relocated to San Luis Potosí; the War Manpower Commission readily agreed.[13]

This was the beginning of what could be termed the maturation of the railroad bracero program. Although it was to have been an extension of the agricultural program, the railroad project achieved virtual autonomy through the separation of recruitment. With this step it went well beyond the plans of the original negotiators, who had thought it would be a temporary footnote to the agricultural program.

The Mexican government also insisted that recruitment procedures be modified to avoid the problems that came to be associated with the bracero program in Mexico City. Therefore, the Mexican government specified that although recruitment headquarters would be located at San Luis Potosí, preliminary selection of candidates would be conducted by recruitment personnel at designated points in central and southern Mexico following a schedule to be developed by the STPS. Mexican labor inspectors were to supervise field operations and determine who would be taken to San Luis Potosí for final examination and processing. The RRB would arrange transportation for prospective braceros[14] and the War Manpower Commission would subsidize it, including return transportation in the event of rejection.[15] Oliver Stevens of the U.S. Railway Mission and the Association of American Railroads both acted as consultants.[16]

In April 1944, recruitment did indeed open in San Luis Potosí, but it only lasted there for two months. In spite of efforts to control the movement of recruits to and within the city, unsupervised groups of would-be braceros collected around San Luis Potosí, creating the same difficulties as in Mexico City. Some observers claimed that crime in the city had already increased due to railroad bracero recruiting.[17] The San Luis Potosí *Heraldo* estimated on June 3, 1944, that at least 5,000 new arrivals to the city were wandering the streets without resources in the hope of joining the program.[18] Many probably came without realizing that under the new procedures they could not initiate the process in San Luis Potosí. At this point, Gonzalo Santos, the governor of the state, requested a meeting with recruitment personnel from both governments; he stressed the severity of the situation and, like others, maintained that crime in the city had increased. Governor Santos offered to help the recruitment headquarters relocate to Querétaro; although Governor Agapito Pozo of Querétaro was none too happy about the prospect of the recruitment center moving to his capital city, Governor Santos had persuaded him to accept it.

By the end of June 1944, the Railroad Retirement Board had located a building in Querétaro and made the necessary arrangements. The Mexican government assured the recruitment staff, both Mexican and U.S., that the railroad program could remain in Querétaro for the duration of the war—and in fact it did.[19]

The decentralized recruitment procedures operated with more success in Querétaro than in San Luis Potosí. Recruitment personnel actually went to rural and semirural points for preliminary selection. Candidates passing the first battery of tests in the field were taken to Querétaro, where they underwent further tests and interrogations. Although a high percentage taken to Querétaro were contracted, those rejected were returned home. Contractees were assigned a northbound train.

The field recruitment schedule that the Secretaría de Trabajo y Previsión Social issued for the summer of 1944 illustrates the pace of recruitment and the quota levels that were anticipated for the summer. From the state of Hidalgo, 6,000 individuals would be hired; from the state of Michoacán, 4,000; from Querétaro, 3,000; and from Guerrero, 2,000 braceros.[20] Since Jalisco was reserved for the agricultural program, it was not included in the schedule.[21]

The railroads requested substantial increases in their allotments of braceros toward the end of 1944, which were approved by Mexico, so the monthly quotas rose from 1,675 to 4,405, a 262 percent increase.[22] Although the Secretaría de Trabajo y Previsión Social revised its preliminary recruitment schedules, the Railroad Retirement Board found it increasingly difficult to fill its quotas.[23] In many instances, the states providing unskilled laborers (Hidalgo, Michoacán, Querétaro, and Guerrero) simply did not have enough laborers available to fill the quotas. In little over a year, almost 100,000 railroad braceros had been hired, not to mention an even larger number of farmworkers. The bracero program had severely depleted local labor markets.

The War Manpower Commission office in Mexico reported, in fact, in January 1945 that railroad recruitment fell short in Zacatecas by some 6,000 workers.[24] The WMC asked the Mexican government to endorse the program more publicly on the assumption that this would encourage additional eligible workers to apply, so President Ávila Camacho urged the state governments to promote recruitment.[25] The WMC also asked the Secretaría de Trabajo y Previsión Social to urge state governments to identify eligible workers.[26] Despite these efforts, the recruitment campaign for April 1945 was only slightly more successful; it fell far short of filling the quotas.[27]

Recruitment continued according to schedule through the summer of 1945, when the conclusion of the war brought the program to an end. Although there were attempts to continue the program, recruitment was formally discontinued at the end of August 1945,[28] and most recruitment personnel were released or transferred.[29]

The Process of Recruitment

Recruitment was intended to be a relatively simple operation, to correspond to contractual obligations, but it soon became painstaking, time-consuming, and expensive. As the program expanded and contractual difficulties arose, recruitment became more complicated and bureaucratic. Contract renewals, increases in quotas, and repatriation of workers required ongoing recruitment drives and supplemental procedures. Moreover, recruitment in Mexico provoked abuses, such as selection-card selling, that were unforeseen by most involved. Some of these abuses, such as bribe-taking, were quite costly for prospective braceros.

Recruitment was a binational process, implemented by representatives of both governments; in addition, the U.S. railroads and the U.S. Railway Mission participated in the process. Basically, the goals were (1) to identify potentially eligible Mexican workers, (2) to conduct a series of examinations to determine if they were qualified, and (3) to complete the formal contracts. Although these goals remained unchanged, the procedures to achieve them were modified many times over the course of the program, and the abuses associated with the program resulted from faulty procedures used to achieve these goals.

When railroad recruitment commenced in 1943, worker eligibility was not an issue; unemployed, unskilled workers living in the Mexico City area could apply at the National Stadium for the program without any intermediaries. As long as they could produce a document showing they were Mexico City residents, they could obtain a selection card that allowed them to enter the stadium. Even for those who had traveled to Mexico City to apply, supplying such proof of residence was relatively easy; a receipt from a rooming house sufficed. However, the greatly increased supply of applicants created competition for the limited number of selection cards to enter the stadium, and therein originated an abuse costly for prospective braceros. Although apparently even at the beginning of the program applicants often gave a tip to the Secretaría de Trabajo y Previsión Social inspectors when they received their selection cards, competition converted the tip into a bribe. The practice soon became a normal part of recruitment. Mexico City residents even complained to President Ávila Camacho of neighborhood disturbances caused by the labor inspectors demanding money for the selection cards. One letter even speaks of violence. Not surprisingly, the documents of the STPS in the Archivo General de la Nación contain no mention of this scandal, but *Excélsior* and the documents of the Ávila Camacho presidency do.

The average applicant paid between Mex$5 and $25 for the selection card, although in one case it was over $100. Some inspectors sold the cards right in front of the stadium, while others positioned themselves on street corners in *colonias* (settlements) where aspirants from outside Mexico City were staying. Moreover, some cards were forged. Although U.S. personnel were aware of the irregularities related to the selection cards, there was little they could do. The problem essentially was internal to the STPS.

One reason, in fact, that both the War Manpower Commission and the Mexican executive branch wanted to take recruitment out of Mexico City was to eliminate card-selling. Many assumed that moving recruitment away from Mexico City would eliminate the corruption associated with selection cards. Although distribution of selection cards was turned over to the municipal authorities when recruitment was transferred to San Luis Potosí and Querétaro, the abuses continued. *Presidentes municipales* (mayors) and apparently some *diputados* (legislative representatives) accepted payment for selection cards; some local residents also tried to use political influence to acquire them.[30] *Ejidatarios* (persons living on government-sponsored communal farms) were technically not eligible for either the agricultural or nonagricultural program. The Mexican government deemed their contribution to Mexican agriculture essential; rural applicants had to prove that they were not *ejidatarios.* Agricultural braceros, who were generally from rural areas, often did not receive proper authorization from their local governments to be recruited; undoubtedly some were *ejidatarios.*[31]

However he got his preliminary selection card, each applicant basically followed the same procedure. The applicant presented himself at recruitment headquarters at the designated time. An inspector for the STPS issued a permanent selection card if he was satisfied that the individual was qualified, and the applicant was vaccinated. The man was then examined by a representative of the railroads—at first by a railroad employee and later generally by someone from the Western Association of Railway Executives—to see if he was fit for railroad work.[32] Then the applicant was screened not for individual railroad companies but for types of work skills he possessed—later in the program, railroad braceros had opportunities to perform tasks other than track maintenance. (This aspect was quite different from the agricultural program, since farmworkers had little chance to do anything semiskilled or skilled.)

At this point, the Railroad Retirement Board started a file on the worker that contained personal data and results of the exams. An identification card was then issued that carried the individual's thumbprint. Provisional acceptees were administered the equivalent of a U.S. Army physical exam, conducted by both Mexican and U.S. public health doctors. For a brief time, applicants were given chest X-rays to detect tuberculosis, but this procedure was discontinued when equipment became unavailable.

Representatives of the two governments then explained the terms of employment to the contractee, at which time the contract was signed. The contract was signed in triplicate by the worker, by a War Manpower Commission representative, and by a Mexican labor inspector. The bracero was assigned to a railroad by the WMC office. The U.S. Immigration Service also prepared in triplicate an entry permit card for the worker (which included a picture) and an alien registration form with the worker's fingerprint.[33]

On any one day, 500 to 700 applicants were normally scheduled to be processed, and the procedures required one full day of each applicant's time. The National Stadium in Mexico City, and later recruitment centers in San Luis Potosí and Querétaro, came to resemble assembly lines for labor contracting. The recruiting teams organized by the two governments were formidable and large: about ten officials from each country, plus support staff and railroad representatives.[34]

What sort of individuals applied to work on the railroads? Fortunately, information from the state archive of Querétaro provides some idea of the program's applicants. When the Secretaría de Trabajo y Previsión Social asked state governors to identify potential applicants for the program, Licenciado Agapito Pozo, governor of Querétaro, instructed the *presidentes municipales* in his state to cooperate. The reports they submitted to Pozo provide historically significant information, and although far from a scientific survey of aspirants, the data provide a general preliminary profile of those who wanted to be braceros.

Some of the *informes* (lists) submitted to Governor Pozo were quite detailed, giving names, ages, and frequently occupations and addresses; often applicants were divided into "preferred" and "alternate" lists. The *presidentes* verified that their nominees were indeed qualified—that is, they were residents of Querétaro, were not skilled workers or *ejidatarios,* and were not necessary to the local economy. Collection of these data functioned also as a way of monitoring the movement of workers, both within the state and to the United States through the bracero program. Mexican government communications show the government thought that the demonstrations and bands of workers roaming the streets of Mexico City and San Luis Potosí resulted from a lack of supervision. Pozo was apparently determined to avoid such disruptions in his state; most towns in Querétaro responded with the requested information.

As might be expected, the bulk of the applicants were in their twenties. The average age of those from Ezequiel Montes, for example, was 24, that of another town, 28. The youngest, most inexperienced workers were in their late teens, but they were not numerous. Since employment as a bracero was evidently desirable, perhaps many younger workers did not have enough position in the community to get on the list. Applicants in their thirties were also represented. For example, the median age of the applicants from Municipio Benito Bocanegro was 31, and of San Juan, 38. Although aspirants over 45 were not encouraged to apply, the documents demonstrate that some were recommended for the program.

The lists also indicate occupation and in some instances if the applicants were *propietarios* (homeowners). Although individuals working on *ejidos* were ineligible to apply for either program, homeowners could and did apply. The *presidente municipal* of Tolíman submitted to the governor a list of twenty-five *propietarios* in his jurisdiction that he considered qualified to be braceros, as well as another list of *suplentes* (alternates).

Although one *presidente municipal* listed twenty-five of fifty recommended individuals as unemployed (*desocupado*), the majority of men listed in these *informes* are described as unskilled laborers (*jornalero, obrero, peón,* etc.). However, there were also semiskilled and skilled workers such as plumbers, bakers, muleteers, hunters, carpenters, *pulque* workers, and *comerciantes en pequeño* (owners of small businesses such as taco stands). On average, among the *informes* that indicated occupations, between 70 percent and 75 percent of the workers were unskilled; the remainder were skilled or had their own small businesses. Although none of the lists indicates whether or not they were actually employed at the time of the report, at least the small businessmen were probably self-employed. Unskilled and casual labor was probably seasonally or irregularly employed, depending upon local industry and agriculture. Since the majority of the applicants for the bracero program were from small towns of a few thousand people with small and vulnerable labor markets, it is safe to conclude that local labor supplies were affected by labor recruitment.[35] As the bracero program grew during World War II, it became increasingly difficult to locate eligible workers.

Transportation

The second phase of program operation in Mexico was the orderly, supervised transport of workers to and from the recruitment centers, as well as to the U.S. border. The Railroad Retirement Board team in Mexico was responsible for planning and executing the transportation of braceros,[36] while the War Manpower Commission financed it. The braceros were transported on trains belonging to the Ferrocarriles Nacionales de

México, and their transportation required close collaboration between Mexican railroad officials, the RRB, and the WMC. Obviously, transportation schedules were designed to dovetail with recruitment activities.

While recruitment was still in Mexico City, contracted workers presented themselves at Buena Vista Station; officials checked to see that their papers were in order and that results of their medical tests were satisfactory. The Southern Pacific claims that early in the program it provided the workers with free blankets. The railroads also provided meals to the workers en route through the services of a commissary company and special train equipment.[37]

Perhaps the most serious problems were delays caused by traffic congestion and mismanagement of railcars, which resulted in expensive and unanticipated stopovers. U.S. railroads were anxious to avoid delays, and the Southern Pacific even dispatched coaches on its Mexican branch to transport workers north. In April 1943, the Ferrocarriles Nacionales agreed to help out, estimating that it could move around 7,000 men a month for both phases of the bracero program without straining its facilities.[38] All workers would ride in first-class cars[39] and the U.S. government would subsidize the transport. From 1943 to 1944, the Ferrocarriles Nacionales did in fact transport 5,000–7,000 men a month, both agricultural and railroad braceros. The largest monthly transport occurred in February 1945, when over 8,000 braceros went north.[40]

Railroad braceros were transported north by a total of 173 trains, the first 55 from Mexico City, the next 15 from San Luis Potosí, and the remaining 103 from Querétaro. Before recruitment was suspended in September 1943, about five trains a month were scheduled. After the end of November, when recruitment resumed, about eight trains were dispatched monthly, transporting an average of 850 men per train. Almost 60 percent of all trains delivered the workers to railroad employers in El Paso, the hub that supplied midwestern railroads and southwestern ones with tributary tracks, such as the Santa Fe. Trains also brought railroad braceros to Nogales, where western and northwestern railroads could pick up their workers. Nogales in fact received almost as many workers as El Paso in the first few months of the program. However, when recruitment resumed, braceros mostly passed through El Paso and Laredo. As the program became increasingly national and supplied roads in the East and Northeast, Laredo became the most convenient port of entry.

Contracted braceros were supposed to be supervised constantly once they were recruited. While waiting to go to the United States after signing their contracts, they were under the supervision of recruitment personnel.

En route to the border, the braceros were under the authority of train riders, Railroad Retirement Board employees who were assigned to accompany the workers and oversee their trip. The workers were supposed to be provided with meals—usually box lunches—and other services while in transit. Generally the role of the train riders seems to have been quite routine,[41] but there were instances when circumstances required extraordinary action, such as when workers became ill or incapacitated en route.[42] Workers were allowed to bring personal belongings they would need, and at least some carried a blanket issued in Mexico.[43]

Problems arose in the transport of workers very early in the program. In 1943, reports in the Mexican press claimed that braceros were being transported in boxcars, even though first-class cars had been negotiated, reserved, and paid for.[44] Indeed, the STPS itself, through its labor inspector Mariano Franco, filed formal written complaints about the extensive use of boxcars and overcrowded conditions.[45] The War Manpower Commission had stipulated that it would tolerate boxcars only under very specific and limited circumstances.[46]

Furthermore, delays in recruitment as early as June 1943 caused reserved coaches to stand idle. In fact, on May 1, 1944, the Mexican government canceled the allocation of two trains to the railroad program and reassigned them to the agricultural program, since there were not enough railroad workers ready to leave. Not surprisingly, the WMC in Mexico was quite upset over the incident.[47] Later a memorandum indicated that Ferrocarriles Nacionales had issued instructions without notifying the WMC that if railroad trains remained idle, they would be reassigned to the War Food Administration and the agricultural program.[48] This matter was of serious concern to Ambassador Messersmith, since the U.S. Embassy had participated in difficult negotiations to arrange the collaboration of Ferrocarriles Nacionales.[49]

Program Administration

The railroad program in Mexico was unusual in that it was essentially an international response to a domestic labor shortage, and its administration illustrates how flexible bureaucracy can be in an emergency. Most of the active government offices, especially the U.S. domestically oriented ones in Mexico, were operating far outside their normal jurisdictions.

From the spring until the fall of 1943, the status of the railroad program was ambiguous, its future uncertain and therefore its bureaucracy ad hoc. Evidently many government officials, both Mexican and U.S., did not anticipate that the project would last more than a few months or even recruit more than the first quota of a few thousand railroad workers. Partly because it was not expected to survive, the railroad program was attached to the agricultural program.[50]

The War Manpower Commission was the agency in charge.[51] It appointed Sam Hough as its first representative in Mexico City in May 1943; a regular WMC employee, Hough at first worked out of the U.S. Embassy.[52] Because the Railroad Retirement Board did not have an independent office at this time, its personnel worked out of the Farm Security Administration facilities. Indeed, personnel from both the WMC and RRB almost packed up and returned to the United States in August when an extension of the program was refused.[53] Once the extension was obtained, however, the WMC decided to establish its own office.[54]

The Railroad Retirement Board dispatched two senior officers, Frank Fleener and Harlon Carter, from its headquarters to Mexico early in 1943 to work out details of the agency's involvement and the terms of collaboration with the FSA and the agricultural program.[55] Both remained in Mexico, and Fleener in particular shaped development of the railroad project.[56] That summer they were joined by more RRB personnel: Raymond Lusk, Manfred Mitchell, and Guillermo Walls.[57]

Although it had been informally agreed earlier in Washington that the RRB in Mexico would be accountable to the WMC, formal instructions were issued to that effect.[58] Although the RRB and the WMC's normal functions had little to do with one another, collaboration in the bracero program created joint interests. Although located in separate offices, the RRB was dependent on the WMC for policy decisions, supplies, and authorizations, including transmitting its communications to the Mexican government[59] and even to its own offices in the United States.[60] While railroad recruitment remained in Mexico City and it was connected with the agricultural program, its status as an extension of the original program persisted.

Relocation of recruitment to San Luis Potosí expanded the program's administration in Mexico. Sam Hough and the WMC recruitment team moved their equipment and activities to that city,[61] while the agency maintained its principal office in Mexico City and dispatched an additional officer, "head of Commission operations," to supervise it. The appointment of Churchill Murray to this post reflects the increasing interest that the WMC was taking in its activities in Mexico. Murray was no ordinary government employee. Although a U.S. citizen, he was born in Mexico City and spent his early childhood there. His family was deeply involved in philanthropic affairs in Mexico, and his father established the YMCA in Mexico. Murray remained with the program for its duration.[62]

In September 1944, the WMC and RRB decided that a shared central office in Mexico City would better serve the interests of the railroad program;[63] this shared facility, staffed by both agencies' highest-placed officials in Mexico, established the program's autonomy. About fifty Mexican nationals were hired to perform much of the routine clerical work. Responsibility for their supervision and financing was split; the WMC paid the rent and the RRB furnished the office,[64] which was about 550 square feet. The office served about fifty repatriated railroad braceros daily who inquired about benefits, back pay, savings accounts, and other unresolved problems.[65]

Not surprisingly, the close collaboration of two normally domestic government agencies in an international context created extraordinary circumstances and unanticipated difficulties. Another source of difficulties was the strict control that the WMC and RRB in the United States tried to maintain over their personnel in Mexico. For instance, in monitoring its Mexico operations, the RRB followed its customary procedures, which could not accommodate the unusual circumstances.[66] An example: even though the two agencies operated from the same office, the RRB people were required to channel communications for WMC colleagues in Mexico through RRB headquarters in Chicago and WMC offices in Washington. This was an absurd waste of time and eventually the RRB modified its procedures.[67]

For its part, the WMC tried to control its agency's activities by maintaining recruitment as a centralized operation in Mexico City. The Foreign Labor Section in Washington, D.C. (in charge of all foreign labor in the United States), tried unsuccessfully to override the decentralization of recruitment and to bring it back to Mexico City, allegedly to simplify the program. Although RRB personnel stopped the move, WMC policymakers neither understood the motives for decentralizing recruitment nor the consequences of reinstituting the old procedures. The RRB claimed with justification that such an action would provoke more expenses and more problems for both governments and would offend the Mexican government.[68]

The railroads were also active participants in recruitment in Mexico City, at first through the Association of American Railroads and later through the Western Association of Railway Executives. Both were industry organizations that represented the interests of railroad management. Representatives from these organizations facilitated the railroads' subsidy of recruitment ($7.50 per recruit), arranged transportation of workers, and were charged "to look after the smooth functioning of the program." WARE also maintained detailed records and later assigned personnel to the border to oversee transportation north and south. The Southern Pacific even assigned some of its personnel who had been their representatives in Mexico to work for WARE for the duration of the program.[69]

Railroads served by the program seem to have been satisfied with the administration of the program in Mexico. Railroad representatives assigned to the program in Mexico—for example, L. J. Benson of the Chicago, Milwaukee, St. Paul and Pacific—particularly acknowledged the RRB's contribution and frequently expressed their company's satisfaction to the WMC. Benson even commended some individual RRB employees.[70] Although in part these expressions of gratitude undoubtedly were attempts to prolong the program after the war, there is sufficient documentation to conclude that they were also responses to the RRB's efforts to supply the industry with workers. The agency's legal responsibilities normally concerned railroad employees, not management; the circumstances of the program altered its obligations.

Daily Routine

As the responsible agency, mostly on an ad hoc basis, the WMC developed standard routines and policies governing the project for its own activities as well as for those of the agencies with which it contracted, such as the RRB and the U.S. Public Health Service.[71]

Because of the international character of the program, the WMC was also responsible for various quasi-diplomatic functions. After the negotiations to establish the railroad program had been completed, the responsibility and participation of U.S. Embassy personnel was reduced to a minimum; hence the WMC performed what logically would have been embassy duties. WMC people routinely met with representatives of several Mexican *secretarías* (secretariats), and the RRB looked to the WMC to act as its intermediary in its dealings with Mexican officials. Murray, in fact, deliberately cultivated working relationships with the Secretaría de Relaciones Exteriores, the Secretaría de Trabajo y Previsión Social, the Secretaría de Gobernación, and the Ferrocarriles Nacionales. Indeed, on one occasion the State Department explicitly told the STPS to deal directly with Murray regarding railroad braceros.[72] Out of necessity and to maintain good relations, the WMC forwarded to the Mexican government data sent by U.S. agencies about the status of the *ferrocarrileros* (railroad workers). The WMC also channeled data and correspondence submitted to it by the Mexican government to the appropriate U.S. offices. For example, the STPS asked the WMC to notify the Immigration Service that a theft of some RRB identification cards had occurred, which greatly complicated Immigration Service procedures at the border.[73] Likewise, Paula Alegría of the STPS's Oficina Investigadora de la Situación de Mujeres y Menores Trabajadores (Investigating Office of Working Women and Minors) periodically contacted Murray on behalf of braceros' dependents to inquire about the workers' status in the United States.[74]

Contractually, the RRB was under the supervision of the WMC and was legally accountable for the recruitment and transportation of workers. An important RRB function was to maintain a large part of the program's records, including separate files for each recruit.[75] The RRB was also the authorized purchasing agent in Mexico for the Immigration Service and the Public Health Service,[76] as well as for the WMC.

A key aspect of the RRB's collaboration with the WMC was its financial function. The WMC did not handle money, accounts, purchasing, or financial vouchers; all financial administration was delegated entirely to the RRB. Selected RRB personnel in Mexico City, and later in the field, were designated agent-cashiers, which enabled them to function as financial officers. The WMC reimbursed the RRB from a President's Emergency Fund allocation.[77] That executive grant expired June 30, 1944, and it appeared that the WMC would no longer be able to finance the railroad bracero program.[78] It will be recalled that at a much earlier point the Department of Agriculture had brought the question of funding the agricultural program to Congress and after some haggling arrived at a funding agreement that gave the United States Department of Agriculture virtually independent moneys. However, no evidence has appeared that such a strategy was ever seriously entertained for the railroad program by either the WMC or the RRB. The WMC did find some unassigned funds in its regular budget with which it continued to reimburse the RRB for its services, and in fact signed a formal agreement to that effect.[79]

The RRB in Mexico also discharged its normal domestic obligation of processing workers' benefits. In February 1944, the RRB office in Mexico City began accepting applications for benefits from repatriated braceros.[80] Although their work time in the United States had been short, deductions had been taken from their pay for RRB benefits and retirement funds (in spite of protests from the Mexican government), which technically entitled them to certain benefits. RRB employees in Mexico were not authorized to actually process the applications, only to accept them, after which the applications were forwarded to RRB headquarters in Chicago.[81]

Auxiliary U.S. Agencies in Mexico

The Immigration Service, which sent inspectors to Mexico to help recruit, did not establish its own office but assigned agents to the program's recruitment staff.[82] Since the contracts specified the workers would maintain their status as temporary contract workers, specific immigration forms were required to process them. These agents provided the forms, and also kept immigration authorities at the border apprised of the movement of railroad workers north. About six inspectors were attached to the recruitment team at any time,[83] and moved with the staff to San Luis Potosí[84] and later to Querétaro. The agricultural program subsidized all Immigration Service activities until railroad recruitment became autonomous; at that time the WMC assumed their expenses.[85]

Prospective braceros' physical exams were the responsibility of the U.S. Public Health Service, which first dispatched physicians to Mexico in May 1943. Public Health doctors were relocated to Mexico from posts in the United States such as Louisiana[86] and Missouri.[87] Using standards established by the U.S. military, Public Health doctors collaborated with Mexican colleagues to determine if the applicants were physically eligible to be braceros. The recruits were required to be in good general health and not be carriers of any infectious diseases such as tuberculosis.[88]

The Public Health Service both encountered and provoked serious difficulties in Mexico. One difficulty related to courtesy. On a couple occasions, U.S. doctors were observed being rude to the applicants they were examining, which prompted Mexican officials to request their release.[89] Another problem arose concerning tuberculosis testing. When the railroad recruitment office left Mexico City for San Luis Potosí, U.S. physicians wanted to move the X-ray equipment to detect tuberculosis with them, but the WMC insisted that X rays be replaced with manual exams to reduce costs.[90] The WMC arranged to have a quiet, isolated room readied for the doctors' chest exams. However, in 1945 the Florida East Coast Railway filed a complaint that it was assigned a bracero with an active case of tuberculosis. Dr. Van Beeck, who was in charge of the team of U.S. physicians, responded that without proper equipment it was impossible to consistently diagnose tuberculosis. Charles Holler of the RRB finally agreed to move the equipment, but Murray of the WMC was adamant about not spending money for medical equipment for tuberculosis examinations.[91]

The agricultural program subsidized Public Health Service expenses until railroad recruitment became independent.[92] Thereafter, the WMC covered Public Health Service costs.[93] At the very end, the State Department paid the bills.[94]

The U.S. Embassy in Mexico City kept a watchful eye on the railroad program throughout the war, although it ceased active participation after its negotiations to initiate the program. The embassy did act as intermediary for U.S. agencies operating in Mexico; government personnel, for example, used the courier service to send supplies and correspondence.[95] Also Ambassador Messersmith on occasion approached the Mexican government, usually President Ávila Camacho, when problems could not otherwise be solved.[96]

Actually U.S. consulates throughout Mexico played a more active role. Their involvement began with the repatriation of the first workers; braceros who left the United States without their final paycheck could claim it at their local consulate. U.S. consulates also served as contacts to distribute accumulated savings accounts, and were equipped to verify repatriation for the railroads and the Immigration Service in cases where railroad braceros returned to Mexico on their own.[97]

The Mexican Government

The railroad bracero program as implemented during World War II could not have been executed without the collaboration of the Mexican government. Indeed, Mexican government actions and policies regarding this phase of the program are of particular significance, since it is the only time Mexico was able to bargain with the United States on basically equal terms. Mexican government agencies—domestic and international, together and separately—monitored and administered the project in collaboration with U.S. agencies.

The Secretaría de Relaciones Exteriores conducted the original negotiations, as well as additional discussions, and often forwarded to the U.S. Embassy information on returning braceros that it received from other Mexican government ministries. Like its counterpart in the United States, after the first negotiations the office maintained a low profile. At times the SRE formally met with U.S. representatives to discuss unusual or difficult problems, such as the Santa Fe incident (see chapter 11). It often served as a conduit for other government bodies; when quotas were revised upward, the SRE engaged in formal communication with the U.S. Embassy on behalf of the Secretaría de Trabajo y Previsión Social.[98]

As the government entity accountable for the welfare of Mexican workers, the Secretaría de Trabajo y Previsión Social logically formed an integral component of railroad program administration. Indeed, the STPS was the most prominent Mexican government agency involved with the program; it participated from the beginning and established most of Mexico's policy regarding the program. The *oficial mayor* (vice secretary) of the STPS, Luis Padilla Nervo, was one of three Mexican representatives in the original railroad program negotiations.[99]

The STPS assigned labor inspectors to the recruitment team. The inspectors issued selection cards for entry into recruitment, conducted preliminary and final interviews with all applicants, determined worker eligibility, and signed contracts on behalf of the Mexican government. The STPS also officially commissioned inspectors for the program; the first was Pablo Ruiz de la Peña, replaced in June 1943 by Lugán Piñeda.[100]

As the most prominent Mexican office in determining policy, the STPS appears to have had the power of veto—the department threatened and almost succeeded in suspending recruitment of railroad workers in December 1943, due to an alleged lack of cooperation from U.S. personnel.[101] It was, moreover, the STPS that ruled in March 1944 that recruitment would be decentralized. Indeed, a committee within the STPS developed the field recruitment schedules.[102]

In response to a deluge of complaints about living and working conditions for railroad braceros, the STPS approached the U.S. government in mid 1944 about beefing up the corps of Mexican labor inspectors assigned to visit U.S. agricultural camps[103] in order to investigate these reports.[104] Some U.S. officials were reluctant to approve more inspectors. Yet, still without formal approval from the U.S. government, the STPS informed the War Manpower Commission in August 1944 that it was sending ten additional labor inspectors to observe the working conditions of railroad braceros. Left with little choice, the WMC endorsed the STPS's actions and later subsidized the inspectors.[105]

The STPS routinely forwarded information to the U.S. government from its offices in Mexico City. Not only did the office receive reports from its labor inspectors in the United States, the Secretaría de Relaciones Exteriores, and the Presidencia (presidency), but railroad braceros frequently contacted the STPS directly. For example, in September 1943 the STPS presented copies of correspondence written by braceros detailing substandard conditions of employment, naming places and names. The information directly contradicted what U.S. personnel had been representing as the living and working conditions of braceros.[106] On another occasion, Padilla Nervo forced a discussion with a reluctant U.S. delegation about a dual-wage structure in the Southwest, which violated the spirit of the international agreement.[107] Moreover, Padilla Nervo alluded to the ambivalent feelings of organized labor in both countries about the administered migration of railroad workers.[108]

Jurisdiction over immigration matters fell to the Secretaría de Gobernación, since its Departamento de Migración was responsible for regulating international migration, developing policy for such, and guarding Mexico's borders. The Departamento de Migración, as part of Gobernación, was long responsible for Mexican immigration policy. Gobernación regulated and monitored movements of people and therefore participated in the bracero programs. Luis Cortines, *oficial mayor* of Gobernación, represented his agency in the preliminary negotiations. Gobernación's primary role was to provide data and appropriate administrative support for the STPS.[109]

Since the braceros as Mexican citizens were obligated to register their labor contracts with Mexican immigration authorities, the Departamento de Migración assigned representatives to the recruitment teams to process the appropriate government forms.[110] Likewise, U.S. citizens assigned to the program in Mexico had to register as nonimmigrant residents with the Departamento de Migración.[111]

The Secretaría de Gobernación's responsibilities in Mexican national life are much broader than its U.S. counterpart (Department of the Interior). Immigration policy is but a small part of Gobernación's role. Other functions oversee the country's political stability and some social programs. Therefore, Gobernación assigned representatives to many aspects of the program, not just from the Departamento de Migración, but also from higher levels.[112]

Of particular interest to the Departamento de Migración was current information about the number of braceros working in the United States at a given time; revising quotas and replacing workers were contingent upon such data. However, since a significant number of braceros abandoned their jobs in the United States for other employment or to return to Mexico on their own, it was difficult for anyone to have accurate statistics. Therefore the office had to depend on RRB data to advise the STPS about further recruitment. Moreover, at that time Mexican law required only that citizens report repatriation, not emigration. Consequently it became standard procedure for the War Manpower Commission to forward current statistical information submitted by the Railroad Retirement Board to the Departamento de Migración.[113] Gobernación received from the Departamento de Migración copies of the transportation reports filed by RRB train riders, since Mexican immigration inspectors were required to sign the forms.[114]

Reports of increased undocumented Mexican migration to the United States abounded after the implementation of the bracero program, contrary to the intentions of the negotiators. Gobernación attributed the increase to higher demands in the United States for workers, as well as to the bracero program itself, which inadvertently publicized the availability of jobs. Gobernación considered the undocumented migration contrary to the letter and spirit of the bracero program and protested to the United States.[115] The issue eventually became so problematic that the Mexican government insisted on high-level binational discussions in Mexico City in May and June 1944. Commissioner Earl Harrison of the Immigration Service and staff traveled to Mexico along with representatives from the State Department to discuss the problem with the Secretaría de Relaciones Exteriores and the Secretaría de Gobernación. At the talks all agreed that stricter vigilance of the border was needed, and the discussions produced an agreement about concrete measures each country would take to tighten the border.[116]

As a government-owned company and the largest railroad company in Mexico, Ferrocarriles Nacionales de México was the logical choice to transport railroad braceros north to the border. The U.S. government was interested in the company anyway, since it also shipped defense-related raw materials to the United States. Indeed, as part of its broader strategy toward Mexico, the United States subsidized a rehabilitation project under the direction of longtime railroadman Oliver Stevens to bring the tracks and other facilities of Ferrocarriles Nacionales up to standard. The U.S. Railway Mission, under the authority of the Office of Inter-American Affairs (Nelson Rockefeller, director), operated out of Mexico City during most of World War II. The mission worked closely with the administration of Ferrocarriles Nacionales to develop a strategy of improving the company's efficiency and capacity. However, many in Mexico roundly criticized Stevens and others in the mission for trying to dominate Ferrocarriles Nacionales.[117]

In his capacity as director of the U.S. Railway Mission, Stevens advocated transporting all braceros to the United States on Ferrocarriles Nacionales to bolster its importance for the war effort. The Southern

Pacific Railroad had proposed sending trains from the United States to bring braceros, in order to save time.[118] The State Department wanted to transport railroad braceros on Ferrocarriles Nacionales and agricultural braceros on U.S. trains,[119] but in the end all braceros traveled on the Mexican railroad.

In 1943, Ferrocarriles Nacionales formally committed itself to transport 12,000 braceros a month, 5,000 of them railroad braceros.[120] Even though Ferrocarriles Nacionales did draw train schedules compatible with both segments of the bracero programs, delays in recruitment activities and occasional shortages caused Ferrocarriles to modify its schedule or even cancel trips.[121]

Ferrocarriles Nacionales used its office in New York City to coordinate its activities related to the bracero program. Ferrocarriles Nacionales employees found it easier to maintain communication with the War Manpower Commission, which financed the braceros' transportation, and the Railroad Retirement Board, which handled the payments, from New York. It was also more efficient to operate accounts in U.S. dollars in New York.[122]

10

Operations in the United States

The program in the United States assumed a form much less centralized and structured than its counterpart in Mexico. Nothing in the original program negotiations specified the role that either government would play in the U.S. phase of the program. Legally, in fact, the bonds that the railroads posted made the railroad braceros their responsibility once delivered to them. Nonetheless, government agencies from both countries monitored the railroads and the workers. Some personnel from both governments were vigilant and occasionally intervened when circumstances warranted it.

Departure Bonds

Once under the supervision of the railroads, the braceros and their welfare were the railroads' responsibility. Both governments wanted formal guarantees from each other and from the employers that the workers would retain their status as unskilled, temporary contract workers while employed as railroad braceros.[1] Indeed, the railroads posted bonds with the Immigration Service for this purpose. The only exceptions were those instances in which a government was the employer, as was the U.S. government, at least technically, in the agricultural program.[2]

The Contract of Employment and Transportation and the Individual Work Agreement were ambiguous with respect to the employer; it could have been the federal government.[3] However, the U.S. government decided (probably at the recommendation of the Immigration Service) to require the railroads to post $500 departure bonds for each bracero. That clarified the issue and clearly demonstrated that the railroads were indeed the legal employers. If a railroad violated the terms of a bond by altering the bracero's status in any way, the railroad would forfeit the bond and pay the penalty of $500 per worker.

The Immigration Service administered and monitored the bonds. Since the quantity of bonds involved was so large and the bonds were something of a novelty for the agency, it developed forms and procedures especially for them. Although the railroads actually bought the bonds from private insurance companies, the Immigration Service had to clear the bonds for each requested bracero before recruitment for any railroad could begin in Mexico.[4] The Southern Pacific, the Santa Fe, and the Western Pacific in May 1943 were the first three railroads to have their bonds processed—in the amount of $30,000 for the Western Pacific, $44,000 for the Santa Fe, and $70,000 for the Southern Pacific.[5] Each of the thirty railroads subsequently participating in the bracero program also had to post bonds and have them cleared by the Immigration Service before their quota of workers was hired. Each time an individual railroad arranged a new quota or an increase in its allotment of braceros, additional bonds were processed.

Any modification of the conditions specified in the bonds were considered a breach of contract and caused the railroad to forfeit the bond. For example, instances of railroad braceros deserting their railroad jobs and taking other employment on their own initiative were clear violations of their immigration status. If the railroads did not locate the workers and return them to their jobs within a specified time period, they forfeited the bonds they had posted for the workers. Likewise, in the course of the program, railroad management sought to transfer braceros to other unskilled and semiskilled job classifications. Early in the program, such actions were also considered violations of the bonds.[6]

The Contracts

Since the administration of the railroad program in the United States fell mostly to the railroads, of necessity the contracts formed a legal basis for its operation. They sketched the legal parameters of the program, especially for nongovernment participants, that is, the railroads and the workers. The contracts that governed the program provided really only a general context for its implementation in the United States.

The Individual Work Agreement was signed at the time of recruitment by a representative of the War Manpower Commission, an agent representing the railroads, and by the worker. The contract recognized the international agreement as its legal precedent. While the document acknowledged the responsibilities of the three entities—the worker, the U.S. government, and the railroad—the text detailed only the obligations of the worker. Few specific data were provided about either the employer or the government. The rights of the Mexican government to directly oversee a Mexican national working on the railroads were virtually ignored.

For its part, the U.S. government guaranteed that the bracero would be transported safely to his work site and back to Mexico after his employment was terminated. The railroad bracero was also guaranteed legal admission into, and departure from, the United States within the bounds of immigration law. The government also guaranteed that the railroad bracero would not be subject to U.S. military service. The government promised assistance in event of emergency health and welfare problems, and pledged to the Mexican government that the contracting railroad would be required to fulfill its contractual obligations.

As a party to the contract, the railroad agreed to employ the worker within contractual guidelines and to reimburse the federal government for expenses incurred in any case where the railroad defaulted on a contract. The railroad agreed to assume responsibility for the bracero when he arrived, and to provide transportation for the worker and his personal belongings to the assigned place of employment, as well as subsistence en route. The railroad also agreed to notify the government should the worker be separated from his job or not work for any reason for seven consecutive days, and to maintain the plethora of detailed records required by the WMC.

By signing the Contract of Employment and Transportation, the worker promised to travel under the jurisdiction of the bracero program to his place of employment in the United States, and to perform his job as directed by his employer. The section of the contract entitled "Terms and Conditions of Employment" detailed the circumstances of his employment. He was to be employed only in nonagricultural work; his wages were to be the same as those paid to U.S. workers "for the same work in the same place of employment," and the railroad was obligated to inform him in detail of the wages and working conditions to which he was entitled. Deductions could not be made that would effectively lower his check below prevailing wages, but a 10 percent deduction was authorized that would be sent to Mexico and deposited in a savings account. The federal government and the employer guaranteed the worker sanitary and medical facilities identical to those available for domestic workers. The normal term of employment was six months. The worker would not be subject to discrimination and would have to perform the tasks assigned him. The worker was guaranteed a certain amount of work and would receive the same pay increases that other railroad workers did. The contract also recognized that the worker had the right to join with other workers and to file grievances with the WMC. Provisions for termination of employment were also included.

Each contracted worker also signed an Individual Work Agreement, which summarized most of the points in the Contract of Employment and Transportation discussed above. More important, it acknowledged the relationship between the worker and the U.S. government and recognized obligations involved therein. A representative of the Mexican government also had to approve and sign the Individual Work Agreement.

The evolution of the program clearly shows that the framework of contracts developed by the negotiators was not adequate. The contracts' ambiguities soon caused serious problems, some enough so as to threaten the program. The questions of job transfers, of quotas, and of the number of workers that needed to be in the United States or in transit at a given time to satisfy quotas all required amended contracts. Moreover, a bitter dispute about a wage differential that involved Santa Fe employees in California led to the establishment of an international ad hoc commission. This matter will be discussed in chapter 11. Despite the failings of the contracts, however, they formed a legal infrastructure for the program that laid the basis for bilateral discussions when modifications were required.

Living and Working Conditions, Wages and Benefits

Government oversight of the program in the United States was particularly concerned with workers' living and working conditions, since direct daily supervision was carried out by the railroads rather than the government. That many railroads customarily furnished their track workers, at least seasonal ones, with living quarters as a normal condition of employment supported their requests for workers from Mexico,[7] but the truth is that much of the housing was extremely substandard. On several occasions, the Mexican negotiators pointedly stipulated that railroad braceros be provided with housing equivalent to or better than that of domestic workers. They wanted to be sure that all facets of the braceros' experience would be protected. Since many domestic track workers, especially seasonal ones, were provided with only minimal housing, the Mexican government's insistence that railroad braceros be provided with housing equivalent to that of the domestic workers was meaningless.

The braceros were specifically guaranteed adequate and fair compensation for their labor, defined as the prevailing wage, that is, the wage received by other workers performing the same work. To avoid a situation in which railroad wages were arbitrarily fixed by the employers, the agricultural agreement was modified for the railroad program to include a clause guaranteeing Mexican workers the prevailing wage in their locale.[8] While the railroad industry and its labor structure were highly diversified, railroad wages were largely determined by collective bargaining, since most employees were covered by a contract. Even though the Mexican railroad workers were temporary and at least theoretically removed from many developments in the industry, they were affected by union activities during their stay in the United States.[9] For the period of World War II, wages negotiated by railroad brotherhoods affected both U.S. workers and Mexican braceros.[10] Even nonunion laborers working for railroad contractors received at least the wages reached by collective bargaining.

In the middle of the bracero program, after a struggle that long antedated the program, the railroad brotherhoods managed to get an industry-wide wage increase. Effective at the beginning of 1944, the minimum wage for all railroad workers was 46 cents an hour, higher than that for agricultural workers (30 cents hourly), although agricultural pay during the war was sometimes higher when calculated on a piece-rate basis.[11]

Payroll amounts generated by the program accumulated quickly; by the end of November 1943, barely seven months after its implementation, $9 million had already been distributed in compensation.[12] Approximately 10 percent of that was forwarded by the WMC to Mexico in the form of bank deposits. An additional undetermined amount was sent by the braceros to their families.

Like those of domestic workers, braceros' paychecks were subject to deductions. Unfortunately, inadequate record keeping makes it difficult to generalize,[13] but some comments are in order. Deductions were made, it seems, for the Victory tax (paid by all U.S. workers except those in agriculture) and for the Railroad Retirement Board, although, as already stated, the program negotiators had informally agreed that the RRB money would be returned to Mexico.[14] Braceros did not pay the 30 percent withholding tax.[15] Since technically braceros were eligible for unemployment benefits, at least some railroads paid federal unemployment tax on their behalf.[16] Moreover, many railroads deducted for room and board. The Southern Pacific, for example, charged $1.29 a day, quite a large amount.[17] The Southern Pacific also deducted for providing shoes and appropriate clothing during transport. This was done through a commissary company at train stops in Los Angeles and Sacramento.[18]

Ten percent of the workers' pay was deducted and deposited in a savings account in the workers' names, a procedure that was stipulated in the international agreement. The agreement specified that the savings were to be pooled in U.S. banks, forwarded in aggregate amounts to Mexico, and distributed to repatriated braceros, presumably to provide them with an incentive to return to Mexico. Specific financial responsibility was left unclear in the agreement, but in the end the War Manpower Commission assumed control while the savings were still in the United States.[19]

Arthur Motley, a WMC bureau chief in Washington, D.C., directed early in the program that accumulated savings be deposited in designated San Francisco and Chicago banks, then forwarded to the Banco de México,[20] usually on a monthly basis. The savings were then transferred to the Banco de Ahorro, which distributed them directly to the repatriated braceros.[21]

The savings accounts occasioned even more paperwork. The WMC in the United States compiled detailed lists of repatriated braceros, along with their savings account numbers, and the number of deposits.[22] These lists were sent to the U.S. Embassy in Mexico to be forwarded to the Secretaría de Trabajo y Previsión Social,[23] for they formed the basis for verifying that the workers received their savings. Having returned to Mexico, the ex-braceros went to the nearest branch of the Banco de Ahorro, where they had to present valid identification.

The WMC had established early in 1943 that all workers in the United States, regardless of occupation or employment status, would receive time and a half for work over eight hours in any day.[24] Until this rule was established, the railroads had customarily paid overtime after eight hours only to regular track workers; seasonal track workers (the classification into which many braceros fell) had received overtime only after ten hours.[25] As a consequence of the WMC order, all railroad braceros were paid time and a half after eight hours. The situation was complicated by a request from the STPS that all braceros be given the opportunity to work ten hours a day; the result was that they could receive time and a half on a daily basis.[26]

The issues of vacation benefits and leaves of absence for railroad braceros were not clear-cut. For personal and work-related reasons, some braceros took unpaid leaves of absence to go to Mexico, often returning to their job shortly thereafter. The Southern Pacific and the Santa Fe both insisted that braceros were not entitled to leaves of absence and vacations, as were domestic workers, and that they were obligated to complete their contract without hiatus. WMC personnel, however, felt that railroad braceros were entitled to some flexibility and the same vacation benefits, since these benefits were usually included in collective bargaining agreements.[27] For a while, it became tacit program policy that braceros would automatically receive five days of paid vacation upon the expiration of their contracts as an incentive for them to renew their employment.[28] Vacations and leaves of absence, nonetheless, remained issues. As late as 1946, the Mexican government was urging Churchill Murray and the WMC to discuss the issue with the Southern Pacific and the Santa Fe.[29]

At the beginning of the program, the Southern Pacific offered unpaid leaves of absence of a month to braceros upon the completion of their contracts as an incentive for them to renew their contracts. The arrangement proved unsatisfactory; most who accepted the leaves of absence did not return. Later in the program, the Southern Pacific allowed short trips within the United States but no long passes.[30]

The disagreement over vacations and unpaid leaves of absence for railroad braceros reflects the conflicts inherent in an international temporary contract labor program. The railroads did not want to extend either leaves of absence or vacations to the braceros, but recognized that to keep them they might have to make some concessions. Normally, seasonal and regular track workers would not take unpaid leaves of absence but were entitled to limited vacation days. The WMC argued that the unique circumstances of the braceros and the need for track workers justified extending planned paid and unpaid absences for the Mexican workers.

Living conditions in the railroad camps became another controversial issue. Government guidelines were distributed to the railroads delineating the minimum acceptable conditions for the camps. In a circular entitled "Hints on the Employment of Mexican Laborers," the Railroad Retirement Board tried to impress upon railroad management the importance of clean, well-equipped camps with the provision for warm clothing in cold weather, adequate food, and other amenities for the braceros' welfare. The railroads were to make sure that the workers enjoyed easy access to Catholic churches, and arrangements were to be made for them to celebrate Mexican holidays. Interaction with local communities was to be encouraged through cultural events and English classes. The RRB recommended that the railroads appoint some Spanish-speaking supervisors to the bracero program.[31]

The Southern Pacific acknowledged that it was responsible for providing decent living conditions for the braceros, and allegedly distributed instructions to those in charge to upgrade living conditions. Living quarters were to have been equipped with amenities such as wood-burning stoves, tables, chairs, a reliable water supply, and tin lamps. The Southern Pacific claims that representatives from both governments inspected its camps, and that they filed only minor complaints about living conditions. Camp maintenance initially fell to the Southern Pacific braceros themselves, but later the company contracted the Threlkeld Company for this assignment.[32]

The quality of living conditions appears to have varied widely from railroad to railroad[33] and from region to region, with periodical reports reaching Mexico of unhealthy, substandard conditions in the camps. While some workers were housed in permanent buildings, others were forced to live in makeshift structures. Since technically the railroads were responsible for camp conditions, government supervision was minimal. In fact when the Mexican government realized in July 1943 that camp inspection was essentially being left to the railroads, and was not effective, it threatened to suspend the program unless Mexican inspectors were granted access to them.[34]

Mexican inspectors already in the United States for the agricultural program received orders to include railroad housing in their schedules, which they did, although their visits were irregular. Not until March 1944 did the inspectors of the agricultural program routinely visit railroad camps and report their findings to the RRB.[35] Erasmo Gamboa, however, states that these inspectors were not taken seriously by U.S. government agencies because, especially at the local and regional levels, the input of Mexican officials was not important. Besides, the War Food Administration associated with the agricultural program was able to control the movements and activities of the agricultural inspectors, thereby rendering them ineffective. Moreover, many inspectors may not have been qualified, being political appointees looking for extended vacations in the United States.[36]

Aside from the fact that the War Manpower Commission was not convinced that its and the railroads' collaborators were failing in their attempts to monitor the railroad camps, the WMC did not have funds to subsidize additional labor inspectors from Mexico. But complaints filed by repatriated and active railroad braceros with Mexican consulates and other Mexican government officials pressured the U.S. government to take the railroad camps more seriously. Ambassador George Messersmith observed officially in August 1944 that the survival of the railroad program was probably contingent on the financing of ten additional inspectors attached specifically to the railroad program.[37] The Secretaría de

Trabajo y Previsión Social went ahead and appointed ten additional labor inspectors for the railroad bracero program without authorization from anyone.[38] The new inspectors were assigned to RRB regional offices around the United States. They worked out of regional RRB offices and were provided support services and supplies by the RRB. Their tours were scheduled and monitored by the RRB, after which the inspectors filed written reports. The RRB covered all the inspectors' expenses.[39]

Because the braceros were living in an economy completely oriented to an international war, their daily life was affected in ways not anticipated by the program's administration. The purchase and consumption of certain commodities by all U.S. residents was regulated by the federal government; foods such as sugar and meat, as well as goods such as gasoline, were in limited supply due to the extraordinary war demand. Braceros were not exempt from these regulations; however, implementation in their case was somewhat different and in some respects questionable. The Office of Price Administration issued ration books and stamps to all residents to cover regulated products; these were submitted to a vendor when a purchase was made. The WMC assumed liability for the stamps and books issued to the braceros,[40] but the OPA shipped the stamps and books directly to Mexico for distribution at the time of recruitment. The OPA allotted books in appropriate numbers according to recruitment schedules furnished by the railroads. All books and stamps were numbered and assigned to particular workers; the OPA tightly controlled their issuance, since they could be sold for high prices on the black market.[41]

At the end of each month, WMC representatives were required to submit to OPA regional headquarters in San Francisco detailed forms that contained the names of all contracted braceros, their social security numbers, the serial number of each book, and quite important, the names of braceros who did not appear for the trip to the United States. RRB representatives at recruitment headquarters in Mexico were to destroy the ration books and stamps that had not been distributed that month and were required to send forms to the OPA certifying their destruction. Despite these measures, there were instances of illegal sales and use of ration books and stamps issued to the railroad program.[42]

It was unusual for the OPA to surrender distribution of its books to another agency, particularly in an international context. The OPA's only leverage was to force the RRB and WMC to account for every ration book and stamp. Although accountability was a serious issue since the black market was quite active, record keeping early in the bracero program was

sloppy. Because the OPA sent ration books to Mexico for both the agricultural and railroad bracero programs in one shipment, separate inven-
tories were not kept and precise statistics were impossible to provide.[43]
However, later in the program the OPA did issue ration books directly to
the WMC for the railroad program.[44]

In their capacity as legal, albeit temporary, residents of the United
States, braceros were entitled to receive their fair share of ration stamps.
Ration books were originally distributed to individual workers at the
time of recruitment based on the OPA's assumption that the braceros
would purchase their own food and supplies. However, seasonal agricultural and railroad laborers were often provided room and board by com-
missaries contracted by the employers. When bracero program administrators determined that issuing the stamps directly to the employers
would simplify the procedure, they bypassed the rights of the braceros to
receive and use their own stamps. Eventually ration books were forwarded directly to employers from the bracero administration in Mexico,
to be distributed to purveyors of food services for the braceros.[45]

This practice raises some issues about the rights of the workers. During World War II, there were many products an individual could not purchase without OPA stamps. Issuing the stamps directly to employers on
the assumption that they would see to the purchase of food clearly shows
the second-class status of the braceros.

Job Transfers

The occupational structure of the railroad industry in the United States
during World War II was complicated, highly unionized, and regulated
by the Interstate Commerce Commission code of occupations, which
covered everything from unskilled seasonal labor to skilled artisans and
workers. At the time, the U.S. railroad industry and its corresponding
unions were among the most powerful and influential in the country.
The railroad braceros, however, entered the structure at the very lowest
level, on seasonal track maintenance gangs, represented by the Brotherhood of Maintenance of Way Employees. Certainly some in Mexico must
have thought that employment by the railroads might have offered the
possibility of transfers to higher-paying jobs. According to some sources,
the Mexican government was keenly interested in the railroad braceros
being offered opportunities to perform work other than track maintenance, so that they could earn more and obtain potentially valuable
experience. Peter Kirstein even alleges that the Mexican government

suspended recruitment in August 1943 not just because of the Santa Fe incident (see chapter 11) but also due to the lack of occupational mobility. Soon thereafter the Justice Department stated that braceros could be employed in other unskilled and some semiskilled jobs.[46]

Further, from time to time certain individuals in the United States discussed transferring both braceros and nonbraceros to different work spheres to maximize efficiency. For example, the possibility of moving agricultural braceros to the railroads or even industry, or assigning domestic railroad workers to mines so the quota of railroad braceros could be increased, appealed to some. Others tried to assign agricultural and railroad braceros to indoor work during the winter, in an effort to keep them in the United States for assignment to tracks and fields in the warm weather.[47]

In fact, in mid May 1943, the Atchison, Topeka and Santa Fe assigned railroad braceros to ice platform work in Needles, California, after consulting with its attorney, who contacted the Immigration Service. The ATSF attorney contended that the transfer was justified because, although it paid more (60 cents an hour compared to 48½ cents), it was similar to track work and the company had often in the past used track labor for ice platform work; in fact, both track and ice platform workers belonged to the same union.[48] By late May, the Immigration Service determined that using railroad braceros for ice platform work was a breach of the bond.[49] But within a couple weeks, the Immigration Service granted the ATSF emergency authorization to assign railroad braceros to ice platform work in Needles, apparently with the understanding that they could petition and secure a blanket authorization for track workers to work on ice platforms.[50] The labor shortage was so acute in a war-essential industry that the Immigration Service could not continue to put aside the request. State Department records indicate that the Mexican government was concerned about the transfers and wanted them made only with its approval, so it could be sure that the pay was the same as for domestic workers.[51]

By September railroad employers could routinely recruit ice platform workers as well as track workers, and the Railroad Retirement Board was already investigating how to broaden the authorization to include employing braceros, at least for short periods, in shops and roundhouses. The WMC claimed it contacted the railroad unions about such "upgrading" and that they consented to it, provided the railroads respect their contracts. The Mexican government also approved, as did the Board of Immigration Appeals and the Attorney General.[52] The broadened authorization was approved in October.[53]

A Southern Pacific report written by company analysts after the war claims that the railroads themselves had to procure written approval from the union involved to be able to assign railroad braceros to tasks other than track maintenance.[54] They clearly understood that such transfers would not include skilled jobs, but rather "so-called unskilled or semi-skilled positions." The transfers would be made "in a limited manner" and quotas would be specified, although the quotas could be renegotiated. From the Brotherhood of Maintenance of Way Employees, the Southern Pacific obtained authorization for 12,750 braceros to be employed in the following jobs:

ICC Job Classifications
- Truck drivers in track department only
- Maintenance-of-way and structure helpers
- Miscellaneous maintenance-of-way work equipment and welding helpers
- Assistant extra gang foremen
- Assistant section foremen
- Miscellaneous maintenance-of-way laborers—snowshed watchmen
- Wood-preserving workers—timber-treating plants
- Miscellaneous work equipment helpers, tie handlers, and common laborers—treating plants
- Truckers[55]

The railroad also requested authorization from the Brotherhood of Maintenance of Way Employees to recruit section foremen, carpenters, and mechanics from among the Mexican workers but without success, although some braceros apparently had experience as mechanics.

From the System Federation no. 114 of the Railway Employee Department of the American Federation of Labor, the Southern Pacific negotiated a quota of 1,500 braceros for the Motive Power and Car Department in the following categories:

ICC Job Classifications
- Coach cleaners
- Classified laborers—Motive Power and Car Department
- General laborers—Motive Power and Car Department[56]

From the Brotherhood of Railway and Steamship Clerks, Freight Handlers, Express and Station Employees, the Southern Pacific negotiated a quota of 500 braceros for the following classifications:

ICC Job Classifications
- Gang foremen—tie-treating plants and store department
- General laborers—stores and timber-treating plants[57]

Some companies were also interested in transferring the workers among themselves once they were in the United States. The Northern Pacific Terminal Company of Portland, Oregon, requested permission from the War Manpower Commission to employ braceros already under contract to the Southern Pacific; such workers would remain technically the employees of the Southern Pacific but would be assigned to the Terminal Company, which would reimburse the Southern Pacific. The WMC did not approve the arrangement.[58] But later, in April 1944, the RRB agreed to a transfer of about twenty-five to thirty braceros from the New York Central to the Chicago River and Indiana Railroad; they were to work as freight handlers.[59] Some agricultural braceros employed in sugar beet fields in Camp Carson, Colorado, asked to be transferred to the railroads, since the railroads had better working conditions. They were successful—some thirty-five agricultural braceros were hired by the Chicago, Burlington and Quincy Railroad.[60]

In May 1944, the WMC finally requested blanket authorization from the Immigration Service to allow transfers and promotions of braceros to skilled positions as conditions warranted, but it was told that such an order would violate the original legal conditions of the bracero program. Such an action would have to fall under the fourth proviso to section 3 of the Immigration Act of 1917 with respect to skilled workers, which required a public hearing. However, the Immigration Service agreed to certify all workers, unskilled and otherwise, under the procedure already established of WMC certification of a need for labor.[61]

Complaints and Grievances

The right and ability to file grievances about working and, as in the case of many railroad braceros, living conditions is vital to any worker. Negotiators did not neglect to address the problem; for its part, the Mexican government had insisted upon regular inspections by labor inspectors to avoid complaints. But the resolution of complaints was not as efficient as it might have been. The international character of the program that incorporated the Mexican government, the ambivalent attitude of many U.S. bureaucrats (particularly those outside the WMC), and the isolated nature of track work all combined to make processing a complaint difficult.

The War Manpower Commission was the only agency authorized to deal with grievances of workers and railroads, although in practice regional WMC or Railroad Retirement Board offices both dealt with complaints. The WMC was required to investigate and evaluate information related to both sides of a dispute and to make an informed decision based on its findings. Either side could appeal a decision made by WMC management. In the event of an appeal, the Area Management-Labor Committee would organize a panel to consider the case. If this committee could not resolve it, the worker could further appeal to the WMC area director, then the regional director. As long as the worker was prompt in his appeals and continued to work, he could pursue his case.[62]

The Southern Pacific report confirms that the U.S. Employment Service, part of the WMC, held hearings periodically to air complaints and often made the final decisions.[63] Many complaints, however, went unresolved. The WMC did at times request that the RRB investigate complaints lodged by braceros against their employers and "take any necessary action."[64] A graphic example is the Santa Fe incident, treated in detail in the next chapter.

On at least two occasions complaints provoked a strike. Details are sketchy, but soon after the first braceros arrived in Wellsburg, New York, to work for the Erie Railroad Company, the workers went out on strike to protest living and working conditions. Apparently the problems were resolved, for the braceros returned to work the day after the strike, following an investigation by the RRB, a Mexican labor inspector, and the WMC.[65]

Although the Southern Pacific report does not mention it in its report, the dismissal of a couple railroad braceros in its employ in Live Oak, California, in December 1943 provoked a strike. On a more basic level, the workers struck to protest the extremely substandard working conditions. They were transported to and from the work site in trucks without roofs, a violation of the international understanding. The braceros were provided with cold lunches instead of hot ones. They were not provided with sanitary toilets or heat in the old motel where they were staying. One Anastasio B. Cortés was fired when he left work early one day to wash his clothes before dark; twenty-nine braceros refused to work unless Cortés and another bracero that was fired, Manuel M. Rivas, were reinstated. Upon investigation, the RRB discovered that Southern Pacific management considered the workers' demands for better housing to be politically inspired and refused to accede. The RRB also found that other Southern Pacific camps lacked electric lights and decent cesspools.[66]

Many braceros complained about the conditions they experienced en route as well as in the camps. Mexican officials notified the U.S. government of crowded conditions on the trains that transported the workers north.[67] In fact, in August 1943, Manuel Tello of the Secretaría de Relaciones Exteriores stated that his secretariat had received so many complaints about the working and living conditions of the railroad workers that the Mexican government might insist that they be assigned to other industries—a reaction that contrasted starkly with early Mexican satisfaction with the agricultural bracero program.[68] A year later, a U.S. official in Mexico would declare, to the contrary, that organized labor in the United States had complained because the Mexican workers were being treated better than domestic railroad workers.[69]

At times, railroad braceros registered their dissatisfaction with Mexican consuls and U.S. government officials about conditions in the camps, such as the bad food, overcrowded conditions, and lack of access to medical care. A private citizen even wrote to Secretary of State Cordell Hull complaining about the living conditions of the braceros in the employ of the Southern Pacific in Nevada: "[They live in] tents, full of holes, and have only very small tin stoves for heating purposes . . . they have no bathrooms."[70] Others complained about the cold weather in some parts of the United States.[71]

Complaints about the quality of the food were common. In August 1943, several braceros, as well as the cook, became sick from consuming rancid turkey meat in a Southern Pacific camp in Manteca, California.[72] Braceros working for the Boston and Maine Railroad in New York complained that the food was substandard and that they could not eat in the restaurants of their choice.[73] The Mexican consul in Salt Lake City, Utah, complained that the Western Pacific and the Southern Pacific did not provide cooks in the camps to which the braceros were assigned, leaving the men to their own devices.[74]

However, the living conditions at New York Central Railroad's Camp 201, in Ypsilanti, Michigan, seemed to have provoked the most serious problem. The camp was established in August 1943 to house railroad braceros, and at that time the company contracted the Colliani and Harding Company of Chicago as the commissary. Numerous complaints about the scarcity and quality of the food finally forced the New York Central to change commissary companies in April 1945. The workers alleged that they had registered their dissatisfaction on several occasions with the local War Manpower Commission office, which claimed that it investigated and remedied the situation upon each complaint.[75] Finally, in April 1945, apparently exasperated with the conditions, the braceros sent a collective letter to the Mexican consul in Detroit, claiming that their grievances had not been resolved. The braceros even complained that the foremen threatened them with the termination of their contracts if they "demanded their rights."[76] Upon investigation, the WMC Foreign Labor Section in Washington, D.C., alleged that the original complaint had been filed with the Pan American Union, a claim that is not consistent with the agency's own regional office.[77] It is known, however, that Dr. Ernesto Galarza, chief of the Division of Labor and Social Information of the Pan American Union, did visit the camp on at least one occasion. Since the organization of the railroad bracero program essentially neutralized the corresponding unions regarding Mexican workers, Galarza sought to fill the vacuum by using his position in the Pan American Union to improve conditions for braceros. But neither Galarza nor the union enjoyed formal affiliation with the bracero program, so it was difficult for them to insist that the braceros be treated better.

Although subsequently Galarza became recognized more for his numerous publications about the bracero program and Mexican farmworkers than for his advocacy work, during World War II he was one of the few in the United States representing the interests of the braceros. Galarza made representations to the U.S. government on behalf of both agricultural and railroad braceros, insisting that in many respects the program did not serve the workers. Early in the program, he determined through conversations with the Department of State that both agricultural and railroad braceros were free to join U.S. unions. He also insisted that grievance machinery did not exist (an assertion later borne out), and that educational and cultural programs were wanting.[78]

The observations that Galarza recorded about a meeting he had with Joseph McGurk of the Department of State and Robert MacLean of the WMC in September 1944 reveal much about the attitude of at least some bureaucrats toward the program. Basically, Galarza again presented his analysis of the lack of grievance machinery. McGurk and MacLean resisted Galarza's criticisms of the program. Galarza claimed his observations were based on "the testimony of several hundred workers," while the WMC people's lack of contact with the workers made their observations suspect. McGurk remarked that after almost two years of successful operation (in the case of the agricultural program) it was no time to "begin any agitation"—an argument similar to that of the railroad companies. Workers who were assertive and insisted that the conditions of their contracts be respected were labeled agitators and returned to Mexico.[79] Galarza himself was seen as a troublemaker by some administrators in the bracero program, although he did manage to force them to resolve some issues.

Other braceros complained about prejudice, discrimination, and bad treatment. Some grievances were resolved quickly, like the case of Camp 23 in Wellington, Ohio, where the cook not only served unacceptable food but physically beat some of the braceros. The individual was promptly fired and replaced with another cook, to the satisfaction of the workers.[80] Another bracero working in Connecticut complained about a foreman who treated Mexican workers badly, even physically abusing them. In this case, the worker abandoned his job and returned to Mexico on his own.[81]

Discrimination against railroad braceros employed by the Texas and Pacific in Midland, Texas, presented another source of grievances. Although the Mexican government did not want railroad workers assigned to Texas because of the state's long history of discrimination against Mexicans, it finally agreed to let them work there, since the braceros would be under the direct supervision of a railroad.[82] But in September 1943, a group of thirty-eight workers presented a formal complaint to the Secretaría de Relaciones Exteriores, citing problems with prejudice and payroll deductions. Their main complaint was that they were not allowed to eat in some restaurants.[83] The workers also complained of excessive payroll deductions for room and board. The unfair deductions were remedied by the War Manpower Commission forthwith,[84] but the discrimination proved more difficult. The case was forwarded to the Good Neighbor Commission of Texas, a state agency supposedly founded to eliminate prejudice. The executive secretary indicated that "unfortunately, matters involving contractual rights do not fall within the province of the Commission."[85] The president's Fair Employment Practices Commission finally intervened and took action.[86]

The organization of the program gave rise to many complaints about the railroads' failure to pay the braceros the full amount of wages due them. If a worker terminated his employment under his own volition, the railroads at times found it difficult to justify payment of wages. In one instance, a worker assigned to New Mexico obtained permission to visit Ciudad Juárez for the day. However, immigration officials would not let him reenter the United States because he did not have the proper documents; his papers were locked up in the office of the railroad he worked for in New Mexico. By the time he returned to the work site the following night, his things had been removed from the sleeping quarters and his contract terminated. He had to pay Mex$126 to return to Mexico, and asked the railroad to reimburse him.[87] Much correspondence was generated among bureaucrats requesting the status of back pay in instances such as this.

The most common reason for a worker to request back pay was leaving the work site, either to return to Mexico, or to seek other work in the United States. Early in the program, the Railroad Retirement Board requested procedures from the Immigration Service to document desertions and resignations, since quitting the job fell outside the normal operations of the program.[88] Some railroads did refer the termination of contracts to regional managers in an attempt to prevent it.[89] The War Manpower Commission tried to prevent migration within the United States of braceros who left their work sites by expediting their paperwork, which could be done for workers who applied at local WMC offices.[90] Workers already in Mexico often approached the local U.S. consul about their back pay.[91]

As contracts expired, many railroads had problems in fulfilling their contractual obligation to provide return transportation to Mexico for the braceros. In many instances, the braceros returned to Mexico on their own after waiting unsuccessfully for return passage. In 1945, for example, the Baltimore and Ohio told twenty-four workers that a shortage of rolling stock prevented the company from setting a date for their return transport. After waiting for six weeks, the workers returned to Mexico on their own[92] and requested reimbursement for the trip from the WMC there. Among those who were returned to Mexico by the railroads, many complained that, contrary to the agreement, they were not returned to their home ("The Point of Origin") but to the place where they signed their contract—Mexico City, Querétaro, or San Luis Potosí. Obviously such an oversight meant added expenses for a returning bracero.[93]

Sickness and Death

It was inevitable in the railroad bracero program that there would be illnesses, both occupational and otherwise, injuries, and death.

For its part, the Southern Pacific, at least formally, recognized its obligation to provide medical care for the braceros equal to that for domestic workers and claimed that its general hospital facilities were made available to them. The railroad even claimed that it hired Mexican doctors to treat the braceros. Convalescing workers returned to their camps and were assigned light duties until they fully recuperated; during convalescence they paid board to the commissary company but not room. Many work-related injuries were treated in the United States, but more seriously injured workers were returned to Mexico under the custody of the railroad.[94]

During the course of the program, the Southern Pacific reported eighty-nine bracero deaths, of which seventy occurred while the workers were off duty. Of the eighty-nine deaths, eighty-one occurred on the Southern Pacific itself, six on the Northwestern Pacific, and two on the San Diego and Arizona Eastern Railway. Off-duty deaths were attributed to natural causes, train and rail accidents, drowning, suicides, fights, and alcohol. Work-related accidents were caused by train accidents[95] and heat prostration.[96] Upon the death of a bracero, the Southern Pacific notified the Railroad Retirement Board and the appropriate Mexican consul; the consul informed the family in Mexico.[97]

The daily files of the War Manpower Commission for the period October 15 to December 31, 1944, include notification that six railroad braceros became ill and eighteen others died throughout the United States. Twelve different railroads were involved. Many of the deaths and injuries were attributed to work activities, reflecting the occupational hazards of railroad employment. Other causes included car accidents, broken appendages, tuberculosis (two cases), insanity, complications from routine medical procedures, and fights.[98] At least one railroad bracero, Máximo Fuentes González from Tlaxcala, employed by the Santa Fe, was killed by a policeman.[99]

The medical costs for treating a worker injured on the job were to be borne by the railroad; when injuries resulted from off-the-job activities, the question of who would pay became less clear-cut. In one instance, the Mexican consul in San Francisco obtained a U.S. lawyer to represent several workers who had suffered injuries. The Southern Pacific openly stated that it resented the intervention of the consul. Apparently, however, some eastern railroads such as the Pennsylvania customarily consulted local consuls for help in processing such claims. It was the Southern Pacific in California that wanted to control the influence of the consul. Of course, the railroads in general feared any precedent that would open the way for unions to intervene.[100]

Unlike the agricultural program, the railroad program paid for funeral expenses. Respecting an informal agreement made when the program was negotiated, employers paid $130 toward funeral expenses and later $130 to the survivors. At first the bodies were returned to Mexico, but this procedure proved expensive and cumbersome because Mexican laws made it difficult to return the corpses. Subsequently the railroads arranged for a local funeral and burial for deceased braceros, and forwarded the date and place to the family, as well as a copy of the death certificate to the Railroad Retirement Board and the Immigration Service so the bond would be canceled.[101]

Contract Renewals

Around October 1943, as the expiration date of the first group's contracts approached, railroad employers as well as the War Manpower Commission were somewhat preoccupied about maintaining the supply of labor. Because bringing workers from Mexico was expensive, the railroads wanted to renew the contracts of working braceros rather than recruit new ones. Therefore the WMC approached the State Department about discussing contract renewals with the Mexican government.[102] Shortly thereafter, the Secretaría de Relaciones Exteriores approved the request, and the Railroad Retirement Board implemented the necessary procedures.[103]

Obviously a large percentage of contract renewals would have minimized the number of replacements needed to maintain the labor quota and thus reduced administrative costs for all. However, few railroad braceros from the first group opted to renew; most returned to Mexico.[104] Little surprise really—many workers suffered through low pay and unsatisfactory living and working conditions, while the program had not yet sought mechanisms to respond to problems and complaints.

Those braceros who, then and later, opted to renew were gathered into large groups and transported to some location where the employers, regional directors of the RRB and WMC, and later local Mexican consuls met with them to explain once again the terms of employment and to elicit the appropriate signatures. Contract renewals became increasingly popular with railroad braceros as camp inspections and grievance machinery were instituted. Lists of renewing braceros were routinely forwarded to the Immigration Service for their quota revisions.[105] The WMC determined that renewals could be arranged for 180, 120, or even 90 days, as agreed upon by the worker and the employer.[106]

11

Administration in the United States

Because the agreements defining the railroad program failed to specify the limits of government responsibility, administration of the program in the United States never functioned as successfully as it did in Mexico. As in the agricultural program, where farmers had virtually total control of the workers, government supervision of railroad braceros was minimal; de jure and de facto supervision mostly fell to the railroads themselves.[1] Many U.S. government agencies did function in some capacity regarding the braceros or the program, but it would be more appropriate to characterize their activities as collaboration rather than administration. Indeed, many problems concerning substandard living and working conditions and unfair wages can be attributed to a lack of accountability in the program's domestic administration.

The War Manpower Commission's function and jurisdiction as the supervising agency were formalized by Executive Order no. 8802. However, implementation of the program required expertise not found in its staff, hence the involvement of other agencies such as the Railroad Retirement Board and the U.S. Public Health Service. Some like the RRB were heavily involved, while others like the Social Security Administration contributed only tangentially.

Because the WMC was the wartime agency that evaluated all U.S. labor's contribution to the war effort and coordinated its national mobilization,[2] it was able to certify that additional labor was required to assure the railroads' contribution to the war effort.[3] This capacity was pivotal to the legal foundation of the bracero program, and the railroad segment in particular, and one that was consistently articulated. The WMC's periodic declarations about the deteriorating condition of southwestern tracks, and the deleterious effect of this situation on the shipment of soldiers and war materiel, sufficed to justify the recruitment of temporary Mexican workers, at least in the eyes of U.S. bureaucrats. Since the Selective Service was legally empowered to declare transportation essential to the prosecution of the war, its declarations often accompanied those of the WMC and played a crucial role in articulating the need for labor.[4]

The Foreign Labor Section of the WMC developed the policies that guided the bracero program in its entirety, as well as policies for the agricultural program until the Department of Agriculture assumed control. At first little relevant WMC policy existed; the government had never before sponsored foreign labor recruitment, so the agency had no precedents to draw upon in shaping its policies. Further, although the WMC did become the U.S. Employment Service at the end of the war, in 1942 and 1943 it was a wartime agency that functioned on an ad hoc basis; it developed procedures and made policy decisions as circumstances warranted. In this manner, for instance, the WMC determined that railroad braceros could not hold second jobs,[5] that they would be exempted from the Victory tax but not the withholding tax,[6] and that the railroads would have to perform an array of administrative services as participants in the bracero program.[7] Moreover, the WMC assumed liability for the braceros' savings that were deducted from their wages and deposited in U.S. banks.[8] And from the Foreign Labor Section came the directives for all members of the U.S. recruitment team to organize the efficient recruitment of workers in Mexico,[9] and to keep government and railroad collaborators abreast of labor mobilization in the United States.[10]

The WMC determined which government offices would be best suited to assist the project. Although the WMC did not appear to have the legal power to force other government offices to cooperate, participants seem to have respected WMC decisions. Thus the WMC involved other offices in the program, delineated their tasks, and modified their assignments to suit changing needs and situations. The Immigration Service was recruited for an obvious reason: it enforced the Immigration Act of 1917 with respect to the bracero program.[11] The WMC also established the boundaries of Railroad Retirement Board activities and jurisdiction within the program, both in the United States and in Mexico.[12]

The WMC in Washington, D.C., obviously maintained constant communication with U.S. government offices in Mexico and coordinated orders and information necessary for the program. A principal WMC function was periodically approving applications with the Immigration Service for increases in quotas. Each time the Mexican government agreed to raise the quota of workers, the WMC wrote legal briefs to justify the increase.[13]

The WMC was often required to resolve complaints and negotiate other issues. Although many problems and complaints filed by both the workers and the Mexican government were resolved at lower levels of the bureaucracy, some reached WMC headquarters in Washington, D.C. Difficult cases of discrimination against railroad braceros, especially if violence was involved, were considered a serious breach of the international agreement. These became more frequent during the course of the program,[14] and the headquarters was required to consider each case. In 1944, the WMC also negotiated with some difficulty the transfer of railroad braceros from track work to station and roundhouse work, some of it semiskilled, which was contrary to the spirit of the Immigration Act of 1917 and of the international agreement.[15]

A delicate, yet necessary role of the WMC was to act as a conduit among government agencies, and between the government and others (the railroad industry, the public). Normally, government offices operate within stable parameters of authority, but the peculiar circumstances of the bracero program required that the WMC continually redefine and expand its functions. The WMC and the State Department had discussed a bracero program long before binational discussions about recruiting Mexican workers were even anticipated.[16] In its representations to the Mexican government, the State Department depended upon WMC data regarding the utilization of labor in the United States.

Throughout the program, the WMC maintained regular contact with the railroad employers, in particular the western and southwestern companies,[17] apparently because they employed the largest number of braceros. In their function as supervisors, the railroads assumed a semiofficial administrative role, with their duties and responsibilities determined by the WMC. The WMC customarily gave written notification to all railroads of new procedures and policy decisions.[18] In 1945, for example, the WMC circulated a letter warning the railroads that the braceros were not to displace domestic workers, that bracero quotas were temporary, and the responsibility to establish need lay with the railroads.[19]

The WMC also maintained communications with the railroad unions, especially the Brotherhood of Maintenance of Way Employees. At the first rumors of a railroad bracero program in early 1943, T. B. Shoemake, the brotherhood's treasurer, formally protested to the WMC that the railroads were using the federal government to find unskilled track labor when domestic workers were available for decent wages.[20] Although at some point the government began to pursue the program without consideration of the unions' position, the WMC apparently felt it prudent to keep the railroad brotherhoods informed and customarily forwarded copies of new and updated policies.[21]

The Railroad Retirement Board

While policy ultimately rested with the WMC, the Railroad Retirement Board more closely monitored the working braceros than any other government agency. From its headquarters in Chicago, the agency constantly monitored all railroad employees, domestic workers and braceros alike, and regularly updated industry information for the WMC.[22] These reports furnished the information necessary to certify labor shortages in its applications to the Immigration Service for additional workers.[23]

The individual folders that RRB personnel started for each recruit in Mexico were sent to Chicago. These folders were complemented by extensive statistical reports submitted by the railroads detailing wages, hours worked, absences, and savings accounts. The accumulated documentation must have been tremendous; the RRB estimated that eight full-time clerks were needed to handle the paperwork in just the first few months of the program.[24] This information was periodically consolidated and forwarded to the WMC in the form of weekly and quarterly reports.[25]

The RRB also dealt with the railroads, clarifying for them the conditions of the program in matters such as living and working conditions, the transportation of workers, and establishing medical and sanitary facilities. It also supervised much of the recruitment process in Mexico and was responsible for the initial allocation of selection cards.[26]

RRB regional offices, located in strategically important cities such as Dallas and Los Angeles, were assigned certain responsibilities. Regional personnel usually investigated complaints from workers about working or living conditions, wages, and so on, particularly before Mexican labor inspectors included railroad camps in their tours. Upon the receipt of a grievance, regional personnel were sent to investigate and submit a written report.[27] From these reports came suggestions for the resolution of individual cases and, at times, official recommendations for program-wide modifications in matters such as forced terminations of contracts[28] and contract modifications.[29] When Mexican labor inspectors were assigned to the railroad bracero program, regional RRB offices organized their tours, supervised their activities, and provided administrative support. Regional personnel also processed contract renewals, following WMC guidelines,[30] and cooperated with the labor inspectors as well as local Mexican consuls.[31] The regional offices compiled lists of braceros who renewed their contracts and distributed them to the agencies involved as well as to the railroads,[32] to be forwarded eventually to the Mexican government.

The expenses the RRB and other agencies incurred through their bracero program activities were subsidized by the WMC. The WMC paid the RRB, which in turn reimbursed the other agencies for their services, the largest payments going to the War Food Administration, Ferrocarriles Nacionales de Mexico, and the U.S. Public Health Service. The War Food Administration made its recruiting team in Mexico available to the RRB at the beginning of the program, with the stipulation that it be reimbursed.[33] The RRB reimbursed Ferrocarriles Nacionales for transporting contracted braceros from the point of origin where they were selected to the contracting center in Mexico City, San Luis Potosí, or Querétaro, and then to the border. Men who were not contracted were returned by Ferrocarriles Nacionales to their home villages. Agents of Ferrocarriles Nacionales in New York billed the RRB at its headquarters in Chicago. Payment was often delayed because Ferrocarriles Nacionales did not submit sufficient documentation or because the RRB needed time to conduct an audit.[34]

The Immigration Service

Although it maintained a low profile in the railroad bracero program, the Immigration Service wielded great power and performed services essential to the program. In fact, the Immigration Service could override the WMC's administrative decisions simply by failing to execute routine procedures. It was the only federal government agency with this power. For example, when the WMC wished to revise bracero quotas, it was obligated to submit certifications of labor and await its approval.[35] Moreover, when the WMC negotiated quota increases with the Mexican government, it had to secure approval from the Immigration Service. The Immigration Service had to grant its approval and authorization before the WMC could recruit additional workers.[36]

The Immigration Service, moreover, approved and processed the bonds the railroads were required to post for each recruited worker, as stipulated by the international agreement. When a railroad wished to hire braceros, it purchased bonds for the number it wanted to contract from a designated insurance company. The insurance company then forwarded copies of the completed bonds to the Immigration Service in Washington, D.C.[37] With the completed bonds in its files, the Immigration Service notified the WMC that a specific number of braceros could be recruited for the railroad.[38]

The bonds that the railroads posted for the braceros were intended to guarantee that the workers would not change their work status while they were in the United States; that is, they were to remain temporary workers employed by railroads as track workers and to return to Mexico at the conclusion of the contract. Any change in their status had to be approved by the Immigration Service. Only a month after the program began, however, the Santa Fe wanted to transfer some braceros to ice platform work. This was also unskilled work, but it was higher-paying and had a different Interstate Commerce Commission job classification. The local Immigration representative declined to approve the transfer,[39] and bureau headquarters thought it would be a breach of bond[40] until the WMC petitioned the Immigration Service on behalf of the railroads with documentation to support such transfers.[41]

Later, in response to the railroads' requests, the WMC approached the Immigration Service about transferring braceros to job classifications more removed from track work than ice platform work.[42] The WMC formally certified that braceros were needed in other job classifications and that such reclassification was necessary for the war effort, and asked that Immigration Service regulations be modified to allow braceros in other jobs.[43] Although the Immigration Service replied that each case would be considered separately,[44] in the end many braceros were transferred. The Immigration Service maintained that the braceros had been brought to the United States as temporary track workers but could be promoted or transferred once they began working in the United States.[45]

The railroads were to apprise the Immigration Service of the workers' whereabouts at all times and to notify it if the braceros left their work sites unsupervised. When they could, Immigration personnel escorted misplaced braceros back to their places of employment. Ultimately, however, it was the railroads' responsibility to supervise the braceros and to inform the Immigration Service of their location.[46]

The Department of State

The State Department was the agency least involved in the program in the United States. Despite the fact that the bracero program was international, the State Department limited its role at the conclusion of negotiations in Mexico City. The WMC assumed much of what might have been the responsibility of the State Department under other circumstances, including a relationship with the Mexican government. The State Department functioned primarily as a link between offices of the WMC in the United States and the WMC office in Mexico City, relaying information, money, and resources. Nonetheless, the secretary of state received reports and observations from Ambassador George Messersmith, which occasionally prompted the State Department to inquire about particular problems or disputes and sometimes intervene in the program.

Upon implementation of the program, the State Department instructed its embassy in Mexico to facilitate the WMC's activities, including forwarding cash to open its office.[47] Thereafter the State Department maintained regular correspondence with the U.S. Embassy staff about the railroad bracero program, receiving reports from it and conveying information and official authorizations from it.[48] At the WMC's request, the State Department on several occasions had Messersmith approach the Mexican government about various issues, including savings funds and renewals.[49] The State Department was also instrumental in getting a commission established to study the wage situation at the Santa Fe and other companies (see discussion below).[50] In response to complaints it received about living and working conditions, the State Department requested the War Food Administration to allow Mexican agricultural inspectors to include the railroad camps in their tours.[51]

The level of bureaucratic cooperation among the agencies varied according to the combination of agencies and the particular phase of the program. Considering the unusual circumstances, the tone of collaboration among the bureaucrats was generally cordial. Although agencies in the United States never functioned as cohesively as their counterparts in Mexico, they functioned adequately. The interests of the workers were not always served, and perhaps never could have been within the parameters of a bracero program.

Mexican Officials in the United States

Early in the bracero program, the Mexican government proposed that a team of inspectors appointed by the Secretaría de Trabajo y Previsión Social be assigned to the United States to periodically review working and living conditions. The formal presence of representatives from the STPS, in fact, would serve not only as a vehicle to monitor the camps but as a constant reminder that the braceros were in the United States thanks to an internationally recognized agreement. The workers would not be completely isolated from their homeland.

Because the first agricultural braceros reported substandard living and working conditions when they returned to Mexico at the end of 1942, the Secretaría de Relaciones Exteriores issued an ultimatum to the Farm Security Administration. If the United States did not agree to the incorporation of Mexican labor inspectors, all recruitment for agricultural labor would stop.[52] By August 1943, Mexican labor inspectors were already touring the agricultural camps and submitting regular reports,[53] their activities subsidized by the War Food Administration. In September, the Mexican government wanted to formally include inspections of the railroad facilities in its schedules. The agricultural program did not object as long as the WMC paid for the inspectors' activities that were connected with the railroad program and the Department of State saw no obstacle.[54] All were in agreement by October 1943.

The WMC formally incorporated the Mexican labor inspectors into its inspections for both the agricultural and railroad segments in March 1944 by issuing instructions about financing their travel and per diem expenses.[55] But these arrangements for the inspectors to include railroad camps in their schedules were only to last until June.

In August, on orders from President Ávila Camacho, the Secretaría de Trabajo y Previsión Social informed the U.S. government that it was sending ten inspectors specifically for the railroad camps. The STPS would pay their salaries, but the WMC was to subsidize their expenses.[56] Ambassador Messersmith opined that if the WMC did not cooperate, the railroad program would be in jeopardy.[57]

The inspectors were assigned to New York, Cleveland, Chicago, Dallas, Kansas City (Missouri), Denver, and California.[58] They were to work in the regional offices of the Railroad Retirement Board and be under the supervision of the RRB. By the end of November, three inspectors were in the United States under the new agreement.[59] Two of the four inspectors assigned to California were located in Los Angeles so they would be near the Mexican Consulate General where the program's regional records were housed.[60] Little is known about these inspectors. One was an attorney with a Ph.D. in economics.[61] Another, the inspector assigned to Chicago, spoke English well, was conscientious, and was educated in the United States (Colorado School of Mines).[62]

Reimbursement from the WMC for the inspectors' expenses was based on the reports that the inspectors submitted. While much disagreement ensued about what constituted an adequate report,[63] these written accounts of what they observed could constitute a significant source of information. Unfortunately, few of their reports have been located.

The attitude of some U.S. bureaucrats surely limited their effectiveness. Messersmith himself claimed that the inspectors were more hindrance than help, even that some were "ex-pistoleros."[64] In conversations with the author, U.S. bureaucrats who had contact with these labor inspectors demonstrated a somewhat cavalier attitude toward the inspectors, who they alleged were wont to seek romantic attachments while in the United States.[65]

Even though the organization of the bracero program made it difficult for the inspectors to function adequately, their presence in the United States unequivocally pointed to the intention of the Mexican government to protect its workers. As representatives of the Mexican government, they also served as a reminder that the bracero program during the war was a bilateral arrangement.

Mexican consuls throughout the United States also collaborated in the railroad program, although their duties were much broader and encompassed all those of Mexican origin in their district. Some aspects of the program such as contract renewals and the death of workers specifically required their attention, but many braceros sought the intervention of local consuls to resolve problems and improve working and living conditions. In fact, in 1942 Mexico and the United States signed a consular convention to more clearly define the roles of both countries' consuls. The convention legally empowered Mexican consuls to receive complaints from all citizens of Mexican origin living in their districts and gave them the right to communicate with those citizens, visit them, and assist them.[66]

At times, local Mexican consuls did act on the complaints lodged by railroad braceros. At the end of 1943, Detroit consul Ernesto Trejo requested an investigation of a camp in Ohio where a cook was serving bad food, a situation that was promptly remedied.[67] On an another occasion, the Mexican consul in El Paso approached R. R. Ball, vicepresident of the Gulf, Colorado and Santa Fe Railroad, about the living conditions of braceros, eliciting a personal promise that he would see to any future complaints.[68] On at least one occasion, a Mexican consul obtained lawyers for railroad braceros so they could sue their employers.[69]

The consuls also acted as representatives of the Secretaría de Relaciones Exteriores by maintaining communications with U.S. agencies involved in the railroad bracero program and collaborating with the committee that resolved the Santa Fe incident. In the case of the Santa Fe incident, the Los Angeles consulate was quite active, although the consular documents have not been located.

The Santa Fe Incident

Complaints lodged by braceros employed by the Santa Fe Railroad in Fullerton, California, in July 1943 occasioned the most difficult and long-standing diplomatic and bureaucratic problem in the railroad bracero program. Railroad braceros contracted directly by the Santa Fe Railroad to perform track maintenance learned that other track workers, U.S. laborers, doing exactly the same work adjacent to their assigned track section were receiving substantially higher wages. The braceros' wages were 48¾ cents an hour, while the U.S. workers were making 86 cents an hour.[70] The braceros immediately protested to their supervisors and refused to work, since, as they understood it, their contract guaranteed them the same wages as those paid domestic workers. The WMC immediately investigated the details of the complaint and verified that the higher-paid domestic workers turned out to be employees of companies subcontracted by the Santa Fe to perform track maintenance. Although the workers were not directly employed by the Santa Fe, the fact that they were paid much more than the braceros was a violation of the spirit of the bracero program. The Mexican government had insisted since the first discussions about a bracero program that the braceros receive wages equal to those of domestic workers. The Mexican government protested immediately, saying that the end result was discrimination, regardless of the special circumstances in Fullerton in July 1943. Not surprisingly, the Mexican government suspended recruitment.

The Mexican government protested this pay differential through all channels at its disposal. At least as early as September 8, 1943, Mexican officials from the Secretaría de Relaciones Exteriores, Secretaría de Gobernación, and Secretaría de Trabajo y Previsión Social met with their U.S. counterparts from the Department of State and WMC at the U.S. Embassy. Adolfo de la Huerta, Mexican consul general, maintained that a slight discrepancy regarding the term *employer* in the English translation of the original contract provided the legal justification for the difference in wages. The term *employer* could be construed to mean the particular employer of each railroad bracero or all railroad employers, which could affect the definition of railroad pay. The U.S. officials denied that such a discrepancy existed, and asserted that in any event it would not affect railroad wages, since they were determined by collective bargaining. They also indicated that employees of subcontractors did not enjoy many of the advantages that the braceros had; their pay was subject to a 20 percent withholding tax[71] and they had no job security. Moreover, an across-the-board raise of 8 cents an hour for all railroad workers had received approval, pending a final okay by President Roosevelt.[72] The Mexican representatives emphasized the result (different wages for the same work in the same place) more than the explanation (the role of subcontractors, conditions peculiar to the railroad industry, pending raises, etc.). Indeed, the Mexican representatives used the discussions to insist that the railroad braceros be given opportunities for higher-paying work on the railroad and in other industries.[73]

Later, the embassy attributed the belligerent attitude of the Mexican officials to Adolfo de la Huerta, the Los Angeles consul who spoke "heatedly" about the difficulties arising from the Santa Fe incident. Apparently some in the Secretaría de Relaciones Exteriores initially felt de la Huerta's position was too militant but subsequently came to agree with him.[74]

U.S. embassy personnel observed that the visit to Mexico in September by U.S. labor leaders complicated the situation. Their insistence that the recruitment of Mexican railroad workers had undermined their attempts to achieve pay raises reinforced Mexican arguments that the railroad braceros receive more appropriate wages.[75]

The suspension of recruitment by the Mexican government in August 1943 to protest poor working conditions had made railroad management nervous. The Santa Fe incident in September greatly complicated their position, and seemed to legitimize the complaints registered by the braceros and the Mexican government. By October, they were pressuring the Office of Defense Transportation for its director, Joseph Eastman, to urge the Department of State to "bring these views forcibly to the attention of the appropriate government officials in Mexico." Eastman felt that since the United States was sending so many men into combat, the least Mexico could do was provide workers for the railroads.[76] The ability of western railroads, in particular, to operate at the capacity required by the war was in jeopardy.[77] Some railroads had already indicated they were prepared to settle with Mexico, but they had to rely upon the WMC to negotiate with the Mexican government.[78]

By October 1943, it had been determined that a binational fact-finding commission[79] would be established to resolve the problem, although the WMC suggested that redefining "place of employment" in paragraph B-1 of the braceros' contract—that is, "wages paid to Mexican workers under this agreement shall be the same as those paid for similar work to domestic workers at the *place of employment*" (author's emphasis)—might avert the necessity of a commission. The Secretaría de Trabajo y Previsión Social wanted to go ahead with a commission, but agreed that it should reach agreement on "place of employment." The commission would also determine whether any discrimination had resulted from the misapplication of paragraph B-1 and, if so, establish a fair compensation for any workers who had been affected. The railroads were eager to resume recruitment and pressured the Department of State to seek a solution. By mid November, the Mexican government agreed that the establishment and operation of such a commission would suffice to renew recruitment.[80]

The concepts of place of employment in the railroad bracero program and prevailing wages in the agricultural program were both manipulated by employers to their advantage. Prevailing wages for agricultural braceros were essentially those established by the growers, not by market forces. However, the wages of unskilled railroad workers in the United States were determined by collective bargaining, since the majority were employed directly by railroads that recognized unions. Wage negotiations in the railroad industry often use roadmasters' districts as a unit to define wages. Regional differences did exist in railroad wages for all job categories, but the geographical extension of many large railroads meant the roadmasters' districts were more appropriate to determine regional differences. Neither the U.S. nor the Mexican negotiators took this into account when they established the railroad program. Consequently, the final agreement did not really incorporate actual industry conditions into guaranteeing wages. A more appropriate agreement may not have prevented the Santa Fe incident, but may have helped to open discussions.

In any event, the Mexican–United States Railroad Worker Commission was functioning by early 1944 and so recruitment resumed. From January to April of that year, members of the four-man commission—two representatives of the WMC (Robert MacLean and Robert Clark), one from the Secretaría de Trabajo y Previsión Social (Luis Padilla Nervo), and one from the Secretaría de Relaciones Exteriores (Los Angeles consul Manuel Aguilar)—met in various cities in the United States to talk with other people and among themselves. By February, they had already met in Los Angeles, El Paso, and Washington, D.C.[81] In El Paso, an official from the Southern Pacific openly declared without thinking that as soon as he could get enough Mexican workers under contract, he would fire all the domestic workers.[82] While it cannot be assumed that the railroad industry as a whole entertained such a plan, it probably reflects the attitude of some in railroad management.

The Southern Pacific report on this meeting, indeed, casually refers to the problems with the individual work contracts, citing the clause about the place of employment "in the region in which they are employed" and admitting that it led to complaints by the Mexican government. According to the report, the contract should have read: "The worker shall receive the same wages as those paid by the employer to domestic workers for the similar work as authorized by the Railway Labor Act, or as those paid by the employer to domestic railroad track Laborers for similar work."[83] However, it is surely not a coincidence that the railroad does not allude to the problems caused by the oversight or their international implications.

The commission's activities confirmed what the Mexican negotiators had contended all along: braceros were performing exactly the same maintenance-of-way work as domestic workers but often at lower pay. The U.S. members then offered to approach the railroads not about increasing wages but about paying a penalty to the Mexican government in recognition of wage discrimination and as a show of good faith to continue the program.[84]

However, in March 1944 the chairman of the WMC, Paul McNutt, rather brusquely stated that, although the Mexican representatives had no legitimate complaint, he was prepared to offer Mex$1 million (about US$250,000) by way of settlement.[85] The manner in which the offer was presented made the commission members uncomfortable and offended the Mexican representatives, since the arrangement was to work strictly through the commission.[86] In fact, the Mexican negotiators claimed they had received claims from braceros that amounted to almost half a million dollars. After some discussion, the Mexican representatives agreed to present an offer of US$300,000 to the Mexican government.[87]

Finally, the commission presented a joint resolution outlining its conclusions. The document included a definition of place of employment as it applied to workers in the United States railroad industry and a statement that the two governments agreed that a payment of $300,000 to Mexico would settle all past complaints about wages in the program. The U.S. representatives wanted a series of clarifications and exceptions included to avoid any future misunderstandings. For their part, the Mexican representatives again alluded to the incident with Governor McNutt; in fact, Padilla Nervo of the Secretaría de Trabajo y Previsión Social indicated that if the negotiations broke off under such circumstances, it would provide him political points on his return to Mexico.[88] Obviously the failure of the negotiations would have reinforced the position of those in the Mexican government opposed to the bracero program. At that moment, it was not clear whether the Secretaría de Trabajo y Previsión Social would accept the proposal for $300,000 but the Secretaría de

Relaciones Exteriores took responsibility for the decision to accept. Nor was it clear who would provide the money, the WMC or the railroads.

In April 1944 a payment of $300,000 was made to the Mexican government, which officially ended the Santa Fe incident, but the significance of the incident transcends the program. Even though the attitude of some U.S. officials was not the most cordial, the bilateral terms of the railroad bracero program within the context of a war emergency forced bilateral discussions to find a solution to this problem. Moreover, U.S. officials recognized among themselves that only a bilateral approach could have worked under the circumstances. The Santa Fe incident was the only occasion when the Mexican government was able to meet the U.S. government on equal terms to resolve a conflict arising from the migration of Mexican workers. A corresponding arrangement did not appear in the agricultural program, either during or after the war; it can be argued, in fact, that the conditions of the agricultural bracero program would never have permitted such a resolution. These binding bilateral discussions enabled the Mexican government to effectively insist on better wages and working conditions for railroad braceros.

Labor Unions, U.S. and Mexican

Since railroad workers in the United States were among the most unionized during World War II and their unions the most powerful, it was inevitable that the railroad unions would lobby for their position during the course of the program. Two overriding factors conditioned the unions' position—their long-term goal of obtaining a pay raise for unskilled railroad workers and the implications of bringing foreign workers into a unionized workforce. The unusual circumstances enabled the government to set aside the objections of the unions to the implementation of the railroad program during the negotiations. It seems, however, that the unions, at least informally, agreed not to press their position before and during the negotiations, contingent on a promise from the War Manpower Commission that under no circumstances would the program be extended beyond the war. But the unions were not altogether silent either.

Some railroad unions recognized very early that railroads in certain parts of the country really were experiencing difficulty in finding workers. In late 1942, the Brotherhood of Railway Trainmen used its own locals to locate trainmen for the Santa Fe Railroad.[89] Like the Railroad Retirement Board, the unions attributed the railroads' problems in hiring to poor distribution and underutilization of unemployed workers. When the WMC proposed to freeze labor in the western states and contract Mexican labor, the Railway Labor Executives Association issued a formal statement suggesting measures to "more fully utilize U.S. manpower," such as employing women and reducing labor turnover. Such a program would "meet our national requirements without resorting to compulsion and abandonment of free labor, free enterprise and democratic process."[90]

Since the pressure from the railroads to recruit workers did not ease, the Brotherhood of Maintenance of Way Employees approached the Department of State in January 1943, insisting that the railroads could not find workers because the wages were so low. The union maintained that the railroads sought temporary workers from Mexico because it would be cheaper. The Department of State backed away from the union, saying that its function as a liaison between the U.S. government and Mexico[91] precluded its drawing such conclusions. The Department of State chose not to deal with the unions.

A couple of weeks later, the same union requested the Management-Labor Policy Committee of the WMC to reconsider the recommendation it had made in December to seek railroad workers in Mexico, again insisting that the railroads were seeking cheap labor. Both Joseph Eastman of the Office of Defense Transportation and a representative of the War Department, as well as representatives from the railroads, argued that offering higher wages had not produced more track workers. The committee continued to support its recommendation, although its AFL and CIO members maintained their veto until May 1943.[92]

In April, the railroad unions analyzed the final agreement outlining the railroad bracero program. They especially took umbrage with the paragraph delineating the workers' right to organize and file grievances. Paragraph 8 of the agreement implied that the spokesmen the braceros elected were entitled to conduct collective bargaining,[93] which undermined the unions' position. Cognizant of the unions' power, the RRB modified the regulations accompanying the agreement to appease them.[94]

U.S. union criticism of the bracero program climaxed in an unofficial, and apparently uncomfortable, visit that union leaders made to Mexico City in September 1943. The Office of the Coordinator of Inter-American Affairs of the Department of State sponsored a tour to acquaint union leaders with labor movements in Latin American countries. Included in the tour were officials from the International Brotherhood of Electrical Workers of the American Federation of Labor, the secretary-treasurer of the United Steel Workers of the Congress of Industrial Organizations, and the vice president of the brotherhoods of Locomotive Firemen and Locomotive Engineers. The U.S. Embassy in Mexico City was instructed to inform the Mexican government of the visit, emphasizing that it was unofficial. These leaders were invited formally to Mexico by Fidel Veláz- quez of the Confederación de Trabajadores Mexicanos.[95]

The activities of the U.S. labor delegation in Mexico City were or- ganized by the CTM and included visits to Ambassador Messersmith, President Ávila Camacho, the Secretaría de Relaciones Exteriores, and the Secretaría de Trabajo y Previsión Social. While the visit was successful in many respects and the embassy itself credited the Mexican government with extending every courtesy to the group, a discussion at STPS about the importation of railroad workers from Mexico created an uncom- fortable feeling. Samuel G. Phillips of the railroad brotherhoods asked openly why the STPS had allowed Mexican workers to be recruited for U.S. work, an action that effectively undermined the unions' long-term efforts to force a wage increase for unskilled railroad workers.[96] In the context of the brewing Santa Fe incident, the STPS complained to the U.S. Embassy. Indeed, it is probably not a coincidence that in September 1943 the Railway Labor Executives Association announced that the orga- nization no longer cooperated with the Office of Defense Transportation in procuring workers in Mexico.[97]

The unions were incorporated into some phases of the program. Or- ders from the Immigration Service authorizing increases or changes in quotas customarily included references to the approval of the Brother- hood of the Maintenance of Way Employees, the Railway Employee De- partment of the AFL, and the Brotherhood of Railway and Steamship Clerks.[98] Also, the railroads ordinarily checked with the appropriate union when a company wanted to transfer track workers to other jobs.[99]

At times the unions became involved through the interpretation of local union contracts. Maintenance employees on the New York Central ordinarily received overtime pay after an eight-hour day, per union con- tract. But the Mexican government insisted that the braceros work ten- hour days at regular pay, a violation of the contract. The WMC indicated to the embassy that overtime regulations were governed by local con- tracts, which in turn reflected local conditions.[100]

The Brotherhood of Maintenance of Way Employees, the union that covers track workers, obviously had a particular interest in the program. Although the union's official history barely acknowledges the recruit- ment of Mexican workers, it could not ignore them. Of the approxi- mately 275,000 maintenance-of-way employees in 1944, around 45,000 (allowing for transfers) were braceros. But the brotherhood continued to insist that no shortage of labor existed, only a "shortage of wages."[101]

The union periodically reminded the WMC that it would continue to present no objections to Mexican labor under certain circumstances: if the rights of U.S. workers were respected, if no domestic workers were available, and if no displacement of domestic workers occurred. In addition, the brotherhood insisted that it be allowed to recruit the braceros as union members, which the WMC permitted, although it could not force the braceros to join the union.[102] The brotherhood also requested that the RRB and the WMC cease recruiting Mexican labor for a period after the long-awaited pay raise was implemented in 1944.[103]

In August 1945, as the war was ending, the unions expressed their opposition to extending the railroad program beyond the war at a meeting with the railroads and government officials.[104] By October, the unions were pressing for prompt repatriation of Mexican railroad workers,[105] a position that became increasingly difficult for the WMC to ignore. The termination of the war and growing domestic unemployment provided the unions with the ammunition to end the bracero program. Even though the repatriation of workers was more gradual than the unions would have liked, the fact that the program was terminated so promptly was due to the unions.

Obviously a review of the program's administration in the United States presents only a limited picture of its domestic phase. To understand the workings of the program more fully, we turn now to the railroads themselves.

12

The Role of the Railroads

The railroad bracero program can be considered a government response to petitions by major western corporations—notably, the Southern Pacific, the Atchison, Topeka and Santa Fe, and the Western Pacific, as well as many other railroads—to supply a commodity they needed to perform the tasks assigned them in a national emergency. Most railroads had previously contracted Mexican immigrant labor, both legal and undocumented, to solve their labor shortages and regarded the program as a reasonable and logical alternative to domestic labor. Indeed, the program largely served the purposes for which it was established; the railroads received significant numbers of track workers as promised.

Nonetheless, while the bracero program supplied the railroads with the workers they so desperately needed, it also burdened them with extensive administrative requirements. The new responsibilities compounded the railroads' existing difficulties—the industry had suffered from poor management for many years, which had resulted in many diverse problems, particularly the distressing condition of the tracks. The addition of the bracero program to an industry as large, powerful, and problematic as the railroads in the 1940s inevitably produced a labor project exhibiting unique characteristics and problems, and very distinctive from the original agricultural program.

At the outset, the U.S. government did not seem to anticipate that the demand for Mexican track workers would expand beyond the West and Southwest. That anyone in the government wanted to limit the geographic boundaries of the program is doubtful; the initial demand simply came from the program's instigators in these regions. However, midwestern and southern roads were equally pressed to find labor and the prospect of temporary foreign contract labor seemed attractive. Thus by 1944 thirty-six railroads throughout the country had working for them at any time around 50,000 Mexican workers contracted through the bracero program.

The daily supervision of braceros fell mostly to the railroads themselves, in part due to the nature of the work—most track maintenance workers, braceros and domestic employees alike, were often assigned to isolated track sections. Although for the purpose of negotiations, the U.S. government through the War Manpower Commission was liable for the railroad braceros, the bonds that the railroads posted forced accountability onto the railroads. Evidently the government felt that the railroads were at least minimally responsible—it did not trust the growers enough to delegate them similar responsibility in the agricultural program.

Peter Kirstein writes that the WMC and the Railroad Retirement Board were both careful about admitting railroad employers into the program; he states that the WMC used strict criteria, including the approval of the Brotherhood of Maintenance of Way Employees, in evaluating their applications.[1] The documents reviewed for this study, however, do not confirm Kirstein's assertion; in fact, there is no evidence that any railroad was rejected once the program was under way.

The WMC and the RRB insisted that the railroads be active and conscientious supervisors and monitored them through extensive paperwork. The railroads were required to maintain detailed individual records as well as individual and collective payroll data, which called for the labor of specialized clerical workers plus additional medical and commissary personnel. Indeed, the RRB used the information generated by the railroads for its own statistical reports.

Unfortunately, I was unable to obtain data from the railroads concerning their participation in the program. On two occasions, I contacted all the railroads involved or their present owners, and only two companies stated that they were even aware of the project. In fact, the first contact with the Southern Pacific several years ago prompted the company historian to respond that to his knowledge the company had not employed Mexican nationals during World War II. Therefore, much relevant archival material remains in private company archives, mostly closed to researchers and probably unidentified.

Administration

Direct railroad supervision of the Mexican workers usually started once the contracted workers arrived at the border. There the braceros were transferred to U.S. railroad equipment. In some cases the employers dispatched their own rolling stock to the border; in others, the railroads picked up their braceros at an intermediate point. In all instances, RRB train riders accompanied the workers until they were delivered to their employers.

The railroads' administrative duties were comprehensive, since technically their responsibility for the braceros included everything from work equipment to medical care and food. Indeed, supervision of the braceros was probably more encompassing than the railroads had ever been required to provide. Most work sites received periodic, usually sporadic, visits from the WMC, the RRB, and, later, Mexican (Secretaría de Trabajo y Previsión Social) labor inspectors, but the railroads dominated the workers' lives, especially in rural areas.

The railroads were particularly obligated to keep government agencies informed about the whereabouts of the braceros. Therefore they maintained regular correspondence with the WMC and RRB, although at times the railroads resented both the paperwork and the intrusion of bureaucrats in their operations. The railroads were divided in their attitudes toward Mexican consuls; for example, the Southern Pacific looked askance at consuls while the Pennsylvania sought their advice.[2]

The Railroads

In 1950, just a few years after the program ended, the Southern Pacific developed a 116-page retrospective about its participation in the bracero program, presumably for its own purposes. Entitled "Historical Data in Connection with Employment of Mexican National Laborers Imported from Mexico," the report must be considered biased, even distorted in some respects, but it nonetheless represents a significant source of information from within the railroad industry regarding the employment of Mexican nationals during World War II. The report does verify many points and includes statistical data generated by the railroad itself. Although the report omits many issues (such as the Santa Fe incident and complaints filed against the company), it does allude to the responsibilities of the railroads in the operation of the program. As a product of the largest and most influential railroad in the program, the report has been invaluable in determining the Southern Pacific's role in the railroad program.[3]

The railroad issued instructions to "Officers in Charge of Mexican workers, to Superintendent for Maintenance of Way and to General Superintendent Motive Power and General Storekeeper" about overseeing the program. The Southern Pacific apparently recognized its obligations to maintain cordial relationships with Mexican consuls and labor inspectors, the Immigration Service, the WMC, and the RRB. Moreover, at least formally, the railroad accepted its responsibility to investigate complaints, to ensure decent housing, and to generally oversee the welfare of the workers. The report also indicates that the company's Mexican Labor Bureau of the General Office maintained individual files on each worker, as well as ledger sheets summarizing the overall dimensions of the program.[4]

The Southern Pacific and its subsidiaries (the Pacific Fruit Express, for example) were consistently the largest and most influential employers. The company's support was crucial to the program's momentum. In fact, it was the Southern Pacific that first formally approached the Office of Defense Transportation in late 1942 about the worsening labor situation in the Southwest, suggesting the possibility of hiring workers in Mexico.[5] The company claimed in December 1942 to have sought labor in Chicago, St. Paul, and Minneapolis for its southwestern tracks but without success.[6] A month later, the railroad suggested to the State Department that the agricultural bracero program be expanded to the railroads.[7] By February 1943 the Southern Pacific was discussing its proposal in detail with the Management-Labor Policy Committee of the WMC.[8]

During the course of the program, the Southern Pacific hired 36,711 railroad braceros, with 32,571 men assigned to the following divisions in California, Oregon, Utah, and Arizona, and 4,140 men to the Motive Power and Store departments throughout the Southern Pacific system.

	Number of Braceros
Division	
Western Division	4,048
Sacramento	3,505
Salt Lake	3,838
Shasta	2,613
Portland	3,965
Coast	2,908
San Joaquin	2,733
Los Angeles	2,691
Tucson	2,896
Rio Grande	3,374
Department	
Motive Power Department	2,964
Store Department	1,176

Assignments to divisions were generally made by carloads when the braceros arrived at the border. The first braceros to work in the Motive Power and Store departments arrived in December 1943.[9]

Of the first approved quota of 6,000 braceros in April–May 1943, some 3,000 were designated for the Southern Pacific system.[10] The WMC allotment specified that they could be assigned to the company's Tucson, Los Angeles, Western, Shasta, and Portland divisions.[11] Importantly, the Southern Pacific was authorized to assign braceros to tracks in Texas. The Mexican government was adamant about not allowing agricultural workers to be contracted by Texas growers for the duration of World War II due to serious problems of discrimination, yet some railroad braceros did work there. These allocations, further, made the railroad program virtually a national one from the beginning.

Anxious to dispense with administrative responsibilities and let the braceros work, the Southern Pacific repeatedly requested, without success, that the bond requirements be eliminated.[12] Southern Pacific management did not even wait for the braceros to be transported by the RRB; with no authorization, in May 1943 the Southern Pacific sent its own equipment to Guadalajara from Nogales to pick up the workers.[13] The company, moreover, sent its own recruiting representatives to Mexico City, not relying on the Western Association of Railway Executives, which represented most of the others.[14]

The Southern Pacific, however, was not careful about its labor policies. In May 1943, the Immigration Service arrested 133 undocumented Mexican citizens working for the company in California;[15] Inspector Del Guernicio reported on May 7 that he had the workers in custody.[16] All but six workers were allowed to voluntarily depart by the Immigration Service; the remainder were held as witnesses against the Southern Pacific.[17] A Mexican citizen employed by the Southern Pacific had recruited the workers in Mexicali for $5.50, leading them to believe that the company would procure the necessary immigration papers for them in the United States.[18]

Complaints about the Southern Pacific's treatment of its braceros abounded, harkening to its previous history of employment of Mexican immigrants. A few examples here will suffice. Carlos Gutiérrez-Macías, consul in Salt Lake City, Utah, reported in August 1943 that numerous complaints about the braceros' working and living conditions were being filed with his office.[19] At the same time, bracero Antonio Mesqueda Delgado complained to the WMC that Extra Gang No. 3 was not being provided with enough meat, and in fact had been given rancid turkey on one occasion, which had made at least fifteen workers ill.[20] Finally, a private citizen took it upon herself to write to Secretary of State Cordell Hull that braceros working in Nevada were struggling through a hard winter in substandard housing, in tents that had holes and were not equipped with adequate heating stoves.[21]

Braceros were critical for the company. The Southern Pacific depended upon the labor of braceros; at the height of the program in December 1944, braceros constituted 72 percent of the company's 11,560 track workers.[22] By July 1945, some 10,802 of the Southern Pacific's maintenance force of 11,889, or a little over 90 percent, were braceros. Braceros even represented over half of the shop laborers (1,191 of 2,121 workers).[23] If the war had not concluded in August 1945, the company probably would have become even more dependent on braceros. Given the company's dominant position in the Southwest and its strategic position in the transport of materials related to the war effort, the significance of the program for the U.S. domestic economy becomes clear. While the bracero program may have caused the company considerable paperwork, it did provide the company with track workers and other laborers that it claimed it could not locate otherwise.

Southern Pacific subsidiaries also participated in the program, most notably the Pacific Fruit Express, which applied to the WMC shortly after the program began. Workers were authorized for Pacific Fruit Express's western division (Oregon, California, Arizona, Texas, Utah, Nevada, Idaho, Wyoming) and its midwestern division (Kansas, Iowa, Nebraska). Although policies and guidelines for the Pacific Fruit Express were cleared through the Southern Pacific, the company had an independent relationship with the bracero program.

Particularly significant about the Pacific Fruit Express was its early request to transfer braceros to ice platform work, a job that involved loading and unloading refrigerator cars. Although the job was classified as being for unskilled labor—a legal requirement for the braceros' work—and in fact was covered by the same union as track work, ice platform work was in a different job category, paid more, and was not specified in the international agreement. The State Department gave preliminary permission for the transfer without the approval of the Mexican government, since it was for unskilled labor.[24] A rider was later attached to the international agreement to cover such transfers; it also extended to other jobs.[25]

The Atchison, Topeka and Santa Fe, another prominent regional railroad in the Southwest and part of the Midwest, also requested Mexican workers early. Organized railroad labor, particularly the Union of Railway Trainmen, had tried to use its national networks to locate workers for the company but without success.[26] Curiously, T. A. Blair, the assistant chief engineer, indicated in a national industrial publication that Mexican workers would be a natural solution, since the railroad had customarily imported Mexican nationals for extra gangs. Language would not even be a problem, since many foremen were from Mexico and obviously spoke Spanish.[27]

In February 1943, the Santa Fe Railway also promoted the importation of Mexican workers with the WMC Management-Labor Policy Committee.[28] The second-largest employer, the Santa Fe, was allotted 30 percent of the first 6,000 braceros, or 1,800,[29] and dispersed them over its extensive territory of Illinois, Missouri, Oklahoma, New Mexico, and California.[30] Like the Southern Pacific, this company wanted to send its own equipment to Mexico to pick up the workers.[31] It was the only company that had a full-time legal representative in Mexico.[32]

Complaints concerning the mistreatment of braceros by the Santa Fe began began to emerge soon after the program began. The Santa Fe incident of September 1943 represents the most obvious major failure of the program, but it could have happened to any railroad in the program. The railroads obviously did not understand the full implications of being employers in an international program, and that such a program required that they be meticulous about maintaining uniform working conditions. The negotiators probably did not know enough about the industry to avoid a Santa Fe incident, nor did the railroads as employers truly understand how to function in such a program.

Like the Pacific Fruit Express, the Santa Fe also wanted to use braceros in ice platform work early, but the company did not seek authorization. Instead, when management decided that the transfer was necessary, it assigned workers before notifying the Immigration Service.[33] Not surprisingly, the Immigration Service served notice that such action was a violation of their bond.[34] Charles Wood, the Santa Fe attorney, however, maintained that it was customary to use track workers for ice platform work when they were needed.[35] In June 1943, the Immigration Service decided to let the Santa Fe use braceros as ice platform workers, since the WMC and the RRB could not find enough workers in the United States for any job category, hardly a ruling consistent with the program's legal basis.[36] The Santa Fe was neither the first nor the last company to use braceros in ice work, but it was the only one not to arrange previous authorization.

The third-largest southwestern railroad to participate was the Western Pacific. The company contacted the Office of Defense Transportation in 1942,[37] and participated in the February discussions of the WMC

Management-Labor Policy Committee with the Southern Pacific and the Santa Fe.[38] Although its share of the first quota was only 350 workers, or 5.8 percent, the percentage it received increased in subsequent recruitment drives.[39]

In August 1943, the quota for the total number of railroad braceros was raised to 10,600, at which point the program became more national in scope. The program came to function as an industry-wide response to chronic unskilled labor shortages, not only for southwestern roads but for companies throughout the country. Midwestern railways in particular sought braceros soon after the program was negotiated; the New York Central was the first, receiving 750 braceros in July 1943 for its Ohio and Michigan tracks.[40] In fact, the company dispatched special equipment to Laredo, Texas, to transport the braceros[41] and made extensive use of them throughout the Midwest.[42] The Chicago, Burlington and Quincy and the Florida East Coast were also allotted braceros (550 and 150 respectively).[43]

Although the WMC assigned priority in the August quota to railroads already participating (Southern Pacific, 4,000; Santa Fe, 2,025), large allocations of braceros were given to the New York Central (500), the New York, New Haven and Hartford (300), and the Western Pacific (300). Several new railroads also were assigned braceros: the Pennsylvania (1,000), the Northern Pacific (200), the Chicago, Rock Island and Pacific (150), the Texas and Pacific (200), Panhandle and Santa Fe (500), Great Northern (225), Pacific Fruit Express (300), North Western Pacific (200), and the San Diego and Arizona (100).

By the end of December 1943, most of the railroads that would become involved in the recruitment of Mexican workers had enrolled in the bracero program. Although the quota was raised several times thereafter and a few additional companies were added, the most important and influential roads were already included. The states in which the braceros were authorized to work encompassed virtually all of the West, Southwest, and Midwest and some in the East. Hardly six months had passed since the first railroad braceros had arrived in the United States.

Early in 1944, the quota was raised to 19,400—almost double the August quota. The March allocations generally followed previous patterns and were mostly filled by April. The Southern Pacific was assigned 4,200 braceros, or 21 percent. The Pennsylvania, an important road bridging the East and Midwest, was allowed 3,200 braceros authorized to work in Pennsylvania, New York, New Jersey, and Delaware. The Atchison, Topeka and Santa Fe received 2,000 and the New York Central, 2,000. Other railroads receiving large numbers of braceros were the Chicago, Burlington and Quincy (1,600), the Union Pacific (1,200), the Baltimore and Ohio (850), and the Chicago, Milwaukee, St. Paul and Pacific (600). Railroads receiving a small number of workers were the Western Pacific (550), the Erie (550), the Delaware, Lackawanna and Western (450), the Panhandle and Santa Fe (300), the New York, New Haven and Hartford (275), the Lehigh Valley (250), the Chicago and North Western (250), the Boston and Maine (250), the Pere Marquette (150), the Illinois Central (125), the Colorado and Southern (75), and, finally, the Peoria and Pekin Union (50). About 1,000 places of the allocation of 19,400 remained. The WMC and the RRB continued to revise quotas for each participating railroad, and to receive requests from new ones.[44] In a month-long recruitment drive, enough workers were contracted to fill most allocations;[45] however, local labor supplies in many rural areas of Mexico were severely depleted and obviously not sufficient to supply the bracero program as well as support local economies.

In mid 1944, the national quota was again raised, to 50,000 braceros for all railroads, an eightfold increase over the original 6,000 workers only a year before. Distribution of the 50,000 workers followed previous patterns: the Southern Pacific, about 12,500, or 25 percent; the Santa Fe, 8,000; the Pennsylvania, 6,800; the New York Central, 3,865; the Chicago, Burlington and Quincy, 2,850; the Baltimore and Ohio, 1,650; the Western Pacific, 1,525; the Chicago, Minneapolis and St. Paul, 1,450; the Pacific Fruit Express, 1,350; and the Northern Pacific, 1,250.[46]

Toward the end of the program in 1945, the WMC and the Immigration Service had already agreed to a final quota of 75,000 Mexican nationals and obtained approval by the Mexican government,[47] but they never carried out the recruitment because the program was dismantled when the war ended. Suffice it to say that the tentative allocations followed already established patterns, with the Southern Pacific being assigned 14,000 braceros.

An overview of the quotas shows that the railroad program quickly came to supply the needs of many railroads besides the original applicants from the Southwest. A couple of examples will illustrate this reliance on the braceros. The Pennsylvania Railroad's original allocations were modest, but the railroad had obviously found braceros to be a valuable source of workers. By the height of the program, from May to July 1945, almost 50 percent of the track workers (8,055 of 17,751) and 20 percent of the shop laborers (1,452 of 5,177) were braceros. An analysis of the Northern Pacific's allocation reveals a similar situation. Between

May and July of 1945, braceros constituted almost 50 percent of the company's track labor (2,600 of 5,800).[48]

Bonds were a major problem for the railroads throughout the program. The railroads' concern with the bond issue was primarily expressed in its communications with the Immigration Service. Although the INS maintained an extensive file for each participating railroad, only a few have surfaced. However, the available INS files clearly demonstrate the agency's preoccupation with monitoring the location and status of the braceros and the railroads' interest in canceling the bonds as soon as possible. Many workers who returned to Mexico on their own claimed their back pay by registering their claims with U.S. consuls, who certified their presence in Mexico and gave them their checks. The consular certification constituted legal justification for the INS to cancel the bonds, thereby releasing large sums of money to the railroads. It seems that at times INS canceled the bonds without appropriate documentation, accepting the word of employers that the workers had picked up their pay.

The question of bonds persisted for many years after the termination of the program and became a delicate issue for the railroads, since so much money was involved. For each worker still charged against a railroad's bond, $50 as a deposit remained in the possession of the insurance company until the return of the bracero to Mexico was verified by the Immigration Service. After the war it became increasingly difficult for the railroads to prove that the workers had returned to Mexico, so the INS began gradually canceling the bonds without proof of return passage. In 1948, for example, the INS reduced the Pennsylvania's bond from $31,000 to $20,000 to cover forty workers still working for the company in the United States.[49] In 1949, the bond was reduced to $12,500 to cover twenty-five Mexican workers.[50] In 1953, some eight years after the program, eighteen workers were still charged against the bond and the company was continuing to report braceros returning to Mexico.[51] By 1956, the Pennsylvania's bond had been reduced to $9,000, but fifteen braceros were apparently still working with the company.[52]

While it participated in the program, the bankrupt Missouri Pacific operated from trusteeship; thus authorization to execute bonds to recruit braceros came from court-appointed trustees.[53] Like many others, the railroad increased its quota in mid 1945, from 300 to 550, which meant a corresponding increase in its bond.[54] But this railroad repatriated its workers more quickly than others; in 1946, there were only nine workers still charged against its bond.[55] A year later, only two Mexican workers remained. To get the amount of the bond reduced, the Missouri Pacific arranged a letter from the INS for the Maryland Casualty Company stating that no more Mexican workers would be recruited.[56] But it was not until 1950 that the bond was finally adjusted to reflect the number of workers repatriated.[57] Unfortunately, in 1951 the INS notified the Missouri Pacific that the conditions of the bond had been breached and asked the company to make full payment for the violation.[58] It seems that one bracero who had been contracted in 1945 returned to Mexico illegally, sold his documentation for the bracero program there, and then immigrated to the United States without papers. The man was apprehended in Chicago in August 1952 and was awaiting deportation hearings in Cook County Jail while the railroad was trying yet again to cancel the bond. The odyssey of this man, still legally a bracero, constituted a breach of the bond because he was not employed as a track worker by the railroad stipulated in the bond.[59] The RRB later supported the railroad's position so as to cancel the bond and release the deposit. Otherwise, the railroad would have had to pay a penalty of $500 to cover just one worker.

The New York, New Haven and Hartford (NY, NH & H), a regional railroad in the Northeast operating from bankruptcy, received in total more than 1,000 workers through allocations of 300 workers. In May 1944, the INS processed a bond bought by the railroad from Aetna Insurance Company with a deposit of $50,000 to cover these workers.[60] The railroad apparently had problems with braceros deserting their jobs, for the INS received numerous telegrams about workers leaving their camps without notice. In January 1946, the NY, NH & H still had 362 braceros charged to them, with thirty workers missing.[61] By March, the workers had mostly been repatriated, with twelve still working and another thirteen unaccounted for.[62] But the records show that it wasn't until February 1946 that the INS authorized cancellation of any of the workers' bonds, thereby releasing bond deposits of $16,500.[63] In July 1950, after clarifying a mistaken assumption that some fifty-seven workers were still working for the NY, NH & H (based on a discrepancy between RRB and INS records), the INS finally authorized cancellation of the last bond.[64]

The New York Central, a major railroad connecting the Northeast and Midwest, passed through New York, Ohio, and Michigan. After receiving 600 braceros,[65] the railroad assigned them throughout its system, averaging around sixty workers per camp:

| | *Number of* |
Location	*Braceros*
OHIO	
Conneaut	59
Ashtabula	60
Unionville	60
Painesville	59
Mentor	60
Amherst	70
Huron	60
Fort Clinton	71
MICHIGAN	
Ypsilanti	50
Francisco	50[66]

Like the other railroads, the New York Central found the bracero program to be a significant source of workers. In May 1945, of 15,958 track workers, about 30 percent, or 5,104, were braceros. The company utilized fewer Mexican nationals for other job categories; of 6,358 freight handlers, only 238 were braceros, and of 3,484 shop laborers, only 239 were Mexican.[67]

However, the New York Central seems to have generated quite a number of complaints from braceros about a variety of issues. Many braceros complained that, contrary to the international agreement, they were not given opportunities to work more than eight hours a day to earn extra money. The company replied that under union contract it could offer employees only eight hours of work a day at regular hourly rates. Further, if the braceros worked additional hours at an increased rate of pay, domestic workers might construe it as favoritism toward the Mexican workers.[68] The Department of State apparently pointed out to the Mexican government that only New York Central and Pennsylvania employees did not work ten-hour days.[69]

Braceros also complained about substandard living conditions, particularly in Ohio and Michigan, and the company's failure to pay back wages. One worker assigned to Dundee, New York, complained that he was not receiving the medical attention he needed.[70] An RRB field representative visited the camp to investigate, but only confirmed that the company doctor's office was two blocks from the camp.[71] In May 1946, another worker developed leprosy while working in Buffalo and had to obtain public assistance to return to Mexico.[72]

The New York Central was not particularly generous in respecting claims for back pay. For example, the management was adamant in not reimbursing workers who left the camps after the expiration of their contracts without waiting the requisite fifteen days to be transported back to Mexico (WMC's field instruction no. 355 [revised] did stipulate that a worker could return to Mexico at any time after waiting fifteen days). The WMC urged the company to be more flexible in reimbursing braceros.[73]

As this brief overview shows, the participation of the railroads varied greatly. Some like the Southern Pacific and the Atchison, Topeka and Santa Fe really depended on the braceros for track labor, shop labor, and other unskilled and some semiskilled job categories; others like the New York Central, the Rock Island, and the Florida East Coast employed braceros mostly for track labor. While Mexican labor came to dominate some track gangs in the Southwest, braceros also made significant contributions in other regions. If the program had lasted longer, braceros would have come to constitute an even larger portion of the unskilled, and even semiskilled, workforce.

Although information about the efficiency of the railroad companies' administration is sketchy, it is safe to conclude that their management of the program was inconsistent. Some companies, such as the Southern Pacific, the Atchison, Topeka and Santa Fe, and the New York Central, generated many complaints from braceros. Others responded more readily to input from the WMC, the RRB, and the Mexican consuls. Regardless of the railroads' response to the program, however, the labor of the braceros was significant, even crucial, to the companies' participation in the war effort.

13

Termination and Repatriation

Like its counterpart, the agricultural bracero program, the railroad program was to be terminated at the conclusion of hostilities. The bracero program was developed during World War II through a bilateral diplomatic agreement with a formal understanding by both Mexico and the United States that it would last only for the duration of the war and that it was a significant Mexican contribution to the war effort. After all, the Mexican government was reluctant to send its citizens to the United States to work, even temporarily, after the unpleasant repatriations of the 1930s and the widely recognized problems of discrimination in the United States. Nor were Mexican decision makers overjoyed at the prospect of draining domestic labor supplies, especially in rural areas. However, the promise of the U.S. government that the bracero program would end at the conclusion of hostilities seemed assurance enough that the program would be controlled and that Mexican workers would be repatriated on schedule.

The termination of the railroad bracero program is of particular interest with regard to the U.S. government's resolve to promptly end the recruitment of Mexican workers after the war, despite pressures to the contrary. The U.S. government considered the positions of organized railroad labor and some agencies more important than those of the railroad companies. Growers, especially those of California, were remarkably successful in promoting their industry after the war,[1] and persuaded the federal government to press the Mexican government for a renewal of the program, at first on an ad hoc basis, later institutionalizing it. Although the railroad industry and even the RRB exerted similar efforts to continue the railroad program after the war, the U.S. government remained firm.

Termination of the Program

Since no one was really sure how long the railroad bracero program would last, U.S. officials had occasionally distributed tentative plans to dismantle the program.[2] Since its inception in May 1943, the WMC developed and circulated in government circles plans for an orderly repatriation of braceros, to be implemented at any time. When the surrender of Japan ended World War II in August 1945, the WMC and other government agencies felt they were prepared to conclude the railroad bracero program.

Therefore, the WMC decided in August 1945 that railroad recruitment in Mexico would be discontinued and that the northbound bracero train of August 24, 1945, would be the last.[3] However, the railroads insisted that the program be extended beyond the end of the war, at least until domestic workers again became available, which they estimated would be in about a year. Not surprisingly, the railroad unions vehemently objected. The WMC sided with the unions and ruled on August 28 that recruitment would cease, contracts of braceros would not be renewed, and the organized repatriation of braceros would begin.[4]

The termination orders issued by the WMC on August 28 decreed that all railroad braceros, numbering around 50,000 and employed throughout the United States, were to be repatriated back home to Mexico within thirty days. As a first step, the WMC refused to finish contracting recruits that had already been transported to Querétaro for final processing, since the program was to be terminated immediately. Understandably, the Mexican government was ambivalent about an abrupt conclusion of the program, and its consequences for Mexico. In response to the Mexican government's concerns, the WMC ruled that a more gradual repatriation would be acceptable. The Immigration Service ruled that railroad braceros could finish their contracts and would be repatriated over a six-month period.[5] Both Mexican and U.S. officials agreed that a gradual repatriation would facilitate the braceros' reintegration into Mexico.

Dismantling the Bureaucracy

Besides repatriating the workers, terminating the program involved dissolving the administrative apparatus developed since April 1943. The domestic portion of the program was easily disassembled. Temporarily assigned employees of participating government agencies simply returned to their normal duties. With the exception of the Immigration Service, agencies absorbed responsibilities that were to continue into their regular postwar routine. Mexican labor inspectors remained in the United States throughout the formal process of repatriation, returning to Mexico upon the completion of their duties.

The Mexico phase of the program was less easy to disassemble. As it became clear that the war was winding down, in July 1945 the U.S. Public Health Service began reassigning its physicians in Mexico to districts in the United States. At about the same time, the RRB issued instructions to its Mexican and U.S. employees to close recruitment headquarters in Querétaro as well as its Mexico City office. On August 16, 1945, WMC representative Churchill Murray was notified that recruitment would cease and no more contracts would be signed. Recruits who had already been examined before termination orders were issued could complete their contracts. The WMC then began to close down its operations in Mexico by dismissing employees, disposing of furniture and other equipment acquired for the program, and arranging for the disposition of its files (some were discarded and destroyed; others were sent to the United States).

On August 22, 1945, railroad management and labor met to discuss the status of the program, and all concurred that the braceros should remain in the United States to complete their contracts. On August 30, the WMC officially notified the railroads that the railroad bracero program was ending, and verified that recruitment had been suspended.

While the Public Health Service had already returned their X-ray equipment and some physicians to the United States in anticipation of the end of the war, in September 1945 the agency was still waiting for official notification of the program's termination. Since the agency's directors wanted to leave some medical equipment and supplies in Mexico, the notification was necessary in order to close operations and transfer the remaining medical supplies to the Mexican government.

The Railroad Retirement Board, however, disposed of most equipment and facilities that were used for the program in Mexico, implementing plans that it had made long before they were needed. In August, the RRB returned several thousand ration books to the Office of Price Administration's regional office in San Francisco.

The U.S. Embassy assisted the RRB by storing its property (supplies, furniture, etc.) and program records until proper disposition could be made. The RRB also received permission to ship what it wished to the United States duty-free. Early in 1946, most of the RRB's property in storage was sold.

Curiously, however, some bureaucrats in the RRB later insisted that since thousands of braceros had contributed to the RRB and were potential receivers of RRB services, it would be appropriate for the RRB to establish Mexico as a district and open a permanent office there. Some in the RRB, it appeared, wanted to use the railroad bracero program as a vehicle to expand the agency's jurisdiction, in the process greatly expanding the agency's power.

Repatriation

The most difficult part of terminating the program was returning the braceros to Mexico in an orderly fashion acceptable to both countries. The original termination orders stipulated that workers would have to leave the country within thirty days after hostilities ended. But the Mexican government objected. For one thing, some contracts had barely begun; those signed in July and August 1945 would not expire until 1946. If the braceros already working in the United States could not finish their contracts, serious legal complications would ensue. Moreover, the Mexican government was concerned that the sudden return of 50,000 workers seeking jobs in a slowing Mexican economy might provoke internal problems. The Mexican government maintained that since the program was international in scope, binational considerations should precede domestic orders.[6]

The U.S. position was not uniform. As late as January 1945, the Immigration Service ruled that only immediate repatriation would be consistent with the bonds and the international agreement.[7] The Department of State, however, maintained that railroad braceros could be repatriated more gradually, at a rate equal to the recruitment rate.[8] The Department of State finally intervened through the embassy in Mexico City and authorized repatriation over a period of six months.[9] The War Manpower Commission notified the railroads in May 1945 that an agreement about repatriation had been reached: the braceros would be returned gradually over six months, proceeding as the contracts expired.[10]

Due to the number of workers involved and bureaucratic requirements, actual repatriation became quite complicated. Once a bracero's contract expired, he was officially eligible to be repatriated. However, since government personnel associated with the railroad bracero program had already been reassigned, the railroads were responsible for getting the workers to Mexico. Railroad management was granted a two-week grace period to arrange transportation to the border for eligible workers at the railroads' expense, while the braceros waited in their camps. U.S. railroads took them to the border, but they traveled without the close supervision of RRB train riders. The Mexican government requested that their labor inspectors remain in the United States and assist in repatriation by verifying expired contracts.[11]

The unions accused the railroads and even the government of trying to keep the braceros in the United States as long as possible. A. E. Lyon, executive secretary of the Railway Labor Executives Association, claimed that the government, in exchange for organized labor's support and co-operation, had promised the immediate repatriation of the Mexican rail-road workers when the conflict ended but was not fulfilling its promise. Further, Lyon claimed that the railroads were trying to prolong the bracero program to suppress domestic rail wages. The Brotherhood of Maintenance of Way Employees even accused the railroads of renewing contracts after V-J Day without verifying the availability of equipment to return the workers. The union also claimed that the 30,000 to 40,000 braceros in the United States as of February 1946 eventually left feeling bitter about the United States because they had been prevented from re-turning to Mexico immediately.[12] Frank Fenton, president of the American Federation of Labor, denounced the government agencies working in the program for not completing their obligations. As Galarza put it, the railroads found it difficult to wean themselves from the employment of braceros.[13]

The Ferrocarriles Nacionales picked up repatriating railroad workers at the border, generally at Ciudad Juárez but also at Nogales and Nuevo Laredo, and transported them to designated places in the interior, at a rate of up to 6,000 monthly.[14] The U.S. Railway Mission, at that time still operating in Mexico City, and the Western Association of Railway Executives assisted in repatriation, collaborating with the War Manpower Commission.[15]

Despite many good intentions and advance planning, numerous prob-lems arose with the repatriation. U.S. railroads were often not able to find enough equipment to move the braceros on schedule as their contracts ended. At times the railroad braceros were forced to wait in their camps for extended periods, much longer than the stipulated two weeks. Some were not afforded an opportunity to work, which Mexico considered to be a breach of contract. Although the Department of Labor (having just absorbed the WMC) tried unsuccessfully to move the braceros to sepa-rate facilities to await repatriation, it reached an agreement with the rail-roads allowing the braceros to work without a contract until they left their work sites.[16] The Mexican government requested that braceros awaiting return home be adequately provided for with amenities such as warm clothing in cold weather.[17]

Administrative procedures documenting repatriation were elaborate and time-consuming; it required about three weeks to process a group of workers. But it was in the interest of railroad management to see to it that this documentation was completed, since the cancellation of a bracero's bond and the subsequent reimbursement to the railroad were contingent on documented repatriation. At the border, the Immigration Service drew up lists of repatriating workers and forwarded them to the Railroad Retirement Board in Chicago to verify against their files. The RRB prepared lists of officially repatriated workers and distributed them to the railroads,[18] which in turn submitted the lists to the Immigration Service for cancellation of the bonds.

Not surprisingly, delays caused frustration for both the braceros and government officials. Immigration Service border personnel were not happy about the additional paperwork they were required to complete for the repatriation process. Not only were their offices understaffed, but the Immigration Service was unwilling to modify any procedures to accommodate the railroad companies. This combination caused trains to become backlogged at the border as the braceros were processed.[19] Once across the border, the railroad braceros often found themselves waiting for the Mexican government to find empty Ferrocarriles Nacionales trains to take them home.[20]

The backlog of braceros, both railroad and agricultural, awaiting return to Mexico created a situation so difficult that John W. Snyder, director of War Mobilization and Reconversion, organized an interagency panel (Office of Defense Transportation, Department of State, Department of Agriculture, War Manpower Commission) to investigate. In the end, Snyder decided to repatriate agricultural braceros from August to November, 1945, railroad braceros from November to December, and the two groups equally thereafter. The following schedule shows the total number of both agricultural and railroad braceros that actually returned to Mexico in the three-month period from December 1945 to February 1946.

Month	Number
December 1945	15,212
January 1946	12,623
February 1946	10,533[21]

While substantial numbers of braceros were officially repatriated to Mexico, other evidence clearly indicates that the railroads did attempt to extend the program beyond the war. The railroads continued to recruit and hire workers through August 1945, when the largest recruitment quota of the program was filled. Many Mexican workers (8,000) who had signed their contracts before V-J Day but had not been transported to the

United States were allowed to go anyway,[22] a clear violation of the spirit of the international agreement.

Some braceros, either through impatience or frustration with the railroads' inaction, returned to Mexico on their own. Upon their arrival home, many filed claims for reimbursement with their former employers to cover expenses they incurred on their trip. Most railroads would not honor their claims, even though WMC field instruction no. 355 stated that a worker could return to Mexico whenever he wished after giving fifteen days' notice. The Southern Pacific, for example, would not reimburse workers unless their contracts had expired at least two weeks before they left.[23] The New York Central followed the same policy for reimbursement.[24] Other major employers—e.g., the Pacific Fruit Express,[25] the Chicago, Rock Island and Pacific, and the Baltimore and Ohio[26]— also received many claims for reimbursement, some submitted without the required documents. Since the Immigration Service would not or could not verify the repatriation of these workers, the bonds that the railroads posted for their return to Mexico could not be released. Likewise, many railroads failed to reimburse individual workers who returned to Mexico on their own for lack of proof.

Cancellation of the Bonds

Officially certified lists of repatriated workers issued by the Immigration Service were the only documents that could be used to cancel the departure bonds posted for the workers at their recruitment and to release the railroads' deposits. The names of workers who returned to Mexico independently did not appear on the lists, which caused many problems for the railroads, even if the braceros' actions were justified. Although in such cases the railroads were not penalized, the bonds were not released for a long time for lack of proof. In fact, the number of workers returning on their own was enough to tie up many railroads' deposits. For instance, of the 3,500 braceros charged against the Southern Pacific's bond in August 1945, approximately 75 percent of the deposits covered braceros actually working. The remaining 25 percent, involving $43,750 in deposits, covered workers who had abandoned their jobs or who had returned to Mexico on their own.[27]

In response to railroad employers' concerns, the Western Association of Railway Executives representative and his assistants stationed in Mexico actually organized house-to-house searches in Mexico City and some states to locate braceros who had returned on their own so the bonds could be canceled. According to the Southern Pacific report, such proof sufficed for the Immigration Service to cancel the bond. WARE's searches continued until 1947.[28]

Many bonds were not canceled until the 1950s, even though technically the contracts had all expired by 1946. While most railroad braceros eventually appeared in Mexico, offering unofficial proof that they had returned to Mexico, others remained in the United States illegally. By 1955, the Immigration Service canceled all the bonds anyway to free the deposits the railroads had made.

14

Corollaries

In spite of efforts in both countries, the railroad bracero program was not as cleanly delineated a project as either would have liked. Unforeseen consequences resulted in some uncomfortable reminders of the program's flaws, and some showed that a temporary labor contract between Mexico and the United States could never function perfectly. In retrospect, it can be seen that the individuals who were most adversely affected by the aftermath of the bracero program were Mexican workers, both those who were contracted as braceros and those who migrated to the United States under other circumstances.

Skilled-Work Program

As part of its overall strategy in the recruitment of workers for the war effort, the Mexican government sought to place its nationals in jobs where they might learn new skills or improve existing ones. Especially in connection with the railroad program, Mexico tried to insist that the braceros be assigned to jobs that would upgrade their skills. Since much of the railroad equipment found in Mexico at the time was from the United States, the position of the Mexican government was understandable, albeit not acceptable within the parameters of the bracero program. The Immigration Act of 1917 clearly stipulated that only unskilled laborers could be employed. However, Mexico's position became more persuasive in early 1944 when rail shipments from Mexico were being delayed because Mexican workers did not know how to operate U.S. equipment.[1]

Although they expressed no interest in providing training, individual U.S. railroads did want to use braceros in certain skilled positions; some braceros had experience the railroads were desperate for. Requests from many participating railroads refer to braceros as carpenters, brakemen, and so forth. The war emergency, however, provided another avenue for training and employing skilled Mexican railroad workers—the U.S. Railway Mission in Mexico City. When the United States established the mission in 1942, it brought U.S. railway maintenance experts to Mexico to advise Mexican railroad personnel and also contracted U.S. firms to actually perform certain maintenance projects.[2] The mission acted in an advisory capacity to the railroad bracero program and sought to promote closer interaction between the railroads of the two countries. As part of the Department of State, the mission served as an indirect conduit between the railway industry in the United States and war-related rail transport in Mexico.

Another division of the State Department in Mexico, the Office of the Coordinator of Inter-American Affairs, proposed a short-term training project, called the Mexican Railroad Workers Project, at least as early as November 1942. This project would have brought Mexican railroad employees to the United States on a thirty-day visit to tour railroad shops and yards and production plants, in collaboration with U.S. railroad unions. The proposal, however, was summarily rejected by the U.S. Embassy in Mexico.[3]

The idea of a training-employment program for skilled railroad workers continued to be discussed in 1943, but no ongoing program took shape until April 1944, when a revised Mexican Railroad Workers Project was initiated. This program was basically under the jurisdiction of the U.S. Railway Mission and its director, Oliver Stevens. The mission, in collaboration with Ferrocarriles Nacionales de México, selected employees of the railroads to go to the United States to train.[4] They were processed separately from the bracero program, and in fact their trips north were not supervised as were the braceros'.

The project was quite small, involving only a few hundred workers, but it offers an interesting contrast to the railroad bracero program. According to the terms under which it was set up, the project was to encompass no more than 1,000 workers.[5] These workers were to learn to use U.S. railway equipment, then return to Mexico and expedite the return of U.S. rolling stock that presumably had not been returned because workers in Mexico did not know how to operate it. These individuals could not become citizens, were not eligible for RRB benefits, and were not to be employees of the railroads to which they were assigned.[6]

From the start it was emphasized that these Mexican workers would present no competition to U.S. workers. Even though they were to perform services for the U.S. railroads to which they were assigned and were to receive a stipend to cover expenses, they would be trainees in modern railroad shop practices. Moreover, while in the United States they would be under the supervision of the U.S. Railway Mission and the Inter-American Training Administration.[7] The terms of the Mexican Railroad

Workers Project made it difficult for U.S. railroad unions to object, since ostensibly the workers were brought to learn, not to work. In June 1944, the Railway Employee Department of the American Federation of Labor officially supported the program through a circular sent to various agencies and offered the union's help in training the workers.

The first contingent of seventy workers was contracted with little formality; in fact, they entered the United States through Laredo with minimum screening and without contracts, having only their I-100 immigration forms marked "trainee." This contingent was sent to the American Refrigeration Transit Company in St. Louis, Missouri.[8] Their stipend was to be equal to the pay of their U.S. counterparts.[9] The Railroad Retirement Board, however, attempted to clarify the status of these workers. Apparently, the railroads took income tax and RRB deductions, which meant that the Mexican workers' financial compensation was not a stipend but a salary. The RRB wanted to amend the Railroad Retirement Act to exclude foreign national trainees from coverage.[10]

The Mexican Railroad Workers Project continued until the end of wartime hostilities. In fact, railroad "trainees" were still being transported to the United States in 1945; in February, seventy workers were dispatched through Laredo.[11]

The status of these workers was ambiguous. They entered the United States as trainees but behaved as employees and were paid the same salaries as regular employees. Because the negotiations to establish their activities were less extensive and less detailed than those creating the bracero program, their working relationship with the U.S. railroads evolved upon their arrival in the United States.

Undocumented Immigration

Even though the Mexican government hoped to use the bracero programs to control, and perhaps even eliminate, undocumented migration to the United States, the fact is that it increased during the war years of the programs. At the beginning of the railroad program, the Secretaría de Trabajo y Previsión Social stated that only workers with official contracts would be allowed to cross the border.[12] But undocumented immigration increasingly became a problem during those years for Mexico and, at a diplomatic level, between the two governments. While the object of this study is not really undocumented migration, it did increase as an effect, albeit unintended, of the bracero programs during World War II. Undocumented Mexican migration to the United States was a response not only to the increased demand for workers in the United States but also to the heightened awareness in Mexico created by the bracero programs. In fact, undocumented migration became apparent shortly after the war began: in April 1942, a local Mexican newspaper reported an increase in migration as a result of the war emergency.[13]

Excélsior reported as early as May 1943 that hundreds of Mexican workers who had illegally crossed the border to the United States were in jail awaiting legal procedures. Many Mexican consuls on the border had communicated their predicament to the Secretaría de Relaciones Exteriores in Mexico City.[14] Indeed, the Secretaría de Gobernación threatened to close the border if undocumented immigration continued; it was contrary to the letter and spirit of the bracero program.[15]

In May 1943, the Southern Pacific itself was discovered by the Immigration Service to have recruited and hired Mexican undocumented workers—individuals who would not have been eligible for the bracero program.[16] Two Mexican citizens in the employ of the railroad recruited about forty Mexican citizens in Mexicali to cross the border and work for the Southern Pacific for $5.50 a day, on the understanding that the employer would procure the appropriate immigration papers. From the testimony of the Mexicans and employees, it would seem that the company had a long-standing network to bring undocumented Mexicans from Mexicali into California through Calexico.[17]

In fact, restricting undocumented immigration was the reason that during the war the Mexican government refused to allow recruiting for the bracero program at or near the border. In 1944, for example, the railroads proposed that recruitment headquarters be moved to Ciudad Juárez, since it and El Paso were so important for the railroad industry. But the Mexican government insisted that recruitment there would encourage movement north of workers seeking jobs; workers not contracted would likely migrate to the United States.[18]

In June 1944, Mexican officials from the Secretaría de Relaciones Exteriores, the Secretaría de Gobernación, and the Secretaría de Trabajo y Previsión Social, as well as U.S. representatives from the Immigration Service and the Department of State, met in Mexico City to discuss the problem of "the clandestine entrance of Mexican laborers." The talks were amiable and the participants arrived at several resolutions: (1) that the Mexican government try to control the emigration of workers, (2) that the INS be reinforced, (3) that both governments launch publicity campaigns about undocumented migration, (4) that undocumented male Mexican workers in the United States be returned to Mexico, and (5) that both governments be stricter in issuing passports, visas, and other forms of identification.[19]

During the bracero programs of World War II, undocumented Mexican immigration to California intensified. The war-related boom throughout California translated into an insatiable demand for workers, especially unskilled. Therefore, the Immigration Service picked up increasingly larger numbers of undocumented Mexicans in Southern California, and routinely returned them to Mexican immigration authorities in Tijuana and Mexicali, regardless of where they were from. But the limited, regional economy of Baja California was not able to absorb them, so local immigration authorities often refused to accept them.[20] In 1945, the Immigration Service agreed to distribute along the U.S.–Mexico border the undocumented Mexicans they picked up in Southern California.[21]

Throughout World War II, the Secretaría de Relaciones Exteriores and the Secretaría de Gobernación wanted to discuss growing undocumented immigration with U.S. government officials. Although it had been a problem since the Mexican Revolution, the information reaching the Mexican government about increasingly sophisticated illegal employment of Mexican nationals in substandard working conditions made binational discussions imperative for them.[22] Mexican officials even proposed that undocumented Mexicans already in the United States be legalized through the bracero program,[23] in an effort to improve their lives. While such a contract would obviously have violated the spirit of the bracero program, the proposal does reflect the desperation of the Mexican government to protect undocumented Mexicans in the United States.

"Clandestine entrance of Mexican laborers" would continue unabated after the war, in many cases following the patterns of migration and employment established by both divisions of the bracero program. It would intensify after the agricultural bracero program was finally dismantled in 1964.[24]

Unfinished Business

For all practical purposes, except for a few workers lingering at their jobs, the railroad bracero program ended in 1946 when the last contracts expired. However, one issue unique to the program remained unresolved for many years. During the negotiations, U.S. officials agreed informally that no deductions for the Railroad Retirement Board would be taken from the braceros' paychecks. What happened subsequently is unclear, but deductions for the RRB were taken from each bracero's checks and deposited in the RRB's general account, along with the deductions from other railroad workers' checks. At the end of the program, the Department of State notified the Mexican government that it would seek authorization for release of the accumulated deductions, which in 1946 amounted to $6,750,000.[25]

The Department of State continued to urge the RRB to release the funds but was not successful. Mexican diplomats occasionally reminded the Department of State after the war that the funds should be returned. The State Department agreed that they should, but since the RRB was not accountable to the Department of State, it had no leverage to force surrender of the funds. The Department of State facilitated the introduction of a bill in the House in 1950 that would have disfranchised ex-railroad braceros of benefits of the Railroad Retirement Act, thereby permitting the release of the accumulated deductions to the Mexican government. Similar bills were introduced in the Senate in 1949 (S. 1852 and S. 2502), 1951 (S. 215), and 1953 (S. 419), and were referred to the Senate Committee on Labor and Public Welfare. None ever passed.[26] Senators Robert Taft and Dennis Chávez were instrumental in the introduction of these bills.

The RRB was reluctant to release the funds. It denied, in the first place, that an informal agreement existed to exempt the braceros from the deductions. More specifically, the RRB asserted that returning the deductions would establish a dangerous precedent. Not only would it be difficult to refund deductions to other short-term workers, but it might encourage the importation of other RRB-exempt foreign railroad workers. Moreover, Mexican railroad braceros had enjoyed certain advantages over domestic workers, such as transportation to the work site (the RRB failed to indicate that the railroads generally hired local laborers). Further, the RRB claimed that $1 million of its own funds had been spent on the program, a sum that had not been reimbursed by the government. Finally, the administrative costs of calculating the correct amount to be reimbursed would be exorbitant. The RRB curtly suggested in 1950 that should the federal government deem such a refund necessary or desirable, the appropriate amount could be taken from the general government account.[27]

However, it was known outside of government circles that the Department of State was trying to get the money refunded. The RRB deductions were discussed, for example, at meetings of the Joint U.S.–Mexican Trade Union Committee from 1953 to 1955. Representatives of the Confederación de Trabajadores Mexicanos prepared a document outlining the problem and soliciting the support of U.S. unions in arranging the refunds. While then President Harry Truman, the Department of State, and the Senate Committee on the Budget all supported the refund, the Senate committee overseeing the railroad retirement fund and Senator John Kennedy opposed it. U.S. unions also opposed it.[28]

The Mexican government continued to press, yet the Department of State could find no strategy to force the RRB to release the money. Neither correspondence between the Department of State and the RRB nor research with related primary documents has confirmed the fate of the accumulated deductions, but there is a likely scenario. Concurrently with the possible return of the RRB deductions, Mexican and U.S. diplomats were discussing Mexican payments arising from the Lend-Lease Agreements of World War II that were coming due in the early and mid 1950s. Around 1956, the U.S. government became more insistent that Mexico pay off Lend-Lease-related war debts, then amounting to around $8 million. Although it is not clear how it happened or who was behind the proposal, apparently Mexico agreed not to pursue its claim to the accumulated RRB deductions in exchange for having its Lend-Lease debts forgiven. Given the evidence, this is the most probable fate of the RRB deductions.[29]

If this is true, the decision that Mexican negotiators made regarding the RRB deductions presents several problems. It is not clear whether the fact that the Mexican government accepted this arrangement means that the ex-railroad braceros (or their widows) are no longer eligible for RRB benefits. The RRB deductions were made from the wages of individual workers toward a general fund for railroad workers, which theoretically entitled them to certain benefits. Since the railroad braceros worked for U.S. railroads such a short time, obviously their benefits would be limited. But for workers who may have returned to the United States to work permanently for a U.S. railroad, would their time as a bracero be counted toward their benefits and ultimate retirement? Did the Mexican government in fact have the right to trade off individual worker benefits?

This situation arises from implementing an international work agreement in an industry whose labor is highly organized within certain parameters. The request from Mexico that the railroad braceros be exempted from RRB deductions is logical, but neither the RRB nor the railroad unions were able or willing to be flexible enough to adapt the program to workers imported from another country.

Conclusion

Although the railroad bracero program of World War II is relatively unknown, analysis of the program clearly shows that the history of Mexican migration to the United States is even richer and more important for the U.S. economy than the literature indicates. The program arose not only out of immediate war-related labor needs in the United States but also from a long tradition of employment of Mexican immigrants, legal and undocumented, on U.S. railroads. The contribution of railroad braceros to their employers' ability to meet war demands is certain: track maintenance gangs on crucial southwestern tracks during World War II were often overwhelmingly Mexican.

The railroad bracero program presents several avenues of analysis. First, the program highlights the historical significance of nonagricultural employment for Mexican immigrants, legal and undocumented alike. Although the waning of U.S. railroads has made the industry seem less important, many early scholars of Mexican immigration, such as Manuel Gamio and Paul Taylor, considered railroad employment essential to understanding the migration of Mexican workers. Indeed, the railroad employers themselves used their traditional employment of Mexican immigrants as justification for an organized program during World War II.

Second, the railroad bracero program is the only example of systematic government-sanctioned importation into the United States of nonagricultural employees. The bracero program is usually associated with the importation of temporary, unskilled agricultural workers. However, the railroad industry was also able to rationalize a temporary contract labor program to acquire workers, especially unskilled ones, justifying it through its previous employment practices.

The railroad bracero program could become a significant precedent should Mexico and the United States negotiate another bracero program; a future temporary contract labor program between the two countries would surely encompass nonagricultural industries. And since the employment patterns of Mexican immigrants have evolved substantially in the last twenty years, a future bracero program would naturally reflect those changes.

Third, the role of powerful U.S. railroad brotherhoods in the railroad bracero program cannot be overemphasized. Although many students of Mexican immigration have assumed that an international temporary contract labor program cannot develop in the presence of strong unions— since unions in effect represent the interests of domestic workers, whose status is inevitably affected by the importation of temporary workers— the World War II experience clearly shows that in the face of a national emergency the most powerful unions can be sufficiently neutralized to allow the recruitment of temporary contract workers.

While the unions agreed to lay aside their objections to the program for the duration of the war, their power was apparent in many areas of the program, including the braceros' pay scale—the railroad unions negotiated braceros' wages, since by definition the collective contracts included bracero wages. Obviously, the unions did not include temporary contract labor recruited in Mexico when they negotiated the contracts; in fact, railroad brotherhood leadership made it patently clear that such recruitment interfered with their long-standing goal of improving the wages of unskilled railroad workers. Nevertheless, the braceros enjoyed some of the benefits the unions had achieved for domestic workers.

Indeed, the attitude of U.S. unions toward Mexican immigration, particularly the railroad bracero program, merits its own study. While the active role of the U.S. brotherhoods in the program appears to have been minimal, even symbolic, their power loomed ever-present in the background, reminding the War Manpower Commission and the Railroad Retirement Board of their obligations to domestic workers. In spite of efforts of the railroads and some U.S. bureaucrats to extend the railroad program beyond the war, for example, the brotherhoods had merely to remind the U.S. government that the negotiators had limited it to the war emergency. A comparative analysis of the unions' relationships with the railroad program and the agricultural program would emphasize the uniqueness of the railroad program and underscore the brotherhoods' challenges in adjusting to a war-oriented economy.

Fourth, the railroad bracero program remains as the only example of a successful binational migration agreement between Mexico and the United States, negotiated on a more or less equal basis and generally respected. The railroad braceros were recruited in Mexico, transported to their work sites, and mostly repatriated to Mexico on schedule after the war. The agricultural bracero program provides a basis for comparison, since it functioned similarly to the railroad segment during World War II, relying on participation from both governments to seek fair working conditions for the farmworkers. But the agricultural program continued willy-nilly until 1964, disintegrating after the war into basically a unilateral seasonal farm labor recruitment program in the hands of the grower employers, with virtually no protection for the workers. Most analyses of the agricultural bracero program attribute its failure not only to the relative power of agribusiness and the complete disenfranchisement of all farmworkers in the United States but also to the debility of the Mexican government in program negotiations after World War II. Only the emergency created by World War II, which made the availability of labor a national obsession in the United States, was sufficient to force the U.S. government to deal with the Mexican government on a more equal basis.

The railroad program, indeed, represents an important precedent for future discussions about migration between Mexico and the United States. Many researchers and policymakers assume that the traditional asymmetrical relationship between the United States and Mexico automatically precludes a bilateral approach to migration policy. While this has generally been true, the railroad program shows that the Mexican government can effectively represent the interests of temporary workers under contract, and it constitutes a point of reference for Mexico in terms of migration policy. Historically, the United States has considered its immigration policy to be strictly a domestic concern; that another country could intervene, at least in one instance, cannot be easily dismissed.

The description of the administration of the program, until now relatively unstudied, provides rich detail about the operation of a binationally administered migration project developed on an ad hoc basis. While the evolution of the bureaucracy may seem irrelevant, its efficacy, or at times lack of, directly influenced the workers' ability to complete their contracts and affected the quality of their living and working conditions. That government agencies settled conflicts and investigated complaints is one measure of the success of the program. Even though the railroad program was imperfect in many respects, its bilateral nature allowed the Mexican government to see that complaints were addressed, which eventually resulted in major modifications of the contract.

A cursory evaluation will place the program's bureaucracy in a more meaningful perspective. In the course of discharging its supervisory duties, the War Manpower Commission developed a network of working relationships among many government and industrial organizations, such as the Railroad Retirement Board, the Office of Price Administration, the railroad labor unions, the Western Association of Railway Executives, the Mexican government, and so on. This patchwork network constituted the railroad bracero program's bureaucracy. Actually, the administration was relatively flexible, given the war emergency and the conditions under which the WMC was working.

By virtue of its position in the program, the WMC office in Mexico assumed quasi-diplomatic status and prestige, an unusual position for a government domestic labor office and one that inevitably caused conflicts. Nonetheless, the U.S. Embassy in Mexico City had no particular problem with limiting its role in the program to that of an observer once the negotiations were completed and recruitment began. Ambassador Messersmith and the embassy staff intervened only in the event of complaints or problems. The WMC office maintained regular communications with the Secretaría de Relaciones Exteriores and the Secretaría de Trabajo y Previsión Social, circumventing the embassy; in turn, the Mexican government normally directed its inquiries about the railroad braceros to the WMC. Although the WMC was never granted any formal recognition for its ad hoc status, the agency successfully maintained its quasi-diplomatic posture throughout the program.

The effect of the railroad bracero program on the Railroad Retirement Board was far more problematic. While many officials were vigilant about protecting the workers' interests, others were equally interested in using the program to expand the agency's power. Some RRB officials considered the agency's collaboration with the railroad bracero program to be justification for establishing a permanent district office in Mexico to service repatriated railroad braceros. Although the move was unsuccessful, it would have meant expanding the RRB's normally domestic role beyond the United States. In addition, the RRB demonstrated an undue interest in holding on to deductions it had received from the braceros' wages, managing to fend off all attempts by the State Department to have them returned to the Mexican government. To this day, the agency has the accumulated deductions in its accounts. Even if the Mexican government did receive a Lend-Lease credit equal to the sum of the RRB deductions, the RRB's till is a dubious final destination for these funds.

The administrative functions of the railroads in the program developed very differently from the way they intended. In 1942 and 1943, railroad management considered a temporary contract labor program to be the most expedient solution to their endemic track labor shortages. The railroads evidently assumed that the program would follow the same casual form that the WWI bracero program had followed, with the RRB assuming the role that railroad employers had played for many years by recruiting track workers in Mexico—in other words, both the WMC and the RRB would act as employment agencies for the railroads. Indeed, the RRB and the WMC did perform pivotal services for the rail companies during the program and were instrumental in the railroads' successful participation in the war effort. In the process, however, the railroads as employers became responsible to the WMC and the RRB, a circumstance they found disagreeable.

Although the railroad bracero program achieved a certain autonomy, its administration remained closely associated with the agencies that participated in it. In time, the railroad bracero program became self-serving for both the WMC and the RRB, since it expanded their functions and their funds beyond their normal scope. The railroad bracero program enabled them to operate outside of the United States, and assume quasi-diplomatic functions. Both agencies' sphere of responsibility basically centered on workers in the United States, but the bracero program greatly altered that.

The Mexican government actively collaborated with the railroad program's administration in certain phases of its operation. Indeed, without its cooperation, recruitment would have been impossible. The conditions that the Mexican government established for recruitment served to delineate clear parameters for the bracero program and prospective employers within Mexico. In spite of bribes and corruption, braceros were more likely to receive fair and consistent treatment during recruitment.

The participation of Mexican government offices and personnel in the bracero program was subsidized by the Mexican government, not the bracero program. Several agencies assigned personnel to the program, at times taking them from other duties. In other words, the Mexican government indirectly financed the bracero program. Although I have no way of estimating how much the program cost the Mexican government, it disrupted many agencies' normal duties.

The railroad program, even though tightly administered, was not without serious domestic consequences in Mexico. The most notorious concerned internal migration to recruitment centers and to the U.S.–Mexico border, as well as undocumented migration to the United States. From this perspective, the bracero program not only failed as a strategy to control labor movements within Mexico but exacerbated them. Moreover, intensive recruitment in rural areas caused labor shortages that occasionally affected local agricultural production, in spite of efforts not to contract *ejidatarios.*

Many railroad braceros complained about the corruption in Mexico during recruitment. At least some applicants were apparently forced to pay a fee to local politicians or to STPS labor inspectors who issued the preliminary recruitment cards to prospective braceros. Although the extent of the practice is still not known, such payments obviously were not consistent with the spirit of the program and implied that the poorest of candidates had less possibility of being contracted.

The long-term effects of the railroad bracero program participants are largely unknown. Upon the conclusion of their contracts, some did remain in the United States to continue working for the railroads. Others, upon their repatriation to Mexico, used the skills they had learned on U.S. railroads to work for the Ferrocarriles Nacionales de México. While I have not found sources to determine the number of braceros who received training, some acquired quite specialized railroad skills that improved their job prospects in Mexico.

In the long run, the experience of the railroad bracero program may be even more valuable than the agricultural component during World War II, not only for students of Mexican migration, but also for those of U.S.–Mexican relations and the Mexican American community. Should the concept of a temporary contract labor program be seriously and formally reintroduced (not as allocation of visas, as is the case now in the H-2 program), it might well be applied to a nonagricultural industry. The demand for seasonal farmworkers in the United States has evolved in the last twenty years, reflecting profound changes within the industry. Other industries, however, particularly in the service sector, have found it increasingly difficult to employ unskilled workers to sustain their growth; some cite geographical location, others low wages, and so on. In any event, the railroad bracero program serves as proof that Mexican immigrants have significantly contributed to nonagricultural enterprises in the United States and that a temporary contract labor program can successfully be implemented for those industries, with the active participation of Mexico and labor organizations.

The railroad bracero program also reaffirms the need to more fully investigate the historical significance of railroad track construction and maintenance to the migration of Mexican American workers. Standard texts of Mexican American history nearly all refer to the importance of railroad employment in determining the settlement and employment patterns of Mexican American settlements throughout the Midwest and Southwest, yet little research has been done. Data gathered for this study suggests that the railroads had been deliberately utilizing Mexican and

Mexican American labor for many, many years before the railroad bracero program, and that railroad management considered the bracero program merely another strategy of locating Mexican labor to which many had become accustomed.

Finally, the railroad bracero program of World War II demonstrates that a bilateral approach to Mexican immigration to the United States is possible. Even though the war emergency that produced it was extreme, the railroad program as a bilateral program introduces a significant new dimension to analyses of Mexican migration and its role in U.S.–Mexican relations. The fact that the Mexican government was able to insist upon an active role establishes an important precedent, one that could serve to open future channels for collaboration between the two countries.

Notes

Abbreviations

INS	Immigration and Naturalization Service
memo	memorandum
Natl Arch., DoS Rec.	National Archives, Department of State Records
Natl Arch., ODT Rec.	National Archives, Office of Defense Transportation Records
Natl Arch., WMC Rec.	National Archives, War Manpower Commission Records
Qrtro, Arch. del Pdr Ejec.	Querétaro (State of), Archivo del Poder Ejecutivo
RRB, Bur. of Law Files	Railroad Retirement Board, Bureau of Law Files
RRB, Exec. Officer's File	Railroad Retirement Board, Executive Officer's File
So. Pac. Intrnl Files	Southern Pacific Internal Files
SRE, Arch. Hist.	Secretaría de Relaciones Exteriores, Archivo Histórico
U.S. Dept of State	U.S. Department of State

INTRODUCTION

1. Robert Jones, *Mexican War Workers in the United States* (Washington, D.C.: Pan American Union, 1945).

2. Ernesto Galarza, *Merchants of Labor: The Mexican Bracero Story* (Santa Barbara, Calif.: McNally & Loftin, 1964).

3. Richard Craig, *The Bracero Program* (Austin: University of Texas Press, 1971).

4. Peter Kirstein, *Anglo over Bracero: A History of the Mexican Worker in the United States from Roosevelt to Nixon* (San Francisco: R&E Research Associates, 1977).

5. Erasmo Gamboa, *Mexican Labor and World War II: Braceros in the Pacific Northwest, 1942–1947* (Austin: University of Texas Press, 1990).

6. So. Pac. Intrnl Files, Historical Labor File, "Historical Data in Connection with Employment of Mexican National Laborers Imported from Mexico," August 1950.

1. THE U.S. GOVERNMENT AND THE RAILROAD INDUSTRY

1. William S. Greever, "A Comparison of Railroad Land-Grant Policies," *Agricultural History* 25 (1951): 83–84.

2. Greever, "Railroad Land-Grant Policies," 83–84.

3. Greever, "Railroad Land-Grant Policies," 83–84.

4. John Stover, *The Life and Decline of the American Railroads* (New York: Oxford University Press, 1970), 118.

5. Gabriel Kolko, *Railroads and Regulations, 1877–1916* (Princeton, N.J.: Princeton University Press, 1965), 3–5.

6. Kolko, *Railroads and Regulations, 1877–1916,* 3–5.

7. Lloyd J. Mercer, "Building ahead of Demand: Some Evidence for the Land Grant Railroads," *Journal of Economic History* 34 (1974): 492.

8. Stover, *Life and Decline,* 113.

9. Walter D. Hines, *War History of American Railroads* (New Haven, Conn.: Yale University Press, 1928), 3.

10. Hines, *War History of American Railroads,* 3.

11. Stover, *Life and Decline,* 164.

12. John Stover, *American Railroads* (Chicago: University of Chicago Press, 1961), 201.

13. Stover, *Life and Decline,* 163.

14. Stover, *Life and Decline,* 163.

15. Stover, *Life and Decline,* 163.

16. Hines, *War History of American Railroads,* 152–186.

17. Stover, *Life and Decline,* 170–177.

18. Julius Parmelee, *A Review of Railway Operations in 1935,* Special Series, no. 59 (Washington, D.C., 1936), 14.

19. Lee G. Lauck, "The Collapse in Railroad Credit," *Barron's* 11 (1931): 15.

20. James C. Nelson, *Railroad Transportation and Public Policy* (Washington, D.C.: Brookings Institution, 1959), 225–226.

21. Ernest T. Clough, "A Crisis in Railroad Finance," *Barron's* 12 (1932): 3, 6.

22. "Government Railroad Loans," *Railway Age* 92 (1932): 948.

23. M. David Gould, "Overinvestment: The Root of Railroads' Trouble," *Barron's* 12 (1932): 10–11.

24. Carlton Corliss, *Main Line of Mid-America: The Story of the Illinois Central* (New York: Creative Age Press, 1950), 438.

25. George Burgess and Miles C. Kennedy, *The Centennial History of the Pennsylvania Railroad* (Philadelphia: Pennsylvania Railroad Company, 1949), 56.

26. Stover, *Life and Decline,* 180.

27. Stover, *Life and Decline,* 180.

28. "Rails' Net Sags: Increase in Gross Revenue Offset by Pressure of Heavier Costs and Taxes in the First Half of 1944," *Business Week,* 14 Aug. 1944, 66.

29. "House in Order? Railroads Hope Their Debt Cuts Have Put Them in

Shape for Postwar Competition Now That Gross Seems to Have Ceilinged," *Business Week*, 14 Aug. 1943, 14.

30. "Resurgent R.R.: Southern System Affords Case Study of What War Traffic and Effective Management Can Do to a Road's Finances," *Business Week*, 31 March 1945, 74–78.

31. "Rail Debt Cut: Southern Pacific Provides Excellent Example of how the War Lines Are Putting Finance to Order," *Business Week*, 28 Oct. 1944, 69.

32. "Rails' Net Slips: Increases in Ton-Miles and Gross Income Aren't Enough to Offset Rising Trend in Operating Costs," *Business Week*, 17 June 1944, 79–80. The ICC divides American railroads into classes, according to size and scope of service. Most large regional and national railroads are Class I railroads. Small or narrow-gauge railroads receive other classifications.

33. "Rails Slump: Most Roads Report Decline in February Earnings despite an Overall Revenue Increase. Net of Pennsylvania Is an Exception," *Business Week*, 1 April 1944, 81.

34. "Rails Are Flush: Comfortable Cash Positions Expected to Provoke Clamor for Retirement of Debt and Payment of Defaulted Interest," *Business Week*, 18 Sept. 1943, 106.

35. Interstate Commerce Commission, *Forty-Seventh Annual Report of the Interstate Commerce Commission* (Washington, D.C.: GPO, 1933), 22.

36. "Year for Ruling: Completion of Four Major Reorganizations Makes 1944 an Eventful Period. Section 77 Is Facilitated by Court Ruling," *Business Week*, 16 Dec. 1944, 66.

37. "Rails Milestone: Western Pacific, When It Emerged from Reorganization, Helped to Settle Some Major Points under Section 77," *Business Week*, 13 Jan. 1945, 75–76.

2. MEXICAN LABOR ON U.S. RAILROADS

1. So. Pac. Intrnl Files, Historical Labor File, "Historical Data in Connection with Employment of Mexican National Laborers Imported from Mexico," Aug. 1950.

2. David Lightner, "Construction Labor on the Illinois Central," *Illinois State Historical Society Journal* 66 (1973): 285–286.

3. Malcolm Clark, "The Bigot Disclosed: Ninety Years of Nativism," *Oregon Historical Quarterly* 75 (1974): 123.

4. John Stover, *The Railroads of the South, 1865–1900* (Chapel Hill: University of North Carolina Press, 1955).

5. George E. Pozzetta, "A Padrone Looks at Florida: Labor Recruiting and the Florida East Coast Railway," *Florida Historical Quarterly* 54 (1975): 74–84.

6. George Kraus, "Chinese Laborers and the Construction of the Central Pacific," *Utah Historical Review* 37 (1969): 42–44.

7. Clark, "Bigot Disclosed," 123.

8. Kraus, "Chinese Laborers," 47–49.

9. James Ducker, *Men of the Steel Rails: Workers on the Atchison, Topeka and Santa Fe Railroad* (Lincoln: University of Nebraska Press, 1983), 27. The Japanese also supplanted Native American (Mojave and Pueblo) workers in Southern California.

10. Ducker, *Men of the Steel Rails,* 28.

11. Denver Hertel, *History of the Brotherhood of Maintenance of Way Employees* (Washington, D.C.: Ransdell, 1955), 10.

12. W. Fred Cottrell, *The Railroader* (Stanford, Calif.: Stanford University Press, 1940), 51–55.

13. Interviews with Crispín del Valle, a long-time resident of Tecate, Baja California, and retired from the San Diego and Arizona Railroad. Don Crispín recalls that when he began working for railroads in that state in the 1920s as a track worker, maintenance gangs attracted criticism and even scorn from local residents.

14. Ducker, *Men of the Steel Rails,* 27.

15. See Rodolfo Acuña, *Occupied America: A History of Chicanos,* 2d ed. (New York: Harper & Row, 1981).

16. See recent studies of local Chicano communities, such as Mario T. García's *Desert Immigrants: The Mexicans of El Paso* (New Haven, Conn.: Yale University Press, 1981); Alberto Camarillo's "The Making of a Chicano Community: A History of the Chicanos in Santa Barbara, California, 1850–1930" (Ph.D. diss., University of California, Los Angeles, 1975); and Antonio Ríos-Bustamante's *Los Ángeles, pueblo y región, 1781–1850* (Mexico City: Instituto Nacional de Antropología e Historia, 1991).

17. See Américo Paredes, *A Texas-Mexican Cancionero: Folksongs of the Lower Border* (Austin: University of Texas Press, 1995). Paredes presents a valuable analysis of the function of *corridos* for Mexican Americans and Mexican immigrants.

18. Although we have many references to this movement of Mexican workers north to the border attendant to the construction of railroads linking northern Mexico with U.S. markets, I have not yet identified the documents necessary to quantify and describe this migration.

19. This is the phase of Mexican employment on U.S. railroads most studied and recognized. In fact, Mexican workers may have been pivotal in the construction of southwestern railroads, which in turn led to further development of many sectors, including mining and agriculture.

20. See Michael C. Meyer and William L. Sherman, *The Course of Mexican History,* 4th ed. (New York: Oxford University Press, 1991).

21. Victor Clark, "Mexican Labor in the United States," *Bulletin of the Bureau of Labor,* no. 78 (1908): 473.

22. John Coatsworth refers to these documents when the Archivo General de la Nación was still located in downtown Mexico City; I have not been able

to identify them in the archive's present location in the former Cárcel de Lecumberri.

23. Clark, "Mexican Labor," 470.

24. Literature about the disintegration of the hacienda system during the *porfiriato* illustrates the increasingly difficult position of Mexican workers.

25. In *Desert Immigrants,* Mario García includes a detailed analysis of how wage and price differentials between Ciudad Juárez and El Paso functioned as part of life on the U.S.–Mexico border. See chapter 3, pp. 33–64.

26. García, *Desert Immigrants,* 36.

27. Vernon Briggs, Walter Fogel, and Fred H. Schmidt, *The Chicano Worker* (Austin: University of Texas Press, 1977).

28. Carey McWilliams, *North from Mexico: The Spanish-Speaking People of the United States* (New York: Greenwood Press, 1968), 186.

29. Roden Fuller, "Occupations of the Mexican-Born Population of Texas, New Mexico, and Arizona, 1900–1920," *Journal of the American Statistical Association* 23 (1928): 67.

30. Robert Divine, *The History of American Immigration Policy* (New Haven, Conn.: Yale University Press, 1957).

31. Clark, "Mexican Labor," 477–478.

32. McWilliams, *North from Mexico,* 169.

33. Charles Wollenberg, "Working on *El Traque,*" in *The Chicano,* ed. Norris Hundley (Santa Barbara, Calif.: Clio Books, 1975).

34. García, *Desert Immigrants,* chapter 4.

35. García, *Desert Immigrants,* 54–55.

36. García, *Desert Immigrants,* 63.

37. Erasmo Gamboa, *Mexican Labor and World War II: Braceros in the Pacific Northwest, 1942–1947* (Austin: University of Texas Press, 1990), 6–9, 13.

3. THE RAILROAD BROTHERHOODS

1. Alexander F. Whitney, *Wartime Wages and Railroad Labor: A Report on the 1942–43 Wage Movement of the Transportation Brotherhoods* (Cleveland: Brotherhood of Railroad Trainmen, 1944), 3.

2. Beulah Amidon, "Trouble on the Railroads," *Survey Graphic* 32 (1943): 493–497.

3. Amidon, "Trouble on the Railroads," 493–497.

4. "Rail Seizure Eases the Strike Menace but Labor Ills Still Plague the Nation," *Business Week,* 3 Jan. 1944, 44–46.

5. Gwendolyn Mink, *Old Labor and New Immigrants in American Political Development: Union, Party, and State, 1875–1920* (Ithaca, N.Y.: Cornell University Press, 1986), 71–112.

6. Philip J. Mellinger, *Race and Labor in Western Copper: The Fight for Equality, 1896–1918* (Tucson: University of Arizona Press, 1995), 1–60.

7. Suzanne LaFollette, "Jim Crow and Casey Jones," *Nation* 155 (1942): 675–677.

8. "FEPC versus the Railroads," *Time,* 27 Dec. 1942.

9. LaFollette, "Jim Crow and Casey Jones," 676–677.

10. Denver Hertel, *History of the Brotherhood of Maintenance of Way Employees* (Washington, D.C.: Ransdell, 1955).

11. Harvey A. Levenstein, "The AFL and Mexican Immigration in the 1920s: An Experiment in Labor Diplomacy," *Hispanic American Historical Review* 48 (1968): 206–219.

12. A translation would be "distributing flyers in this consul's district attacking those Mexicans that work for the railroads in this country." SRE, Arch. Hist., IV-708-12, April 1935.

13. Carey McWilliams, *North from Mexico: The Spanish-Speaking People of the United States* (New York: Greenwood Press, 1968), chapter 8.

14. Rodolfo Acuña, *Occupied America: A History of Chicanos,* 2d ed. (New York: Harper & Row, 1981).

15. Charles Wollenberg, "Working on *El Traque,*" in *The Chicano,* ed. Norris Hundley (Santa Barbara, Calif.: Clio Books, 1975).

16. Mario T. García, *Desert Immigrants: The Mexicans of El Paso* (New Haven, Conn.: Yale University Press, 1981), 107.

17. Acuña, *Occupied America,* 87.

18. Hertel, *Maintenance of Way Employees,* 61–62.

4. WORLD WAR II AND U.S.–MEXICO RELATIONS

1. Richard Craig, *The Bracero Program* (Austin: University of Texas Press, 1971), xi.

2. See Frederick B. Pike, *FDR's Good Neighbor Policy: Sixty Years of Generally Gentle Chaos* (Austin: University of Texas Press, 1995), for a provocative and highly readable revisionist history of this cornerstone of U.S. policy toward Latin America.

3. Samuel Flagg Bemis, *The Latin American Policy of the United States* (New York: Norton, 1943), 257.

4. David Green, *The Containment of Latin America: A History of the Myths and Realities of the Good Neighbor Policy* (Chicago: Quadrangle Books, 1971), 19.

5. Percy Wells Bidwell, *Economic Defense of Latin America* (Boston: World Peace Foundation, 1941), 41.

6. Bidwell, *Economic Defense of Latin America,* 41.

7. Green, *Containment of Latin America,* 42.

8. Bidwell, *Economic Defense of Latin America,* 55.

9. Bidwell, *Economic Defense of Latin America,* 55.

10. Edwin Lieuwen, *Arms and Politics in Latin America* (New York: Praeger, 1960), 212.

11. Stephen R. Niblo, *War, Diplomacy, and Development: The United States and Mexico, 1938–1954* (Wilmington, Del.: Scholarly Resources, 1995), 77–80.

12. Niblo, *War, Diplomacy, and Development,* 35–55, 283–284.

13. J. Lloyd Mecham, *The United States and Inter-American Security, 1889–1960* (Austin: University of Texas Press, 1961), 217.

14. Betty Kirk, *Covering the Mexican Front: The Battle of Europe versus America* (Norman: University of Oklahoma Press, 1942), 31.

15. Daniel James, *Mexico and the Americans* (New York: Praeger, 1963), 353.

16. Carmela Elvira Santoro, "United States and Mexican Relations during World War II" (Ph.D. diss., Syracuse University, 1967), 16.

17. Santoro, "United States and Mexican Relations," 18.

18. Santoro, "United States and Mexican Relations," 19.

19. Kirk, *Covering the Mexican Front,* 292.

20. Santoro, "United States and Mexican Relations," 18.

21. Santoro, "United States and Mexican Relations," 10.

22. Niblo, *War, Diplomacy, and Development,* 92.

23. Santoro, "United States and Mexican Relations," 11–12.

24. Santoro, "United States and Mexican Relations," 24.

25. Santoro, "United States and Mexican Relations," 46.

26. Santoro, "United States and Mexican Relations," 6.

27. Even though this skilled-workers program was quite limited, it involved the Railway Mission in the recruitment and contracting of workers as well as supervision—activities completely unanticipated.

28. Santoro, "United States and Mexican Relations," 6.

29. Oliver M. Stevens, "How Not to Operate a Railroad," *Railway Age* 120 (1946): 672–673. See also an editorial entitled "Unions in the Saddle" in the same issue (p. 665), applauding Stevens's assessment of Mexican railways and opining that U.S. railroads must do whatever is necessary to prevent something similar from happening in the United States. Basically, Stevens and U.S. railroads feared the potential strength of the railroad brotherhoods.

30. The historical archives of the Secretaría de Relaciones Exteriores in Mexico City house several files about this railroad car embargo.

31. Craig, *The Bracero Program,* 23.

5. PRIOR MEXICAN MIGRATION TO THE UNITED STATES

1. Although little documentation remains to analyze the program, Lawrence Cardoso, in *Mexican Emigration to the United States, 1897–1931: Socio-Economic Patterns* (Tucson: University of Arizona Press, 1980), provides a balanced and detailed account. Mark Reisler's version in *By the Sweat of Their Brow: Mexican Immigrant Labor in the United States, 1900–1940* (Westport, Conn.: Greenwood Press, 1976) is also helpful.

2. These articles are reprinted in *Mexican Workers in the United States: Historical and Political Perspectives,* ed. George C. Kiser and Martha Woody Kiser (Albuquerque: University of New Mexico Press, 1979), 9–32.

3. Mario T. García, *Desert Immigrants: The Mexicans of El Paso* (New Haven, Conn.: Yale University Press, 1981), 47–63.

4. Cardoso, *Mexican Emigration.*

5. Manuel Gamio, *Mexican Immigration to the United States: A Study of Human Migration and Adjustment* (New York: Dover Publications, 1971), 181–186.

6. Individuals who had acquired legal U.S. visas often rented them for a fee to others for easy entry into the United States. Since border officials did not have databases to check against, the same visa could be used time and again.

7. Abraham Hoffman, *Unwanted Mexican Americans in the Great Depression: Repatriation Pressures, 1929–1939* (Tucson: University of Arizona Press, 1974), 36.

8. Hoffman, *Unwanted Mexican Americans,* 37.

9. Hoffman, *Unwanted Mexican Americans,* 39–40.

10. Hoffman, *Unwanted Mexican Americans,* 172–173. See *In Defense of La Raza: The Los Angeles Mexican Consulate and the Mexican Community, 1929 to 1936* by Francisco E. Balderrama (Tucson: University of Arizona Press, 1982) for a discussion about the role of the Mexican consulate.

11. George Kiser and David Silverman, "Mexican Repatriation during the Depression," in Kiser and Kiser, *Mexican Workers,* 45–66.

12. Kiser and Silverman, "Mexican Repatriation," 59–61.

13. Hoffman, *Unwanted Mexican Americans,* 174–175.

14. Laurence Ilsley Hewes, Jr., "Some Migratory Problems in California's Specialized Agriculture" (Ph.D. diss., George Washington University, 1946), 129–130. See also Blanca Torres, *Historia de la Revolución Mexicana, 1940–1952: Hacia la utopía industrial* (Mexico City: Colegio de México, 1984), 236.

6. THE AGRICULTURAL PROGRAM

1. Robert C. Jones, *Mexican War Workers in the United States* (Washington, D.C.: Pan American Union, 1945), 24.

2. Laurence Ilsley Hewes, Jr., "Some Migratory Problems in California's Specialized Agriculture" (Ph.D. diss., George Washington University, 1946), 159.

3. Harry Schwartz, *Seasonal Farm Labor in the United States (with Special Reference to Hired Workers in Fruit and Vegetable and Sugar Beet Production)* (New York: Columbia University Press, 1945).

4. Ernesto Galarza, *Strangers in Our Fields* (Washington, D.C.: Fund for the Republic, 1956), 43.

5. Hewes, "Migratory Problems," 123.

6. Galarza, *Strangers in Our Fields,* 42.

7. Richard Craig, *The Bracero Program* (Austin: University of Texas Press, 1971), 38.

8. Schwartz, *Seasonal Farm Labor,* 24.

9. Erasmo Gamboa, *Mexican Labor and World War II: Braceros in the Pacific Northwest, 1942–1947* (Austin: University of Texas Press, 1990), 15–35.

10. Gamboa, *Mexican Labor,* 39–40; Peter Kirstein, *Anglo over Bracero: A His-*

tory of the Mexican Worker in the United States from Roosevelt to Nixon (San Francisco: R&E Research Associates, 1977), 12–14.

11. Carey McWilliams, *North from Mexico: The Spanish-Speaking People of the United States* (New York: Greenwood Press, 1968), 215.

12. See Richard Mines and Ricardo Anzaldúa, *New Migrants versus Old Migrants: Alternative Labor Market Structures in the California Citrus Industry* (La Jolla, Calif.: Program in United States–Mexican Studies, University of California, San Diego, 1982). For a historical study of the effects of the bracero program on local Mexican American workers, see Lisbeth Haas, "The Bracero in Orange County: A Work Force for Economic Transition," Working Papers in U.S.–Mexican Studies, no. 29 (La Jolla, Calif.: Program in United States–Mexican Studies, University of California, San Diego, 1981).

13. Craig, *Bracero Program,* 37.

14. Hewes, "Migratory Problems," 124.

15. Craig, *Bracero Program,* 124; Ernesto Galarza, *Merchants of Labor: The Mexican Bracero Story* (Santa Barbara, Calif.: McNally & Loftin, 1964), 43–44.

16. Craig, *Bracero Program,* 40.

17. Schwartz, *Seasonal Farm Labor,* 120.

18. Hewes, "Migratory Problems," 125–126.

19. During World War II, the U.S. Employment Service was part of the War Manpower Commission. After the war, the entire agency became known as the U.S. Employment Service to reflect the return to peacetime, and then was absorbed by the Department of Labor.

20. Jones, *Mexican War Workers,* 1.

21. Jones, *Mexican War Workers,* 1; Galarza, *Merchants of Labor,* 46–47.

22. Kirstein, *Anglo over Bracero,* 18.

23. If the Mexican government was impressed with the FSA, the growers were not, and in fact, distrusted the agency (Hewes, "Migratory Problems,"150).

24. Hewes, "Migratory Problems," 146, 165. Hewes claims that the county associations assumed the duties of employer, as opposed to the FSA, which would have required a huge bureaucracy to oversee.

25. See Gamboa, *Mexican Labor,* 48–51.

26. Gamboa, *Mexican Labor,* 112.

27. Galarza, *Merchants of Labor,* 48.

28. Kirstein, *Anglo over Bracero,* 18–19.

29. Julia Henderson, "Foreign Labour in the United States during the War," *International Labour Review* 52 (1945): 610–611.

30. Henderson, "Foreign Labour," 627.

7. THE RAILROADS' CAMPAIGN

1. "Southern Pacific Would Bring in Mexican Laborers," *Railway Age* 111 (1941): 386.

2. "Southern Pacific," 386.

3. *New York Times,* 24 March 1942.

4. "How Can Shortage of Manpower Be Overcome?" *Railway Engineering and Maintenance* 44 (1941): 124.

5. The Association of American Railroads, with headquarters in Washington, D.C., represents the railroad industry, and at times acts on its behalf.

6. *New York Times,* 28 Feb. 1942.

7. *New York Times,* 15 April 1942.

8. *New York Times,* 16 April 1942.

9. So. Pac. Intrnl Files, Historical Labor File, "Historical Data in Connection with Employment of Mexican National Laborers Imported from Mexico," August 1950, 62–65.

10. *New York Times,* 9 May 1942. The Southern Pacific itself claims that it spent $135,000 to bring 2,896 workers from the Mississippi Valley in June 1942, only about half of whom actually began work. Later in the year, the company again brought another 3,201 men, of whom only 1,847 began work. Only 428 were still working in March 1943.

11. *New York Times,* 21 July 1942.

12. "Southern Pacific Again Asks to Import Mexicans Laborers," *Railway Age* 113 (1942): 146.

13. *New York Times,* 2 Oct. 1942.

14. *New York Times,* 13 Aug. 1942.

15. *New York Times,* 6 Sept. 1942.

16. *New York Times,* 3 Nov. 1942; Peter Kirstein, *Anglo over Bracero: A History of the Mexican Worker in the United States from Roosevelt to Nixon* (San Francisco: R&E Research Associates, 1977), 19.

17. Natl Arch., DoS Rec., RG 59, V. V. Boatner to Otto Beyer, 10 Nov. 1942.

18. INS, memo from Bert Fraser to Immigration Bureau, n.d., file 56135/227.

19. The Railroad Retirement Board is the New Deal government agency that was established to manage the pension fund of railroad workers, and to oversee other matters pertinent to them. In the United States, railroad workers belong not to the Social Security System but to the Railroad Retirement Board. They are the only workers who have their own system outside of Social Security.

20. Natl Arch., DoS Rec., RG 59, Murray Latimer to Paul McNutt, 13 Nov. 1942.

21. Natl Arch., DoS Rec., RG 59, Murray Latimer to Paul McNutt, 13 Nov. 1942.

22. Kirstein, *Anglo over Bracero,* 23.

23. George Q. Flynn, *The Mess in Washington: War Manpower in World War II* (Westport, Conn.: Greenwood Press, 1979), 117.

24. Natl Arch., DoS Rec., RG 59, Paul McNutt to Cordell Hull, 26 Dec. 1942. The War Manpower Commission was established in Executive Order no. 9279, signed by FDR on 5 December 1941, as the agency to oversee all wartime man-

power mobilization, including the Selective Service. McNutt, a New Dealer, was regarded with suspicion by Congress, and especially the military. See Flynn, *Mess in Washington.*

25. INS, Paul McNutt to Earl Harrison, 7 Jan. 1943, file 56135/227.

26. INS, memo of conversation, 7 Jan. 1943, file 56135/227.

27. Natl Arch., WMC Rec., RG 211, "Recommendation of the Management-Labor Policy Committee with respect to the Railroad Track Maintenance in the Southwest," 5 Feb. 1943.

28. Natl Arch., DoS Rec., RG 59, memo of conversation, 7 Jan. 1943. See also Ernesto Galarza, *Merchants of Labor: The Mexican Bracero Story* (Santa Barbara, Calif.: McNally & Loftin, 1964), 54.

29. Galarza, *Merchants of Labor.*

30. Natl Arch., DoS Rec., RG 59, Labor-Management Policy Committee Hearings, 5 Feb. 1943.

31. INS, William Milroy to Dr. William Leiserson, 16 March 1943, file 56135/227.

32. Natl Arch., DoS Rec., RG 59, Cordell Hull to George Messersmith, 20 March 1943.

8. NEGOTIATIONS

1. Natl Arch., DoS Rec., RG 59, Ambassador Messersmith to Cordell Hull, 9 Jan. 1943.

2. In response to criticism and complaints, the Mexican government suspended the agricultural program shortly thereafter.

3. Natl Arch., DoS Rec., RG 59, memo from Joe McGurk, 11 Jan. 1943.

4. Natl Arch., DoS Rec., RG 59, Ambassador Messersmith to Cordell Hull, 8 March 1943.

5. INS, Commissioner Earl Harrison to Paul McNutt, 18 Jan. 1943, file 56135/227.

6. Natl Arch., DoS Rec., RG 59, Herbert Bursley to Secretary Hull, 19 Jan. 1943.

7. Natl Arch., DoS Rec., RG 59, Herbert Bursley to Cordell Hull, 29 Jan. 1943.

8. Natl Arch., DoS Rec., RG 59, Herbert Bursley to Cordell Hull, 5 Feb. 1943.

9. Natl Arch., DoS Rec., RG 59, Ambassador Messersmith to Cordell Hull, 8 March 1943.

10. Natl Arch., DoS Rec., RG 59, Ambassador Messersmith to Sumner Welles, 23 March 1943.

11. Natl Arch., DoS Rec., RG 59, Ambassador Messersmith to Sumner Welles, 23 March 1943.

12. Natl Arch., DoS Rec., RG 59, Ambassador Messersmith to Sumner Welles, 23 March 1943.

13. Natl Arch., DoS Rec., RG 59, memo, 24 March 1943.

14. Natl Arch., DoS Rec., RG 59, George Messersmith to Sumner Wells, 30 March 1943.

15. Natl Arch., DoS Rec., RG 59, memo by Robert McGregor, Jr., 6 April 1943.

16. Natl Arch., DoS Rec., RG 59, George Messersmith to Joseph R. McGurk, 5 April 1943.

17. A high-level appointed position peculiar to the Mexican political system, *oficial mayor* is roughly equivalent to vice secretary. It carries more power and prestige than undersecretary, and its functions encompass the whole agency, from administration to finance.

18. The legal precedent that governed the entrance of Mexican workers during World War II was the same as for the first bracero program of World War I. Proviso 9 in section 3 of the Immigration Act of 1917 stipulated that unskilled workers could emigrate temporarily to work. No provision was made in this clause for skilled workers.

19. Natl Arch., DoS Rec., RG 59, memo by Robert G. McGregor, Jr., 6 April 1943.

20. Natl Arch., DoS Rec., RG 59, Herbert Bursley to Cordell Hull, 8 April 1943.

21. Natl Arch., DoS Rec., RG 59, Adolf Berle to George Messersmith, 7 April 1943.

22. Natl Arch., DoS Rec., RG 59, Herbert Bursley to Cordell Hull, 8 April 1943.

23. Natl Arch., DoS Rec., RG 59, Herbert Bursley to Cordell Hull, 8 April 1943.

24. Natl Arch., DoS Rec., RG 59, Herbert Bursley to Cordell Hull, 8 April 1943.

25. Natl Arch., DoS Rec., RG 59, Paul McNutt to Cordell Hull, 15 April 1943.

26. Natl Arch., DoS Rec., RG 59, George Messersmith to Cordell Hull, 14 April 1943.

27. George Messersmith to Cordell Hull, 26 April 1943, in U.S. Dept of State, *Foreign Relations of the United States: Diplomatic Papers, 1943* (Washington, D.C.: GPO, 1963), 6: 546–547. In spite of the significant progress toward a railroad program, Messersmith was still worried that serious problems in the agricultural program could stop an extension to the railroads.

28. INS, memo, 21 April 1943, file 56135/227.

29. U.S. Dept of State, *Treaties and Other International Agreements of the United States of America, 1776–1949* (Washington, D.C.: Department of State Publications, 1972), 9: 1136.

30. U.S. Dept of State, *Treaties and Other International Agreements,* 9: 1136.

31. U.S. Dept of State, *Treaties and Other International Agreements,* 9: 1136.

32. U.S. Dept of State, *Treaties and Other International Agreements,* 9: 1136.

33. U.S. Dept of State, *Treaties and Other International Agreements,* 9: 1136.

34. Peter Kirstein, *Anglo over Bracero: A History of the Mexican Worker in the United States from Roosevelt to Nixon* (San Francisco: R&E Research Associates, 1977), 24.

35. So. Pac. Intrnl Files, Historical Labor File, "Historical Data in Connection with Employment of Mexican National Laborers Imported from Mexico," Aug. 1950, 7.

9. OPERATIONS IN MEXICO

1. *Excélsior,* 14 May 1943, 8.

2. INS, Joseph Savoretti to Ugo Carusi, 23 April 1943, file 56135/227.

3. Natl Arch., DoS Rec., RG 59, Cordell Hull to George Messersmith, 8 May 1943.

4. So. Pac. Intrnl Files, Historical Labor File, "Historical Data in Connection with Employment of Mexican National Laborers Imported from Mexico," Aug. 1950, 7–8.

5. Natl Arch., DoS Rec., RG 59, Arthur Motley to William MacLean, 1 May 1943.

6. Natl Arch., DoS Rec., RG 59, George Messersmith to Cordell Hull, 28 May 1943.

7. Natl Arch., DoS Rec., RG 59, Sam Hough to Arthur Motley, 18 June 1943.

8. INS, Lawrence Appley to Joseph Savoretti, 17 Sept. 1943, file 56135/227.

9. Natl Arch., DoS Rec., RG 59, Joseph McGurk to Robert Clark, 24 Dec. 1943.

10. Natl Arch., DoS Rec., RG 59, Sam Hough to Robert Clark, 7 Jan. 1943.

11. National Archives, Department of States Records, RG 59, George Messersmith to Cordell Hull, 8 Jan. 1944.

12. Natl Arch., DoS Rec., RG 59, Sidney O'Donoghue to Cordell Hull, 13 April 1944; Ernesto Galarza, *Merchants of Labor: The Mexican Bracero Story* (Santa Barbara, Calif.: McNally & Loftin, 1964), 52.

13. Natl Arch., DoS Rec., RG 59, Cordell Hull to George Messersmith, 24 March 1944.

14. Natl Arch., DoS Rec., RG 59, Sidney O'Donoghue to Cordell Hull, 13 April 1944.

15. RRB, Exec. Officer's File, Joseph McGurk to John Coates, 2 May 1944.

16. RRB, Exec. Officer's File, P. A. Holler to Frank Squire, 12 May 1944.

17. RRB, Exec. Officer's File, Raymond Lusk to Harlon Carter, 3 June 1944.

18. RRB, Exec. Officer's File, Raymond Lusk to Harlon Carter, 3 June 1944.

19. RRB, Exec. Officer's File, Harlon Carter to Robert LaMotte, 23 June 1944. See also *Segundo informe constitucional rendido ante la H. XXXIV Legislatura del Estado,* given by C. Gobernador Lic. Agapito Pozo, 16 Sept. 1945.

20. Natl Arch., DoS Rec., RG 59, Sidney O'Donoghue to Cordell Hull, 13 April 1944.

21. RRB, Exec. Officer's File, Sam Hough to Charles Holler, 18 Aug. 1944.

22. Natl Arch., WMC Rec., RG 211, Charles Holler to Churchill Murray, 7 Nov. 1944.

23. Natl Arch., WMC Rec., RG 211, Churchill Murray to John Coates, 3 Jan. 1945.

24. Natl Arch., WMC Rec., RG 211, Churchill Murray to Charles Holler, 17 Jan. 1945.

25. Natl Arch., WMC Rec., RG 211, Churchill Murray to John Coates, 2 March 1945.

26. Natl Arch., WMC Rec., RG 211, Churchill Murray to Jorge Medellín, 8 March 1945.

27. Natl Arch., WMC Rec., RG 211, Churchill Murray to John Coates, 2 March 1945.

28. RRB, Exec. Officer's File, memo of conversation between John Coates and Mr. Robson, 23 Aug. 1945.

29. Natl Arch., WMC Rec., RG 211, John Coates to Churchill Murray, 30 Aug. 1945.

30. References to the practice of card selling in Querétaro can be found in Qrtro, Arch. del Pdr Ejec., file 4.31.

31. Erasmo Gamboa, *Mexican Labor and World War II: Braceros in the Pacific Northwest, 1942–1947* (Austin: University of Texas Press, 1990), 51.

32. According to the Southern Pacific, they as well as other railroads at first assigned personnel to the program in Mexico. Later, the railroads participating in the bracero program contracted the Western Association of Railway Executives to oversee their interests in the recruitment process.

33. General information that described the process of recruitment and was deemed essential for recruitment personnel is contained in RRB, Exec. Officer's File, "General Information for Railroad Representatives in Recruitment Activities in Mexico City."

34. Natl Arch., WMC Rec., RG 211, Churchill Murray to Sidney O'Donoghue, 8 Jan. 1945.

35. Information for this overview of the applicants to the bracero program is taken from Qrtro, Arch. del Pdr Ejec., files 37/1.27–45, 191/4.31.

36. Natl Arch., DoS Rec., RG 59, John Coates to Joseph McGurk, 6 May 1944.

37. So. Pac. Intrnl Files, "Historical Data," 11.

38. Natl Arch., DoS Rec., RG 59, George Messersmith to Cordell Hull, 2 April 1943.

39. Natl Arch., WMC Rec., RG 211, Churchill Murray to Luis del Campo, 25 Jan. 1945.

40. Natl Arch., WMC Rec., RG 211, Churchill Murray to John Coates, 27 Feb. 1945.

41. No formal policy existed regarding the duties or responsibilities of RRB train riders.

42. Natl Arch., WMC Rec., RG 211, Sam Hough to Robert Clark, 17 Jan. 1944.

43. Natl Arch., WMC Rec., RG 211, ruling by John Sullivan, May 1943.

44. Natl Arch., WMC Rec., RG 211, Churchill Murray to Luis del Campo, 25 Jan. 1945.

45. Natl Arch., WMC Rec., RG 211, Churchill Murray to Luis del Campo, 25 Jan. 1945.

46. Natl Arch., DoS Rec., RG 59, Paul McNutt to Cordell Hull, 11 May 1943.

47. Natl Arch., WMC Rec., RG 211, Charles Hay to Joseph McGurk, 25 May 1944.

48. Natl Arch., DoS Rec., RG 59, memo of conversation between Sidney O'Donoghue and William MacLean, 1 May 1944.

49. Natl Arch., DoS Rec., RG 59, George Messersmith to Cordell Hull, 19 June 1943.

50. RRB, Exec. Officer's File, Jay L. Taylor to Mary B. Linkins, 19 May 1943.

51. Peter Kirstein, *Anglo over Bracero: A History of the Mexican Worker in the United States from Roosevelt to Nixon* (San Francisco: R&E Research Associates, 1977), 27.

52. Natl Arch., WMC Rec., RG 211, War Manpower Commission to Joseph McGurk, 4 May 1943.

53. Natl Arch., DoS Rec., RG 59, Cordell Hull to the American Embassy, 31 Aug. 1943.

54. Natl Arch., DoS Rec., RG 59, Herbert Bursley to Cordell Hull, 6 Aug. 1943.

55. Natl Arch., DoS Rec., RG 59, Herbert Bursley to Cordell Hull, 27 April 1943.

56. RRB, Exec. Officer's File, L. J. Benson to Nick Carter, 28 Dec. 1944.

57. Natl Arch., WMC Rec., RG 211, Arthur Motley to Sam Hough, 8 May 1943.

58. Natl Arch., WMC Rec., RG 211, Sam Hough to [?], 4 May 1943; Kirstein, *Anglo over Bracero*, 27.

59. Natl Arch., WMC Rec., RG 211, Churchill Murray to Charles Holler, 8 Nov. 1944.

60. Natl Arch., WMC Rec., RG 211, Churchill Murray to Guillermo Salazar, 29 Nov. 1944.

61. Natl Arch., WMC Rec., RG 211, John Coates to Sam Hough, 21 July 1944.

62. RRB, Exec. Officer's File, Sam Hough to John Coates, 7 Aug. 1944.

63. RRB, Exec. Officer's File, Harlon Carter to Charles Hodge, 20 Sept. 1944.

64. RRB, Exec. Officer's File, itemized statement (A), "Division of expenses for joint office of WMC and RRB in Mexico City."

65. RRB, Exec. Officer's File, Churchill Murray to John Coates, 9 Oct. 1944.

66. Natl Arch., DoS Rec., RG 59, George Messersmith to Cordell Hull, 8 Jan. 1944. Messersmith's reports and memos provided much information for policymakers in Washington. His observations about the bracero program during World War II provide some valuable insights not available elsewhere. For instance, Messersmith's remarks about the tension between RRB and WMC operatives are especially interesting, for they highlight the program's conflicts.

67. RRB, Exec. Officer's File, Robert LaMotte to Charles Hodge, 20 March 1944.

68. RRB, Exec. Officer's File, Sam Hough to Charles Holler, 18 Aug. 1944.

69. So. Pac. Intrnl Files, "Historical Data," 26–28.

70. RRB, Exec. Officer's File, L. J. Benson to Nick Carter, 28 Dec. 1944.

71. Natl Arch., DoS Rec., RG 59, Herbert Bursley to Cordell Hull, 6 Aug. 1943.

72. Nelson Rockefeller to George Messersmith, 22 Jan. 1945, in U.S. Dept of State, *Foreign Relations of the United States: Diplomatic Papers, 1945* (Washington, D.C.: GPO, 1963), 9: 1141–1142.

73. Natl Arch., WMC Rec., RG 211, Churchill Murray to Charles Holler, 14 Dec. 1944.

74. Natl Arch., WMC Rec., RG 211, box 3, series 196.

75. Allegedly, the board is still in possession of many, if not all, of these individual folders, but under the terms of the Freedom of Information Act researchers do not have access to them.

76. RRB, Exec. Officer's File, Paul R. Langdon to John Coates, 19 Jan. 1945.

77. RRB, Exec. Officer's File, Arthur Motley to Charles Hodge, 29 April 1944.

78. RRB, Exec. Officer's File, Charles Hodge to Robert LaMotte, 30 May 1944.

79. RRB, Exec. Officer's File, John Coates to Sam Hough, 21 July 1944.

80. RRB, Exec. Officer's File, Harlon Carter to Robert LaMotte, 23 Feb. 1944.

81. RRB, Exec. Officer's File, Robert LaMotte to Harlon Carter, 7 March 1944.

82. During World War II, the Immigration Service, the equivalent of the Immigration and Naturalization Service, fell under the jurisdiction of the attorney general's office.

83. RRB, Exec. Officer's File, Charles Hodge to Harlon Carter, 25 April 1944.

84. RRB, Exec. Officer's File, Robert Clark to Joseph McGurk, 11 April 1944.

85. RRB, Exec. Officer's File, Charles Hodge to Harlon Carter, 17 Nov. 1944.

86. Natl Arch., WMC Rec., RG 211, Office for Emergency Management, travel authorization form, 1 July 1943.

87. Natl Arch., WMC Rec., RG 211, Office for Emergency Management, travel authorization form, 5 May 1943.

88. Natl Arch., WMC Rec., RG 211, Churchill Murray to John Coates, 28 May 1945.

89. Natl Arch., WMC Rec., RG 211, Churchill Murray to Luis Trujillo, 6 March 1945.

90. RRB, Exec. Officer's File, Robert Clark to Joseph McGurk, April 11, 1944.

91. Natl Arch., WMC Rec., RG 211, Dr. Van Beeck to E. N. Sunderland, 13 March 1945.

92. RRB, Exec. Officer's File, agreement between the Railroad Retirement Board and the War Food Administration, 10 May 1943.

93. RRB, Exec. Officer's File, Paul R. Langdon to John Coates, 19 Jan. 1945.

94. RRB, Exec. Officer's File, Paul R. Langdon to Harry J. Sassaman, 23 June 1945.

95. Natl Arch., DoS Rec., RG 59, Robert La Motte to Charles Hodge, 6 April 1943.

96. RRB, Exec. Officer's File, Arthur Motley to Joseph McGurk, 9 May 1944.

97. Natl Arch., WMC Rec., RG 211, payee's receipt.

98. Natl Arch., DoS Rec., RG 59, George Messersmith to Cordell Hull, 29 Feb. 1944.

99. Natl Arch., DoS Rec., RG 59, Herbert Bursley to Cordell Hull, 6 April 1943.

100. RRB, Bur. of Law Files, Harlon Carter to the Bureau of Law, 24 June 1943.

101. Natl Arch., DoS Rec., RG 59, Joseph McGurk to Robert Clark, 24 Dec. 1943.

102. Natl Arch., DoS Rec., RG 59, Sam Hough to Robert Clark, 10 March 1944.

103. Natl Arch., DoS Rec., RG 59, Paul Reveley to William MacLean, 16 June 1944.

104. Natl Arch., DoS Rec., RG 59, William MacLean to Sidney O'Donoghue, 12 Aug. 1944.

105. George Messersmith to Cordell Hull, 24 Aug. 1944, in U.S. Dept of State, *Foreign Relations of the United States: Diplomatic Papers, 1944* (Washington, D.C.: GPO, 1963), 7: 1321–1322.

106. Natl Arch., DoS Rec., RG 59, memo no. 1745, 10 Sept. 1943.

107. Natl Arch., DoS Rec., RG 59, Arthur Motley to Sam Hough, 28 June 1943.

108. Natl Arch., DoS Rec., RG 59, Sidney O'Donoghue to Cordell Hull, 13 April 1943.

109. Natl Arch., DoS Rec., RG 59, Herbert Bursley to Cordell Hull, 6 April 1943.

110. Natl Arch., WMC Rec., RG 211, Charles Holler to Churchill Murray, 9 Jan. 1945.

111. Natl Arch., DoS Rec., RG 59, Herbert Bursley to Cordell Hull, 7 Aug. 1943.

112. Natl Arch., DoS Rec., RG 59, Sidney O'Donoghue to Cordell Hull, 13 April 1944.

113. Natl Arch., WMC Rec., RG 211, Churchill Murray to John Coates, 15 Nov. 1943.

114. Natl Arch., WMC Rec., RG 211, Churchill Murray to Charles Holler, 3 Nov. 1944.

115. Natl Arch., WMC Rec., RG 211, George Messersmith to Cordell Hull, 19 May 1943.

116. M. L. Stafford to Cordell Hull, 6 June 1944, in U.S. Dept of State, *Foreign Relations 1944,* vol. 7.

117. The United States was desperate to improve the efficiency of Mexican railroads to assure the delivery of raw materials. Such enthusiasm undoubtedly became interference.

118. Natl Arch., DoS Rec., RG 59, George Messersmith to Cordell Hull, 23 March 1944.

119. Cordell Hull to George Messersmith, 26 May 1943, in U.S. Dept of State, *Foreign Relations of the United States: Diplomatic Papers, 1943* (Washington, D.C.: GPO, 1963), 6: 553–554.

120. Natl Arch., DoS Rec., RG 59, memo of conversation between Sidney O'Donoghue and William MacLean, 3 May 1944.

121. Natl Arch., DoS Rec., RG 59, memo of conversation between Robert McGregor and William MacLean, 29 April 1943.

122. RRB, Exec. Officer's File, A. Frías Beltrán to Charles Hodge, 11 Dec. 1944.

10. OPERATIONS IN THE UNITED STATES

1. INS, T. B. Shoemake to Thomas G. Finucane, 1 May 1943, file 56135/227.

2. Natl Arch., DoS Rec., RG 59, Claude Wickard to Cordell Hull, 4 April 1943.

3. INS, memo from A. M., 21 April 1943, file 56135/227.

4. INS, memo for the file from A. M., 21 April 1943, file 56135/227. While the bond was $500 per contracted bracero, the actual deposit made by a railroad for any recruited worker was $50, or 10 percent of the total bond.

5. INS, Earl Harrison to Thomas G. Finucane, 8 May 1943, file 56135/227.

6. INS, Earl Harrison to Charles H. Woods, 29 May 1943, file 56135/227.

7. Natl Arch., DoS Rec., RG 59, George Messersmith to Cordell Hull, 4 Dec. 1943.

8. Natl Arch., WMC Rec., RG 211, folder on the Northern Pacific, n.d.

9. Natl Arch., DoS Rec., RG 59, William Haber to Rafael de la Colina, 16 Sept. 1943.

10. Natl Arch., DoS Rec., RG 59, memo no. 1745 of the American Embassy in Mexico City, 10 Sept. 1943.

11. Natl Arch., DoS Rec., RG 59, memo of conversation between Robert McGregor and William MacLean, 15 April 1943.

12. RRB, Exec. Officer's File, "Compensation Reported from Mexican National Contract Workers during the Period May–November 1943, Inclusive."

13. Natl Arch., DoS Rec., RG 59, Rafael de la Colina to Arthur Motley, 25 Aug. 1943.

14. RRB, Bur. of Law Files, A. M. Kobrick to Joseph H. Freehill, 25 Sept. 1943.

15. Natl Arch., DoS Rec., RG 59, Adolf Berle to George Messersmith, 7 April 1943.

16. Natl Arch., DoS Rec., RG 59, Frank Squire to Edward Stettinius, 4 Feb. 1944.

17. RRB, Exec. Officer's File, Murray Latimer to Paul V. McNutt, 13 Nov. 1942.

18. So. Pac. Intrnl Files, Historical Labor File, "Historical Data in Connection with Employment of Mexican National Laborers Imported from Mexico," Aug. 1950, 15.

19. Natl Arch., WMC Rec., RG 211, Arthur Motley to G. H. Muckley, 14 May 1943.

20. Natl Arch., DoS Rec., RG 59, Samuel Hough to Frank Fleener, 24 May 1943.

21. Natl Arch., WMC Rec., RG 211, Arthur Motley to G. H. Muckley, 14 May 1943.

22. Natl Arch., DoS Rec., RG 59, Joseph McGurk to Arthur Motley, 5 May 1943.

23. Natl Arch., DoS Rec., RG 59, George Messersmith to Cordell Hull, 3 June 1943.

24. INS, William Milroy to William Leiserson, 25 March 1943, file 56135/227.

25. RRB, Exec. Officer's File, Railroad Retirement Board to William H. Leiserson, n.d.

26. Cordell Hull to Herbert Bursley, 28 Oct. 1944, in U.S. Dept of State, *For-*

eign Relations of the United States: Diplomatic Papers, 1944 (Washington, D.C.: GPO, 1963), 7: 1329–1330.

27. Natl Arch., WMC Rec., RG 211, report from Delfino Aguilera and Pablo Ávila, n.d.

28. Natl Arch., WMC Rec., RG 211, Churchill Murray to John Coates, 16 Jan. 1946.

29. Natl Arch., WMC Rec., RG 211, Luis Fernández del Campo to Churchill Murray, 23 Jan. 1946.

30. So. Pac. Intrnl Files, "Historical Data," 46.

31. RRB, Exec. Officer's File, "Hints on the Employment of Imported Mexican Laborers," n.d.

32. So. Pac. Intrnl Files, "Historical Data," 32.

33. So. Pac. Intrnl Files, "Historical Data," 32.

34. George Messersmith to Cordell Hull, 28 July 1943, in U.S. Dept of State, *Foreign Relations of the United States: Diplomatic Papers, 1943* (Washington, D.C.: GPO, 1963), 6: 563.

35. RRB, Exec. Officer's File, Robert Clark to Charles Hodge, 2 March 1944.

36. Gamboa, *Mexican Labor,* 53. Personnel of the Railroad Retirement Board in Chicago who were familiar with the bracero program have commented informally to the author about the amorous adventures of the Mexican labor inspectors assigned to the program.

37. Natl Arch., DoS Rec., RG 59, George Messersmith to Cordell Hull, 24 Aug. 1944.

38. Natl Arch., DoS Rec., RG 59, William MacLean to Sidney O'Donoghue, 12 Aug. 1944.

39. RRB, Exec. Officer's File, Harlon Carter to Regional Directors, 20 Feb. 1945.

40. Natl Arch., WMC Rec., RG 211, John Coates to Churchill Murray, 18 Dec. 1944.

41. Natl Arch., WMC Rec., RG 211, William A. Orth to Samuel Hough, 14 Aug. 1943.

42. Natl Arch., WMC Rec., RG 211, Churchill Murray to Regional Rationing Statistician, Aug. 1944.

43. Natl Arch., WMC Rec., RG 211, Edgar Sinton to William Hopkin, 5 Nov. 1943.

44. Natl Arch., WMC Rec., RG 211, monthly reports of the OPA, 1945.

45. Natl Arch., WMC Rec., RG 211, John Coates to Churchill Murray, 13 June 1945.

46. Peter Kirstein, *Anglo over Bracero: A History of the Mexican Worker in the United States from Roosevelt to Nixon* (San Francisco: R&E Research Associates, 1977), 37.

47. Natl Arch., DoS Rec., RG 59, Arthur Motley to Joseph McGurk, 28 July 1944; Natl Arch., DoS Rec., RG 59, Herbert Bursley to Secretary of State, 25 Aug. 1943.

48. INS, Charles H. Woods to Herman Landon (INS), 20 May 1943, file 56135/227.

49. INS, Earl Harrison to Charles H. Woods (ATSF), 29 May 1943, file 56136/227.

50. INS, Charles H. Woods to Arthur Motley, 5 June 1943, file 56135/227. Although not generally known, the Railroad Retirement Board conducted a recruitment drive among Native Americans during World War II to work in various unskilled and semiskilled railroad jobs. At the time of the ATSF labor crisis in Needles, Native Americans were leaving their ice platform jobs to return to their reservations, helping to create the crisis alluded to above.

51. Natl Arch., DoS Rec., RG 59, Herbert Bursley to Secretary of State, 25 Aug. 1943.

52. RRB, Exec. Officer's File, Lawrence Appley to Joseph Savoretti, 17 Sept. 1943.

53. INS, Thomas G. Finucane to Ugo Carusi, 2 Oct. 1943, file 56135/227.

54. Part of the information regarding the Southern Pacific comes from an internal report produced by the company after the war. "Historical Data in Connection with Employment of Mexican National Laborers Imported from Mexico," dated August 1950, represents one of the very few available sources of information about Mexican immigrant workers written by an employer. While the report does not address problems, it does confirm some data.

55. So. Pac. Intrnl Files, "Historical Data," 38.

56. So. Pac. Intrnl Files, "Historical Data," 39.

57. So. Pac. Intrnl Files, "Historical Data," 39.

58. RRB, Exec. Officer's File, Emory Worth, Director for Oregon (WMC), to F. N. Finch, 24 Jan. 1944.

59. RRB, Exec. Officer's File, RRB internal memo, from H. L. Carter to Executive Officer, 1 April 1944.

60. Natl Arch., WMC Rec., RG 211, Mexican Embassy in Washington, D.C., to Secretaría de Trabajo y Previsión Social, 21 Nov. 1944; Natl Arch., WMC Rec., RG 211, Churchill Murray to John Coates, 24 Nov. 1944.

61. INS, Thomas G. Finucane to T. B. Shoemake, 31 May 1944, file 56135/227; INS, T. B. Shoemake to Thomas G. Finucane, 15 June 1944, file 56135/227. See chapter 7 for a detailed analysis of WMC procedures for certifying a need for labor.

62. Kirstein, *Anglo over Bracero,* 31.

63. So. Pac. Intrnl Files, "Historical Data," 6.

64. RRB, Exec. Officer's File, Robert Clark to Charles L. Hodge, 3 April 1944.

65. Natl Arch., WMC Rec., RG 211, John Coates to Churchill Murray, 8 June 1943.

66. Kirstein, *Anglo over Bracero,* 38.

67. Natl Arch., WMC Rec., RG 211, report from Luis Merino Fuentes, n.d. See also Natl Arch., WMC Rec., RG 211, Churchill Murray to Luis Fernández del Campo, 24 Jan. 1945.

68. Ambassador Messersmith to Secretary of State, 20 Aug. 1943, in U.S. Dept of State, *Foreign Relations 1943*, 6: 569–570.

69. Natl Arch., WMC Rec., RG 211, Churchill Murray to Luis Fernández del Campo, 13 Nov. 1944.

70. Natl Arch., DoS Rec., RG 59, Neiola Barley to Cordell Hull, 31 Dec. 1943.

71. Natl Arch., WMC Rec., RG 211, memo, Department of State, 12 Dec. 1944.

72. Natl Arch., DoS Rec., RG 59, Macklin to Hopkins, 19 Aug. 1943.

73. Natl Arch., WMC Rec., RG 211, Churchill Murray to John Coates, 28 March 1945.

74. Natl Arch., DoS Rec., RG 59, Carlos Gutiérrez to WMC Regional Director, 5 Aug. 1943.

75. Natl Arch., WMC Rec., RG 211, J. J. Finnerty (RRB) and Ricardo B. Pérez (Mexican labor inspector) to P. F. Murphy, 12 May 1945.

76. Natl Arch., WMC Rec., RG 211, Ernesto Veirya Avendano et al. to Napoleón Alcocer Mazatán, 21 April 1945.

77. Natl Arch., WMC Rec., RG 211, John Coates to Churchill Murray, 9 July 1945.

78. Natl Arch., DoS Rec., RG 59, Ernesto Galarza to James Patton (National Farmers' Union), 27 Dec. 1943. The letter was also sent to James Carey (CIO), Matthew Woll (AFL), E. E. Milliman (Brotherhood of Maintenance of Way Employees), and George Harrison (Brotherhood of Railway and Steamship Clerks, Freight Handlers, Express and Station Employees).

79. Natl Arch., DoS Rec., RG 59, memo from Ernesto Galarza to Dr. Rowe, 5 Sept. 1944.

80. Natl Arch., WMC Rec., RG 211, Samuel Hough to Robert Clark, 11 Nov. 1943.

81. Natl Arch., WMC Rec., RG 211, memo from Pablo Ruiz de la Peña, 11 Jan. 1946.

82. Agricultural braceros were *not* assigned to Texas during the war precisely due to problems of prejudice.

83. Natl Arch., DoS Rec., RG 59, Herbert Bursley to Cordell Hull, 17 Sept. 1943.

84. Natl Arch., DoS Rec., RG 59, Robert Clark to Joseph McGurk, 11 Nov. 1943.

85. Natl Arch., DoS Rec., RG 59, Pauline R. Kibbe (Executive Secretary, Good Neighbor Commission) to Cordell Hull, 19 Nov. 1943.

86. Natl Arch., DoS Rec., RG 59, William P. Blocker to Cordell Hull, 25 Oct. 1943.

87. Natl Arch., WMC Rec., RG 211, memo from Churchill Murray to John Coates, 11 Dec. 1945.

88. INS, Arthur Motley to Joseph Savoretti, 12 July 1943, file 56135/227.

89. RRB, Exec. Officer's File, RRB memo from Regional Director of Region 9 to Regional Director of Minneapolis, 27 Dec. 1943.

90. RRB, Exec. Officer's File, WMC memo to Regional Manpower Directors (WMC Field Instruction no. 187, supplement no. 1), Feb. 1944.

91. Natl Arch., WMC Rec., RG 211, Churchill Murray to John Coates, 19 July 1945.

92. Natl Arch., WMC Rec., RG 211, Churchill Murray to John Coates, 13 Nov. 1945.

93. Natl Arch., WMC Rec., RG 211, Churchill Murray to John Coates, 3 Nov. 1946.

94. So. Pac. Intrnl Files, "Historical Data," 32–33.

95. So. Pac. Intrnl Files, "Historical Data," 14.

96. So. Pac. Intrnl Files, "Historical Data," 5.

97. So. Pac. Intrnl Files, "Historical Data," 34–36.

98. Natl Arch., WMC Rec., RG 211, WMC daily files.

99. Natl Arch., WMC Rec., RG 211, Churchill Murray to John Coates, 11 April 1946.

100. Natl Arch., DoS Rec., RG 59, memo from William MacLean, 10 Aug. 1944; Natl Arch., DoS Rec., RG 59, William MacLean to Sidney O'Donoghue, 12 Aug. 1944.

101. So. Pac. Intrnl Files, "Historical Data," 36.

102. Natl Arch., DoS Rec., RG 59, Edward Stettinius to Joseph Eastman, 4 Nov. 1943.

103. Natl Arch., DoS Rec., RG 59, memo of conversation between Sidney O'Donoghue and William MacLean, 11 Nov. l943.

104. RRB, Exec. Officer's File, Director of Employment to Purchasing Agent, 31 Dec. 1943.

105. RRB, Exec. Officer's File, Harlon Carter to RRB Regional Offices, 27 Aug. 1945.

106. RRB, Exec. Officer's File, John K. Collins to Regional Manpower Director, 24 Aug. 1944.

11. ADMINISTRATION IN THE UNITED STATES

1. Erasmo Gamboa, *Mexican Labor and World War II: Braceros in the Pacific Northwest, 1942–1947* (Austin: University of Texas Press, 1990), 53.

2. See George Q. Flynn, *The Mess in Washington: War Manpower in World War II* (Westport, Conn.: Greenwood Press, 1979).

3. RRB, Exec. Officer's File, Lawrence Appley to Joseph Savoretti, 17 Sept. 1943.

4. Natl Arch., ODT Rec., RG 219, memo from the Selective Service System, 17 Sept. 1942.

5. RRB, Exec. Officer's File, George W. Cross to Regional Directors, 30 May 1944.

6. Natl Arch., DoS Rec., RG 59, Cordell Hull to the American Embassy, 10 April 1943.

7. RRB, Exec. Officer's File, John D. Coates to A. W. Motley, 18 Aug. 1944.

8. INS, George Messersmith to the State Department, 30 April 1943, file 56135/227.

9. INS, T. B. Shoemake to Thomas G. Finucane, 1 May 1943.

10. RRB, Exec. Officer's File, Lawrence Appley to Joseph Savoretti, 17 Sept. 1943.

11. INS, memo for the file from A. C. Devaney, file 56135/227.

12. RRB, Exec. Officer's File, John Coates to Murray Latimer, 10 Nov. 1944.

13. INS, order approved by Francis Biddle, 15 June 1943, file 56135/227.

14. Natl Arch., DoS Rec., RG 59, memo of conversation between Stephen Wood and William MacLean, 21 July 1943.

15. INS, Thomas Finucane to T. B. Shoemake, 31 May 1944, file 56135/227.

16. Natl Arch., DoS Rec., RG 59, Joseph McGurk to Paul McNutt, 30 March 1943.

17. INS, William Milroy to William Leiserson, 16 March 1943, file 56135/227.

18. RRB, Exec. Officer's File, Charles Hodge to Harlon Carter, 22 Nov. 1943.

19. Natl Arch., DoS Rec., RG 59, WMC letter sent to all railroads, 3 Jan. 1945.

20. Natl Arch., DoS Rec., RG 59, memo of conversation between Elmer Milliman, T. B. Shoemake, Joseph McGurk, and William MacLean, 7 Jan. 1943.

21. RRB, Bur. of Law Files, letter from Charles Hodge, 18 May 1943.

22. INS, A. W. Motley to Elmer Milliman, n.d., file 56135/227.

23. INS, Thomas Finucane to Ugo Carusi, 19 Aug. 1943, file 56135/227.

24. RRB, Exec. Officer's File, Harlon Carter to Charles Hodge, 8 Dec. 1943. The individual RRB folders for railroad braceros still exist and are housed at RRB headquarters in Chicago, but are not available to researchers.

25. RRB, Exec. Officer's File, Robert LaMotte to Charles Hodge, 20 March 1944.

26. Peter Kirstein, *Anglo over Bracero: A History of the Mexican Worker in the United States from Roosevelt to Nixon* (San Francisco: R&E Research Associates, 1977), 28.

27. Natl Arch., WMC Rec., RG 211, Robert Clark to Samuel Hough, 11 Nov. 1943.

28. RRB, Exec. Officer's File, Regional Director, Region no. 9, to the Regional Director in Minneapolis, 27 Dec. 1943.

29. From RRB, Exec. Officer's File, "Excerpts from the Resolution of the Special Commission established to determine the meaning of the phrase 'place of employment' as used in section III B-I of the Agreement of April 29, 1943, for the contracting of non-agricultural workers."

30. RRB, Exec. Officer's File, Harlon Carter to Regional Directors, 12 Nov. 1943.

31. Natl Arch., DoS Rec., RG 59, Robert Clark to Joseph McGurk, 22 Dec. 1943.

32. RRB, Exec. Officer's File, Harlon Carter to Regional Directors, 19 Nov. 1943.

33. RRB, Exec. Officer's File, agreement between the War Food Administration and the Railroad Retirement Board, 22 June 1944.

34. RRB, Exec. Officer's File, Robert LaMotte to Salvador García, 15 June 1945.

35. INS, T. B. Shoemake to Thomas Finucane, 24 Jan. 1943, file 56135/227.

36. INS, order of Board of Immigration Appeals, 6 May 1943, file 56135/227.

37. INS, Earl Harrison to Thomas Finucane, 8 May 1943, file 56135/227.

38. Natl Arch., WMC Rec., RG 211, Samuel Hough to Arthur Motley, 10 May 1943.

39. INS, Charles Wood to Herman Landon, 20 May 1943, file 56135/227.

40. INS, Earl Harrison to Charles H. Woods, 29 May 1943, file 56135/227.

41. INS, Arthur Motley to Joseph Savoretti, 23 June 1943, file 56135/227.

42. INS, Lawrence Appley to Joseph Savoretti, 17 Sept. 1943, file 56135/227.

43. INS, Lawrence Appley to Joseph Savoretti, 17 Sept. 1943, file 56135/227.

44. INS, Thomas Finucane to Lawrence Appley, 25 Sept. 1943, file 56135/227.

45. INS, Lawrence Appley to Thomas Finucane, 30 Sept. 1943, file 56135/227.

46. INS, "Advice on Mexican National Repatriation," n.d., file 56135/227.

47. Natl Arch., WMC Rec., RG 211, WMC to Joseph McGurk, 4 May 1943.

48. RRB, Bur. of Law Files, A. W. Motley to G. E. Muckley, 15 May 1943.

49. Natl Arch., DoS Rec., RG 59, A. W. Motley to Joseph McGurk, 5 Oct. 1943.

50. Memo by Philip Bonsal, 5 Nov. 1943, in U.S. Dept of State, *Foreign Relations of the United States: Diplomatic Papers, 1943* (Washington, D.C.: GPO, 1963), 6: 572–575.

51. RRB, Exec. Officer's File, Paul C. Daniels to Colonel Philip G. Burton, 9 Oct. 1943.

52. George Messersmith to Cordell Hull, 28 July 1943, in U.S. Dept of State, *Foreign Relations 1943*, 6: 563.

53. Natl Arch., DoS Rec., RG 59, Rafael de la Colina to Arthur Motley, 25 Aug. 1943.

54. Natl Arch., DoS Rec., RG 59, memo of a long-distance conversation between Sidney O'Donoghue and Robert MacLean, 25 Sept. 1943.

55. RRB, Exec. Officer's File, WMC Instruction, March 1944.

56. George Messersmith to Cordell Hull, 24 July 1944, in U.S. Dept of State, *Foreign Relations of the United States: Diplomatic Papers, 1944* (Washington, D.C.: GPO, 1963), 7: 1347–1348.

57. Natl Arch., DoS Rec., RG 59, George Messersmith to Cordell Hull, 24 Aug. 1944.

58. RRB, Exec. Officer's File, Harlon Carter to John Coates, 25 Oct. 1944.

59. RRB, Exec. Officer's File, John Coates to Robert LaMotte, 25 Nov. 1944.

60. Natl Arch., WMC Rec., RG 211, Churchill Murray to John Coates, 28 Nov. 1944.

61. I am referring to Andrés Iduarte, inspector for the New York region. RRB, Exec. Officer's File, R. R. McCurry (RRB Regional Director) to Harlon Carter, 2 Dec. 1944. The other inspectors were Carlos Terrazas (Chicago); Juan Trujillo (Dallas); Francisco Casillas Huerta (Kansas City); Guillermo Díaz and his wife, Carmen Amparrán de Díaz (Denver); and Pablo Ávila and Delfino Aguilera (San Francisco). Natl Arch., WMC Rec., RG 211, Churchill Murray to Walter J. Linthicus (Second Secretary of the American Embassy), 26 Dec. 1944.

62. Natl Arch., WMC Rec., RG 211, John Coates to Churchill Murray, 16 March 1945.

63. Natl Arch., WMC Rec., RG 211, Churchill Murray to John Coates, 7 July 1945.

64. Natl Arch., DoS Rec., RG 59, George Messersmith to Joe McGurk, 11 Sept. 1944.

65. As late as the 1980s, bureaucrats at the national office of the Railroad Retirement Board in Chicago who had collaborated with or observed the railroad bracero program still commented on the activities of the Mexican labor inspectors.

66. For a more detailed analysis of Mexican consuls and the legal framework within which they worked, see *México y la protección de sus nacionales en Estados Unidos* by Remedios Gómez Arnau (Mexico City: Centro de Estudios sobre Estados Unidos de América, Universidad Nacional Autónoma de México, 1990).

67. Natl Arch., WMC Rec., RG 211, Samuel Hough to Robert Clark, 11 Nov. 1943.

68. Natl Arch., WMC Rec., RG 211, Álvaro Domínguez V. (Acting Consul General of El Paso) to Fred C. Werdt, 9 Aug. 1945.

69. Natl Arch., DoS Rec., RG 59, Robert MacLean to Sidney O'Donoghue, 12 Aug. 1944.

70. Natl Arch., DoS Rec., RG 84, memo for the files from Sidney O'Donoghue, 29 Sept. 1943.

71. Here the U.S. negotiators were mistaken, for the braceros' paycheck was subject to the 20 percent withholding tax. It was the Victory tax from which they were exempt.

72. During World War II, all wages were frozen by the government. Any raise would have required approval from the government, a point that was probably not considered in the negotiations for the bracero program.

73. Natl Arch., DoS Rec., RG 84, memo of conversation, attachment 1 to despatch 12,987, 13 Sept. 1943. Unsigned [probably written by Robert McGregor].

74. Natl Arch., DoS Rec., RG 84, memo by Sidney O'Donoghue, 29 Sept. 1943.

75. Natl Arch., DoS Rec., RG 84, memo for the file from Sidney O'Donoghue, 29 Sept. 1943. The visit of U.S. labor leaders to Mexico will be analyzed further below.

76. Natl Arch., DoS Rec., RG 59, Joseph Eastman to Edward Stettinius, 13 Oct. 1943.

77. Natl Arch., DoS Rec., RG 59, Joseph Eastman to Cordell Hull, 2 Sept. 1943.

78. Natl Arch., DoS Rec., RG 84, memo by Sidney O'Donoghue, 8 Nov. 1943.

79. Ambassador Messersmith made the original suggestion of a fact-finding commission to resolve the wage dispute. Natl Arch., DoS Rec., RG 84, memo by Sidney O'Donoghue, 8 Nov. 1943.

80. Natl Arch., DoS Rec., RG 84, memo for the files, Sidney O'Donoghue, 8 Nov. 1943.

81. Natl Arch., DoS Rec., RG 84, memo by Sidney O'Donoghue, 18 Feb. 1944.

82. Natl Arch., DoS Rec., RG 59, William MacLean to Joseph McGurk, 29 Jan. 1944.

83. So. Pac. Intrnl Files, Historical Labor File, "Historical Data in Connection with Employment of Mexican National Laborers Imported from Mexico," Aug. 1950, 40–41. The report indicates that the company had, and may still have, a special file on the incident in the chief engineer's office.

84. Natl Arch., DoS Rec., RG 59, William MacLean to Joseph McGurk, 29 Jan. 1944.

85. Natl Arch., DoS Rec., RG 59, memo of conversation regarding Mexican government claims on behalf of Mexican railroad workers, 3 March 1944.

86. Natl Arch., DoS Rec., RG 59, Laurence Duggan to Edward Stettinius, 6 March 1944.

87. Natl Arch., DoS Rec., RG 59, memo of conversation from meeting of Special Railroad Worker Commission, 6 March 1944.

88. Natl Arch., DoS Rec., RG 59, memos of conversation from meeting of Special Railroad Labor Commission to discuss terms of agreement, 7 March 1944.

89. Natl Arch., ODT Rec., RG 219, V. V. Boatner to A. F. Whitney, 14 Oct. 1942.

90. Natl Arch., ODT Rec., RG 219, statement issued by the Railway Labor Executives Association, 2 Nov. 1942.

91. Natl Arch., DoS Rec., RG 59, memo of conversation between Joseph McGurk, William MacLean, and the president and secretary-treasurer of the Brotherhood of Maintenance of Way Employees, Elmer E. Milliman and T. B. Shoemake, 7 Jan. 1943.

92. Natl Arch., DoS Rec., RG 59, memo from William MacLean, 5 Feb. 1943. See also INS, memo from Board of Immigration Appeals, file 56135/227.

93. Natl Arch., DoS Rec., RG 59, Paul McNutt to Cordell Hull, 14 June 1943. See also Natl Arch., DoS Rec., RG 59, Herbert Bursley to Cordell Hull, 26 July 1943.

94. RRB, Bur. of Law Files, Marjorie Marshall to Charles Hodge, 18 May 1943.

95. Natl Arch., DoS Rec., RG 84, Sumner Welles to U.S. Embassy, 21 Aug. 1943.

96. Natl Arch., DoS Rec., RG 84, W. K. Ailshie to Cordell Hull, 21 Sept. 1943. See also Natl Arch., DoS Rec., RG 59, Herbert Bursley to Cordell Hull, 14 Sept. 1943.

97. "Unions Jilt Joe," *Railway Age* 115 (1943): 27.

98. An example would be the order signed by Finucane of the Board of Immigration Appeals to increase the quota to 19,660. INS, order, 2 Oct. 1943, file 56135/227.

99. RRB, Exec. Officer's File, John Coates to D. F. Stevens (B&O), 27 Dec. 1944. The same letter was sent to all participating railroads. See also INS, "Approval of War Manpower Commission for Permission to Import 20,000 Unskilled Mexican Laborers," 30 March 1944, file 56135/227.

100. Natl Arch., DoS Rec., RG 59, John Coates to John Carrigan, 14 Oct. 1944.

101. Denver Hertel, *History of the Brotherhood of Maintenance of Way Employees* (Washington, D.C.: Ransdell, 1955), 165–194.

102. INS, A. W. Motley to E. E. Milliman, 26 Jan. 1944, file 56135/227.

103. RRB, Exec. Officer's File, E. E. Milliman to A. W. Motley, 28 Jan. 1944.

104. INS, Paul McNutt to Ugo Carusi, 28 Aug. 1945, file 56135/227.

105. Natl Arch., WMC Rec., RG 211, John Coates to Churchill Murray, 11 Oct. 1945.

12. THE ROLE OF THE RAILROADS

1. Peter Kirstein, *Anglo over Bracero: A History of the Mexican Worker in the United States from Roosevelt to Nixon* (San Francisco: R&E Research Associates, 1977), 28.

2. Natl Arch., DoS Rec., RG 59, Robert MacLean to Sidney O'Donoghue, 12 Aug. 1944.

3. Interestingly, I received this report anonymously, mailed from the Southern Pacific's headquarters in San Francisco.

4. So. Pac. Intrnl Files, Historical Labor File, "Historical Data in Connection with Employment of Mexican National Laborers Imported from Mexico," Aug. 1950, 18–19. This means that the company probably still houses considerable information about the braceros, possibly even about their employment after World War II.

5. RRB, Exec. Officer's File, Murray Latimer to Paul McNutt, 13 Nov. 1942.

6. Natl Arch., WMC Rec., RG 211, A. T. Mercier to J. M. Baths, 1 Dec. 1942.

7. Natl Arch., DoS Rec., RG 59, William MacLean to Joseph McGurk, 14 Jan. 1943.

8. INS, Lawrence Appley to Management-Labor Policy Committee, 4 Feb. 1943, file 56135/227.

9. So. Pac. Intrnl Files, "Historical Data," 21.

10. INS, memo from E. B., 14 April 1943, file 56135/227.

11. INS, G. C. Wilmoth to Immigration Service, 27 May 1943, file 56135/227.

12. INS, memo to A. C. Devaney, 21 April 1943, file 56135/227.

13. Natl Arch., WMC Rec., RG 211, Arthur Motley to Sam Hough, 4 May 1943.

14. Natl Arch., WMC Rec., RG 211, Arthur Motley to Sam Hough, 14 May 1943.

15. INS, Albert Del Guernicio to Immigration Service, 17 May 1943, file 56135/227.

16. INS, memo from Herman Landon, 7 May 1943, file 56135/227.

17. INS, memo from Herman Landon, 17 May 1943, file 56135/227.

18. INS, Albert Del Guernicio to Joseph Savoretti, 8 May 1943, file 56135/227.

19. Natl Arch., DoS Rec., RG 59, Carlos Gutiérrez-Macías to WMC Regional Director, 5 Aug. 1943.

20. Natl Arch., DoS Rec., RG 59, Mr. Macklin to W. K. Hopkins, 19 Aug. 1943.

21. Natl Arch., DoS Rec., RG 59, Neiola Barley to Cordell Hull, 31 Dec. 1943.

22. *Business Week,* 15 Oct. 1944, 54.

23. RRB, Exec. Officer's File, Placement of Mexican Nationals File, Southern Pacific Company, "Data on Occupations in Which Largest Number of Mexican Nationals Employed, Months May through October, 1945," n.d.

24. Natl Arch., DoS Rec., RG 59, Cordell Hull to the American Embassy, 27 July 1943.

25. RRB, Exec. Officer's File, Robert Clark to G. H. Muckley, 14 Oct. 1943.

26. Natl Arch., ODT Rec., RG 219, V. V. Boatner to A. F. Whitney, 14 Oct. 1942.

27. *Railway Engineering and Maintenance,* April 1944, 347.

28. INS, Lawrence Appley to Management-Labor Policy Committee, 4 Feb. 1943, file 56135/227.

29. INS, memo from E. B., 14 April 1943, file 56135/227.

30. Natl Arch., WMC Rec., RG 211, Arthur Motley to Sam Hough, 29 June 1943.

31. Natl Arch., DoS Rec., RG 59, memo of telephone conversation between William MacLean and Joseph McGurk, 29 April 1943.

32. Natl Arch., WMC Rec., RG 211, Sam Hough to Arthur Motley, 11 Aug. 1943.

33. INS, Charles Wood to Herman Landon, 20 May 1943, file 56135/227.

34. INS, Thomas Shoemake to Charles Wood, 2 June 1943, file 56135/227.

35. INS, order from the Board of Immigration Appeals, Department of Justice, 6 July 1943, file 56135/227.

36. Natl Arch., WMC Rec., RG 211, Arthur Motley to Charles Wood, 5 June 1943.

37. Natl Arch., ODT Rec., RG 219, V. V. Boatner to O. S. Beyer, 28 Nov. 1942.

38. Natl Arch., WMC Rec., RG 211, Lawrence Appley to Management-Labor Policy Committee, 4 Feb. 1943, file 56135/227.

39. INS, Arthur Motley to Thomas Finucane, 4 May 1943, file 56135/227.

40. Natl Arch., WMC Rec., RG 211, Sam Hough to Arthur Motley, 2 Aug. 1943.

41. Natl Arch., WMC Rec., RG 211, Sam Hough to Arthur Motley, 2 Aug. 1943.

42. RRB, Exec. Officer's File, General Counsel to Robert LaMotte, 6 June 1944.

43. RRB, Exec. Officer's File, WMC Field Instruction no. 187, supplement no. 1, Feb. 1944.

44. RRB, Exec. Officer's File, Charles Hodge to Herman Landon, 17 March 1944.

45. RRB, Exec. Officer's File, "Some Points as to Whether Unemployment Compensation Should Be Paid Mexicans That Were Imported for War Emergency," n.d.

46. RRB, Exec. Officer's File, Charles Hodge to Herman Landon, 5 Aug. 1944.

47. RRB, Exec. Officer's File, Charles Hodge to Herman Landon, 15 July 1945.

48. RRB, Exec. Officer's File, Placement of Mexican Nationals File, Book no. 2, "Data on Occupations in Which Largest Number of Mexican Nationals Employed, Months May through October, 1945, Northern Pacific Railway Company," n.d.

49. INS, bond, signed 24 June 1948, file 56135/686-A.

50. INS, W. F. Kelly to J. L. Gressitt, 10 Oct. 1949, file 56135/686-A.

51. INS, J. L. Gressitt to A. C. Devaney, 10 Sept. 1953, file 56135/686-A.

52. INS, Henry to A. C. Devaney, 15 Nov. 1956, file 56135/686-A.

53. INS, H. E. Roll to L. Paul Winings, 10 April 1945, file 56180/313.

54. INS, H. E. Roll to L. Paul Winings, 20 June 1945, file 56180/313.

55. INS, H. E. Roll to L. Paul Winings, 27 March 1946, file 56180/313.

56. INS, J. Crockett to Curtin, 21 April 1947, file 56180/313.

57. INS, James E. Riley to Adjudications Division, 5 Dec. 1950, file 56180/313.

58. INS, District Director of Kansas City to L. Paul Winings, 10 Sept. 1951, file 56180/313.

59. INS, C. C. Davis to INS Commissioner, 29 Aug. 1952, file 56180/313.

60. INS, Filer to Herman Landon, 12 June 1944, file 56135/680.

61. INS, A. C. Devaney to E. B. Perry, 16 Jan. 1946, file 56135/680.

62. INS, Joseph Savoretti to E. B. Perry, 20 March 1946, file 56135/680.

63. INS, order, 23 Sept. 1946, file 56135/680.

64. INS, W. F. Kelly to E. B. Perry, 21 July 1950, file 56135/680.

65. Natl Arch., WMC Rec., RG 211, Robert Clark to Sam Hough, 20 Nov. 1943.

66. INS, S. E. Atromstron to Herman Landon, 13 Sept. 1943, file 56135/227.

67. RRB, Exec. Officer's File, Placement of Mexican Nationals File, New York Central Railroad Company, "Data on Occupations in Which Large Number of Mexican Nationals Employed Months May through October, 1945," n.d.

68. Natl Arch., DoS Rec., RG 59, John Coates to John Carrigan, 14 Oct. 1944. However, I should note that apparently the New York Central did publish its employee publication *The Headlight* in Spanish for the duration of the bracero program.

69. Secretary of State to Herbert Bursley, 28 Oct. 1944, in U.S. Dept of State, *Foreign Relations of the United States: Diplomatic Papers, 1944* (Washington, D.C.: GPO, 1963), 7: 1329.

70. Natl Arch., WMC Rec., RG 211, Luis Merino Fuentes to Churchill Murray, 18 July 1945.

71. Natl Arch., WMC Rec., RG 211, John Fetter to R. R. McCurry, 31 Aug. 1945.

72. Natl Arch., WMC Rec., RG 211, Churchill Murray to Luis Fernández del Campo, 15 May 1946.

73. Natl Arch., WMC Rec., RG 211, John Coates to L. W. Horning, 27 March 1946.

13. TERMINATION AND REPATRIATION

1. Ernesto Galarza, *Merchants of Labor: The Mexican Bracero Story* (Santa Barbara, Calif.: McNally & Loftin, 1964), 55.

2. Natl Arch., DoS Rec., RG 59, Herbert Bursley to Cordell Hull, 6 Aug. 1943. The archives of the War Manpower Commission and other agencies are replete with repatriation plans.

3. INS, Sanderson to R. H. Robinson, 24 Aug. 1945, file 56135/227.

4. INS, Paul McNutt to Ugo Carusi, 28 Aug. 1945, file 56135/227.

5. George Messersmith to Cordell Hull, 28 Aug. 1945, in U.S. Dept of State, *Foreign Relations of the United States: Diplomatic Papers, 1945* (Washington, D.C.: GPO, 1963), 9: 1147–1148.

6. INS, John Coates to Herman Landon, 4 Dec. 1944, file 56135/227.

7. INS, memo of discussion in the Department of Justice, 5 Jan. 1945, file 56135/227.

8. INS, Joseph Savoretti to Thomas Finucane, Dec. 1944, file 56135/227.

9. Herbert Bursley to Cordell Hull, 2 May 1945, in U.S. Dept of State, *Foreign Relations 1945,* 9: 1143.

10. Natl Arch., WMC Rec., RG 211, John Coates to G. H. Minchin, 3 May 1945.

11. Natl Arch., WMC Rec., RG 211, John Coates to Churchill Murray, 31 Aug. 1945.

12. Peter Kirstein, *Anglo over Bracero: A History of the Mexican Worker in the United States from Roosevelt to Nixon* (San Francisco: R&E Research Associates, 1977), 34; Blanca Torres, *Historia de la Revolución Mexicana, 1940–1952: Hacia la utopía industrial* (Mexico City: Colegio de México, 1984), 237.

13. Galarza, *Merchants of Labor,* 54.

14. Natl Arch., WMC Rec., RG 211, Churchill Murray to John Coates, 30 Aug. 1945.

15. Natl Arch., WMC Rec., RG 211, E. V. Vandercook to Churchill Murray, 2 Oct. 1945.

16. Memo of conversation of William MacLean, 14 Nov. 1945, in U.S. Dept of State, *Foreign Relations 1945,* 9: 1151–1152.

17. Antonio Espinosa de los Monteros to Cordell Hull, 26 Nov. 1945, in U.S. Dept of State, *Foreign Relations 1945,* 9: 1153.

18. RRB, Exec. Officer's File, Robert LaMotte to Harlon Carter, 17 Nov. 1945.

19. Natl Arch., WMC Rec., RG 211, Churchill Murray to John Coates, 13 Nov. 1945.

20. Natl Arch., WMC Rec., RG 211, John Coates to Churchill Murray, 1 Feb. 1946.

21. Kirstein, *Anglo over Bracero,* 34.

22. Kirstein, *Anglo over Bracero,* 34.

23. Natl Arch., WMC Rec., RG 211, John Coates to Churchill Murray, 20 March 1946.

24. Natl Arch., WMC Rec., RG 211, John Coates to L. W. Horning, 27 March 1946.

25. Natl Arch., WMC Rec., RG 211, John Coates to Churchill Murray, 2 April 1946.

26. Natl Arch., WMC Rec., RG 211, John Coates to Churchill Murray, 10 April 1945.

27. INS, Archibald to Edward Shaughnessy, 18 Aug. 1945, file 56135/227.

28. So. Pac. Intrnl Files, Historical Labor File, "Historical Data in Connection with Employment of Mexican National Laborers Imported from Mexico," Aug. 1950, 29.

14. COROLLARIES

1. Natl Arch., DoS Rec., RG 59, R. J. de Camp to J. G. Luhrsen, 20 May 1944.

2. The moneys for the U.S. Railway Mission in Mexico, some $7 million, came from the President's Emergency Fund through the intercession of Nelson Rockefeller, the coordinator of inter-American affairs, and the War Production Board. The chief of the mission for most of its existence was Oliver Stevens, a well-known if somewhat controversial U.S. railroad man. See U.S. Dept of State, *Foreign Relations of the United States: Diplomatic Papers, 1944* (Washington, D.C.: GPO, 1963), 7: 1234–1275. See also *Excélsior,* 5 April 1943, 1, and Manuel Aguilar Uranga, "El señor O. M. Stevens y los ferrocarriles nacionales," *Revista de Economía,* 31 Aug. 1946, 11–13.

Interestingly, some mechanics employed by Ferrocarriles Nacionales had already gone to the United States in November 1943 at that company's expense to learn some U.S. equipment, obviously a sign that Ferrocarriles Nacionales was interested in training their employees. See *Excélsior,* 20 Nov. 1943, front page. Also, see *Railway Age* 114 (1943): 1945, for a story about the refurbishment of locomotives by Chicago, Burlington and Quincy for Ferrocarriles de México in June of 1943 that Carlos Rosales, a master mechanic from Mexico, observed.

3. Natl Arch., DoS Rec., RG 59, John C. McClintock to Emilio G. Callado, 19 Nov. 1942.

4. INS, Joseph Savoretti to William Whalen, 3 Feb. 1945, file 56211/216.

5. However, the attorney general signed a certification in July 1944 that would have allowed 5,000 skilled Mexican railroad workers in the United States at any one time. INS, Thomas G. Finucane to Ugo Carusi, 27 July 1944, file 56211/216.

6. RRB, Bur. of Law Files, circular no. 1351 from the Railway Employee Department of the American Federation of Labor, 10 June 1944. The same document is also found in INS file 56211/216.

7. Natl Arch., DoS Rec., RG 59, R. J. de Camp to J. G. Luhren, 20 May 1944.

8. INS, R. J. de Camp to INS Commissioner, 20 July 1944, file 56211/216.

9. INS, Joseph Savoretti to Cordell Hull, 3 Aug. 1944, file 56211/216.

10. RRB, Exec. Officer's File, Washington Representative to the Railroad Retirement Board, 30 Nov. 1944.

11. INS, R. H. Robinson, memo for the file, 30 Jan. 1945, file 56211/216.

12. Natl Arch., DoS Rec., RG 59, Cordell Hull to George Messersmith, 18 May 1943.

13. Natl Arch., DoS Rec., RG 59, Harold Finley to Cordell Hull, 14 April 1942.

14. *Excélsior,* 12 May 1943, front page.

15. Natl Arch., DoS Rec., RG 59, George Messersmith to Cordell Hull, 19 May 1943.

16. INS, memo for the file from Herman Landon, file 56135/227, 7 May 1943.

17. INS, Albert Del Guercio to Joseph Savoretti, 8 May 1943, file 56135/227.

18. Natl Arch., DoS Rec., RG 59, Sidney O'Donoghue to William MacLean, 31 July 1944.

19. M. L. Stafford to Cordell Hull, 6 June 1944, in U.S. Dept of State, *Foreign Relations 1944,* 7: 1314.

20. A. A. Berle to Cordell Hull, 14 Oct. 1944, in U.S. Dept of State, *Foreign Relations 1944,* 7: 1325.

21. Grew to Herbert Bursley, 8 May 1944, in U.S. Dept of State, *Foreign Relations 1944,* 7: 1144.

22. Sidney O'Donoghue to Joseph McGurk, 28 March 1944, in U.S. Dept of State, *Foreign Relations 1944,* 7: 1306.

23. Sidney O'Donoghue to Cordell Hull, 18 April 1944, in U.S. Dept of State, *Foreign Relations 1944,* 7: 1311.

24. This is especially true for parts of the Midwest where the bracero program introduced Mexican workers to large growers and other employers. Undocumented Mexican immigrants and Mexican American workers used the networks created by the bracero program to seek jobs on their own after World War II until 1964, and even thereafter. See Dennis Nodín Valdés, *Al Norte: Agricultural Workers in the Great Lakes Region, 1917–1970* (Austin: University of Texas Press, 1991).

25. RRB, Exec. Officer's File, R. R. Rubottom to William J. Kennedy, 18 Feb. 1946.

26. Bill Poulos, Director of Public Affairs, Railroad Retirement Board, to the author, 16 Dec. 1986.

27. RRB, Exec. Officer's File, internal board report, 1950.

28. "International Conference of Trade Unions of Mexico and the United States Convened by the O.R.I.T.," document submitted by Alfonso Sánchez Madariaga, Francisco J. Macín, and Hermenegildo J. Aldana of the CTM, 14–16 Dec. 1953, Folder U.S.–Mexico Trade Union Committee, Irwin de Shetler Collection, Box 47, Archives of Labor and Urban Affairs, Wayne State University, Detroit.

29. See U.S. Dept of State, *Foreign Relations of the United States: Diplomatic Papers, 1951* (Washington, D.C.: GPO, 1979), 2: 1470–1513; *Foreign Relations of the United States: Diplomatic Papers, 1952–54* (Washington, D.C.: GPO, 1983), 4: 1324–1368; *Foreign Relations of the United States: Diplomatic Papers, 1955–57* (Washington, D.C.: GPO, 1987), 6: 649–776.

Bibliography

BOOKS

Acuña, Rodolfo. *Occupied America: A History of Chicanos.* 2d ed. New York: Harper & Row, 1981.

Association of American Railroads. *Railways of the United States: Their Plant Facilities and Operation.* Washington, D.C.: AAR, 1940.

Balderrama, Francisco E. *In Defense of La Raza: The Los Angeles Mexican Consulate and the Mexican Community, 1929 to 1936.* Tucson: University of Arizona Press, 1982.

Bemis, Samuel Flagg. *The Latin American Policy of the United States.* New York: Norton, 1943.

Bernard, William S. *American Immigration Policy: A Reappraisal.* New York: Harper & Row, 1950.

Bernstein, Irving. *A History of the American Worker, 1933–1941: Turbulent Years.* Boston: Houghton & Mifflin, 1970.

Bidwell, Percy Wells. *Economic Defense of Latin America.* Boston: World Peace Foundation, 1941.

Brandenburg, Frank. *The Making of Modern Mexico.* Englewood Cliffs, N.J.: Prentice-Hall, 1964.

Briggs, Vernon, Walter Fogel, and Fred H. Schmidt. *The Chicano Worker.* Austin: University of Texas Press, 1977.

Burgess, George, and Miles Kennedy. *Centennial History of the Pennsylvania Railroad.* Philadelphia: Pennsylvania Railroad Company, 1949.

Cardoso, Lawrence. *Mexican Emigration to the United States, 1897–1931: Socio-Economic Patterns.* Tucson: University of Arizona Press, 1980.

Cline, Howard. *The United States and Mexico.* Cambridge, Mass.: Harvard University Press, 1953.

Conne, Stetson, and Byron Fairchild. *The Framework of Hemisphere Defense.* Washington, D.C.: Department of the Army, 1950.

Corliss, Carlton. *Main Line of Mid-America: The Story of the Illinois Central.* New York: Creative Age Press, 1950.

Corson, John J. *Manpower for Victory: Total Mobilization for Total War.* New York: Farrar & Rinehard, 1943.

Cottrell, W. Fred. *The Railroader.* Stanford, Calif.: Stanford University Press, 1940.

Craig, Richard. *The Bracero Program.* Austin: University of Texas Press, 1971.

Divine, Robert. *The History of American Immigration Policy.* New Haven, Conn.: Yale University Press, 1957.

Ducker, James H. *Men of the Steel Rails: Workers on the Atchison, Topeka and Santa Fe Railroad, 1869–1900.* Lincoln: University of Nebraska Press, 1983.

Elkins, Stanley. *Slavery: A Problem in American Institutional and Intellectual Life.* Chicago: University of Chicago Press, 1969.

Fernández, Raúl A. *The United States–Mexico Border: A Politico-Economic Profile.* Notre Dame, Ind.: University of Notre Dame Press, 1977.

Flynn, George Q. *The Mess in Washington: Manpower Mobilization in World War II.* Westport, Conn.: Greenwood Press, 1979.

Fraser, Cecil E., and Stanley F. Teele. *Industry Goes to War: Readings in American Rearmament.* Freeport, N.Y.: Books for Libraries Press, 1941.

Fuess, Claude M. *Joseph B. Eastman: Servant of the People.* New York: Columbia University Press, 1952.

Galarza, Ernesto. *Strangers in Our Fields.* Washington, D.C.: Fund for the Republic, 1956.

———. *Merchants of Labor: The Mexican Bracero Story.* Santa Barbara, Calif.: McNally & Loftin, 1964.

Gamboa, Erasmo. *Mexican Labor and World War II: Braceros in the Pacific Northwest, 1942–1947.* Austin: University of Texas Press, 1990.

Gamio, Manuel. *Mexican Immigration to the United States: A Study of Human Migration and Adjustment.* New York: Dover Publications, 1971.

García, Mario T. *Desert Immigrants: The Mexicans of El Paso, 1880–1920.* New Haven, Conn.: Yale University Press, 1981.

Garis, Roy L. *Immigration Restriction: A Study of the Opposition to and Regulation of Immigration into the United States.* New York: Macmillan, 1927.

Gil, Federico G. *Latin American–United States Relations.* New York: Harcourt Brace Jovanovich, 1971.

Gómez Arnau, Remedios. *México y la protección de sus nacionales en Estados Unidos.* Mexico City: Centro de Estudios sobre Estados Unidos de América, Universidad Nacional Autónoma de México, 1990.

Graebner, Norman A., ed. *An Uncertain Tradition: American Secretaries of State.* New York: McGraw-Hill, 1961.

Green, David. *The Containment of Latin America: A History of the Myths and Realities of the Good Neighbor Policy.* Chicago: Quadrangle Books, 1971.

Haber, William, John Carroll, Mark Kahn, and Metton Peck. *Maintenance of Way Employment of U.S. Railroads: An Analysis of the Sources of Instability and Remedial Measures.* Detroit: Brotherhood of Maintenance of Way Employees, 1954.

Harvey, Ray F. *The Politics of This War.* New York: Harper & Brothers, 1943.

Hertel, Denver. *History of the Brotherhood of Maintenance of Way Employees.* Washington, D.C.: Ransdell, 1955.

Hines, Walker D. *War History of American Railroads.* New Haven, Conn.: Yale University Press, 1928.

Hoehling, A. A. *Home Front, U.S.A.* New York: Thomas Y. Crowell, 1966.

Hoffman, Abraham. *Unwanted Mexican Americans in the Great Depression: Repatriation Pressures, 1929–1939.* Tucson: University of Arizona Press, 1974.

James, Daniel. *Mexico and the Americans.* New York: Praeger, 1963.

Jones, Robert C. *Mexican War Workers in the United States.* Washington, D.C.: Pan American Union, 1945.

Kirk, Betty. *Covering the Mexican Front: The Battle of Europe versus America.* Norman: University of Oklahoma Press, 1942.

Kirstein, Peter N. *Anglo over Bracero: A History of the Mexican Worker in the United States from Roosevelt to Nixon.* San Francisco: R&E Research Associates, 1977.

Kiser, George C., and Martha Woody Kiser, eds. *Mexican Workers in the United States: Historical and Political Perspectives.* Albuquerque: University of New Mexico Press, 1979.

Kolko, Gabriel. *Railroads and Regulations, 1877–1916.* Princeton, N.J.: Princeton University Press, 1965.

Langer, William L., and S. Everett Gleason. *The Challenge to Isolation: The World Crisis of 1937–1940 and American Foreign Policy.* New York: Harper & Row, 1964.

Licht, Walter. *Working for the Railroad: The Organization of Work in the Nineteenth Century.* Princeton, N.J.: Princeton University Press, 1983.

Lieuwen, Edwin. *Arms and Politics in Latin America.* New York: Praeger, 1960.

Lipshultz, Robert J. *American Attitudes toward Mexican Immigration, 1924–1952.* San Francisco: R&E Research Associates, 1971.

Lyon, Peter. *To Hell in a Day Coach.* Philadelphia: Lippincott, 1968.

McWilliams, Carey. *North from Mexico: The Spanish-Speaking People of the United States.* New York: Greenwood Press, 1968.

Mecham, J. Lloyd. *The United States and Inter-American Security, 1889–1960.* Austin: University of Texas Press, 1961.

Mellinger, Philip J. *Race and Labor in Western Copper: The Fight for Equality, 1896–1918.* Tucson: University of Arizona Press, 1995.

Meyer, Michael C., and William L. Sherman. *The Course of Mexican History.* 4th ed. New York: Oxford University Press, 1991.

Mines, Richard, and Ricardo Anzaldúa. *New Migrants versus Old Migrants: Alternative Labor Market Structures in the California Citrus Industry.* La Jolla, Calif.: Program in United States–Mexican Studies, University of California, San Diego, 1982.

Mink, Gwendolyn. *Old Labor and New Immigrants in American Political Development: Union, Party, and State, 1875–1920.* Ithaca, N.Y.: Cornell University Press, 1986.

Moore, Joan. *Mexican Americans.* Englewood Cliffs, N.J.: Prentice-Hall, 1970.

Nelson, James C. *Railroad Transportation and Public Policy.* Washington, D.C.: Brookings Institution, 1959.

Niblo, Stephen R. *War, Diplomacy, and Development: The United States and Mexico, 1938–1954.* Wilmington, Del.: Scholarly Resources, 1995.

Palmer, Thomas W., Jr. *Search for a Latin American Policy.* Gainesville: University of Florida Press, 1957.

Paredes, Américo. *A Texas-Mexican* Cancionero: *Folksongs of the Lower Border.* Austin: University of Texas Press, 1995.

Phillips, Cabel B. H. *The 1940's: Decade of Triumph and Trouble.* New York: Macmillan, 1975.

Pike, Frederick B. *FDR's Good Neighbor Policy: Sixty Years of Generally Gentle Chaos.* Austin: University of Texas Press, 1995.

Portes, Alejandro, and Robert L. Back. *Latin Journey: Cuban and Mexican Immigrants in the United States.* Berkeley: University of California Press, 1985.

Rauch, Basil. *Roosevelt: From Munich to Pearl Harbor.* New York: Creative Age Press, 1950.

Rayback, Joseph G. *A History of American Labor.* New York: Free Press, 1966.

Reisler, Mark. *By the Sweat of Their Brow: Mexican Immigrant Labor in the United States, 1900–1940.* Westport, Conn.: Greenwood Press, 1976.

Ríos Bustamante, Antonio José. *Los Ángeles, pueblo y región, 1781–1850: Continuidad y adaptación en la periferia del norte mexicano.* Mexico City: Instituto Nacional de Antropología e Historia, 1991.

Schmitt, Karl M. *Mexico and the United States, 1821–1973: Conflict and Coexistence.* New York: Wiley, 1974.

Schwartz, Harry. *Seasonal Farm Labor in the United States (with Special Reference to Hired Workers in Fruit and Vegetable and Sugar Beet Production).* New York: Columbia University Press, 1945.

Stover, John. *The Railroads of the South, 1865–1900.* Chapel Hill: University of North Carolina Press, 1955.

———. *American Railroads.* Chicago: University of Chicago Press, 1961.

———. *The Life and Decline of the American Railroad.* New York: Oxford University Press, 1970.

Taylor, Paul S. *Mexican Labor in the United States.* Vol. 1. Berkeley: University of California Press, 1930.

———. *Mexican Labor in the United States.* Vol. 2. Berkeley: University of California Press, 1932.

Torres, Blanca. *Historia de la Revolución Mexicana, 1940–1952: Hacia la utopía industrial.* Mexico City: Colegio de México, 1984.

Tulchin, Joseph S. *The Aftermath of War: World War I and U.S. Policy toward Latin America.* New York: New York University Press, 1971.

Valdés, Dennis Nodín. *Al Norte: Agricultural Workers in the Great Lakes Region, 1917–1970.* Austin: University of Texas Press, 1991.

Whitney, Alexander F. *Wartime Wages and Railroad Labor: A Report on the 1942–43 Wage Movement of the Transportation Brotherhoods.* Cleveland: Brotherhood of Railroad Trainmen, 1944.

William, Dean L. *Political and Economic Aspects of Mexican Immigration into California and the U.S. since 1941.* San Francisco: R&E Research Associates, 1973.

Wittke, Carl. *We Who Built America.* Cleveland: Case Western Reserve University Press, 1939.

Wood, Bryce. *The Making of the Good Neighbor Policy.* New York: Columbia University Press, 1961.

ARTICLES AND WORKING PAPERS

Aguilar Uranga, Manuel. "El señor O. M. Stevens y los ferrocarriles nacionales." *Revista de Economía,* 31 August 1946, 11–13.

Álvarez del Vayo, Julio. "Mexico Left and Right." *Nation* 158 (1944): 621–623.

———. "Mexico's War-Time Book." *Nation* 158 (1944): 560–563.

Amidon, Beulah. "Trouble on the Railroads." *Survey Graphic* 32 (1943): 493–497.

Andreas, Peter. "U.S.–Mexico: Open Markets, Closed Border." *Foreign Policy,* no. 103 (1996): 51–69.

"Antitrust Suits as Propaganda." *Saturday Evening Post* 213 (1944): 108.

"Behind the Railroad Strike." *New Republic* 109 (1943): 902–903.

Block, Harry. "Mexico's Home Front." *Nation* 155 (1942): 406–408.

Carson, Robert B. "Railroads and Regulation Revisited: A Note on Problems of Historiography and Ideology." *Historian* 34 (1972): 437–446.

Chalker, Russell. "Irish Catholics in the Building of the McOcmulgee and Flint Railroad." *Georgia Historical Quarterly* 59 (1970): 507–514.

Clark, Malcolm, Jr. "The Bigot Disclosed: Ninety Years of Nativism." *Oregon Historical Quarterly* 75 (1974): 109–190.

Clark, Victor. "Mexican Labor in the United States." *Bulletin of the Bureau of Labor,* no. 78 (1908): 466–522.

Clough, Ernest T. "A Crisis in Railroad Finance." *Barron's* 12 (1932): 3, 6.

Coatsworth, John. "Railroads, Landholding, and Agrarian Protest in the Early Porfiriato." *Hispanic American Historical Review* 59 (1974): 48–71.

"Coming Out into the Open." *Commonweal* 39 (1943): 244–245.

Controneo, Ross R. "Western Land Marketing by the Northern Pacific." *Pacific Historical Review* 37 (1968): 299–320.

Daniels, Jonathan. "Brotherhood except for Negroes." *Nation* 153 (1941): 513.

DeGolyer, Everett L., Jr. "Texas Railroads: The End of an Era." *Southwestern Historical Quarterly* 73 (1970): 1969–1979.

"Dr. Padilla in Washington." *Bulletin of the Pan American Union* 78 (1944): 486–489.

Eastman, Joseph B. "Public Administration of Transportation under War Conditions." *American Economic Review* 34 (1944): 86–93.

"Extent of Federal Control over Labor in America Today." *Congressional Digest* 23 (1944): 106.

Farrar, Larston D. "Paul McNutt's First Sergeant." *Nation's Business* 31 (1943): 26, 62.

Flandrau, Grace. "Fiesta in St. Paul." *Yale Review* 33 (1944): 69–76.

Francaviglia, Richard V. "Some Comments on the Historical and Geographical Importance of Railroads in Minnesota." *Minnesota History* 43 (1972): 58–62.

Fuller, Helen. "Manpower, McNutt, and Politics." *New Republic* 106 (1942): 855–856.

Fuller, Roden. "Occupations of the Mexican-Born Population of Texas, New Mexico, and Arizona, 1900–1920." *Journal of the American Statistical Association* 23 (1928): 64–67.

Gould, M. David. "Overinvestment: The Root of Railroads' Trouble." *Barron's* 12 (1932): 10–11.

Greever, William S. "A Comparison of Railroad Land-Grant Policies." *Agricultural History* 25 (1951): 83–90.

Haas, Lisbeth. "The Bracero in Orange County: A Work Force for Economic Transition." Working Papers in U.S.–Mexican Studies, no. 29. La Jolla, Calif.: Program in U.S.–Mexican Studies, University of California, San Diego, 1981.

Handley, Lawrence R. "Settlement across Northern Arkansas As Influenced by the Missouri and North Arkansas Railroad." *Arkansas Historical Quarterly* 33 (1974): 273–292.

Harbeson, Robert Willis. "The Emergency Railroad Transportation Act of 1933." *Journal of Political Economy* 42 (1934): 106–126.

Henderson, Julia. "Foreign Labour in the United States during the War." *International Labour Review* 52 (1945): 609–631.

Kraus, George. "Chinese Laborers and the Construction of the Central Pacific." *Utah Historical Quarterly* 37 (1969): 41–57.

LaFollette, Suzanne. "Jim Crow and Casey Jones." *Nation* 155 (1942): 675–677.

Lauck, Lee G. "The Collapse in Railroad Credit." *Barron's* 11 (1931): 15.

Levenstein, Harvey A. "The AFL and Mexican Immigration in the 1920s: An Experiment in Labor Diplomacy." *Hispanic American Historical Review* 48 (1968): 206–219.

Lightner, David L. "Construction Labor on the Illinois Central." *Illinois State Historical Society Journal* 66 (1973): 285–301.

McWilliams, Carey. "A Tear for José Dávila." *Nation* 159 (1944): 587.

Mercer, Lloyd J. "Building ahead of Demand: Some Evidence for the Land Grant Railroads." *Journal of Economic History* 34 (1974): 492–500.

Middleton, Kenneth A. "Wartime Labor Productivity in Railroad Transportation." *Monthly Labor Review* 57 (1943): 444–451.

Murkland, Harry Banta. "Mexico and the United States Agree." *Current History* 1 (1942): 459–461.

Pozzetta, George E. "A Padrone Looks at Florida: Labor Recruitment and the Florida East Coast Railway." *Florida Historical Quarterly* 54 (1975): 74–84.

Rico, Carlos. "Migration and U.S.–Mexican Relations, 1966–1986." In *Western Hemisphere Immigration and United States Foreign Policy,* edited by Christopher Mitchell. University Park: Pennsylvania State University, 1992.

Roller Issler, Anne. "Good Neighbors Lend a Hand." *Survey Graphic* 32 (1943): 389–394.

Snell, Joseph W., and Don W. Wilson. "The Birth of the Atchison, Topeka and Santa Fe Railroad." *Kansas Historical Quarterly* 34 (1968): 113–142, 325–356.

Taylor, Frank J. "Brother, Can You Spare a Locomotive?" *Saturday Evening Post* 215 (1943): 25–27, 73, 75.

Taylor, Philip B., Jr. "Hemisphere Defense in World War II." *Current History* 56 (1969): 333–339.

Venable, Charles Leslie. "Chicago Mexicans Meet Synarchism." *Christian Century* 61 (1944): 1183.

Weiner Greenwald, Maurine. "Women Workers and World War I: The American Railroad Industry, a Case Study." *Journal of Social History* 9 (1975): 154–177.

Wollenberg, Charles. "Working on *El Traque.*" In *The Chicano,* edited by Norris Hundley. Santa Barbara, Calif.: Clio Books, 1975.

THESES AND DISSERTATIONS

Camarillo, Albert. "The Making of a Chicano Community: A History of the Chicanos in Santa Barbara, California, 1850–1930." Ph.D. diss., University of California, Los Angeles, 1975.

Hewes, Laurence Ilsley, Jr. "Some Migratory Labor Problems in California's Specialized Agriculture." Ph.D. diss., George Washington University, 1946.

Laird, Judith Fincher. "Argentine, Kansas: The Evolution of a Mexican-American Community, 1905–1940." Ph.D. diss., Denison University, 1975.

Lamb, Helen Boyden. "Industrial Relations in the Western Lettuce Industry." Ph.D. diss., Radcliffe College, 1943.

Rutter, Larry G. "Mexican Americans in Kansas: A Survey and Social Mobility Study, 1900–1970." Master's thesis, Kansas State University, 1972.

Santoro, Carmela Elvira. "United States and Mexican Relations during World War II." Ph.D. diss., Syracuse University, 1967.

Taylor, Nelson. "The Associations of American Railroads: Government and Politics in the Railroad Industry, 1934–1952." Ph.D. diss., Harvard University, 1956.

Vargas y Campos, Gloria R. " El problema del bracero México." Licenciatura thesis, Universidad Nacional Autónoma de México, 1964.

PUBLIC DOCUMENTS

Interstate Commerce Commission. *Forty-Seventh Annual Report of the Interstate Commerce Commission.* Washington, D.C.: GPO, 1933.

Parmelee, Julius H. *A Review of Railway Operations in 1932.* Special Series no. 59. Washington, D.C.: Bureau of Railway Economics, 1933.

———. *A Review of Railway Operations in 1933.* Special Series no. 59. Washington, D.C.: Bureau of Railway Economics, 1934.

———. *A Review of Railway Operations in 1935.* Special Series no. 59. Washington, D.C.: Bureau of Railway Economics, 1936.

———. *A Review of Railway Operations in 1936.* Special Series no. 59. Washington, D.C.: Bureau of Railway Economics, 1937.

Segundo informe constitucional rendido ante la H. XXXIV Legislatura del Estado. Rendido por el C. Gobernador Agapito Pozo, 16 September 1945.

U.S. Department of State. *Foreign Relations of the United States: Diplomatic Papers, 1941.* Vol. 6. Washington, D.C.: GPO, 1963.

———. *Foreign Relations of the United States: Diplomatic Papers, 1942.* Vol. 6. Washington, D.C.: GPO, 1963.

———. *Foreign Relations of the United States: Diplomatic Papers, 1943.* Vol. 6. Washington, D.C.: GPO, 1963.

———. *Foreign Relations of the United States: Diplomatic Papers, 1944.* Vol. 7. Washington, D.C.: GPO, 1963.

———. *Foreign Relations of the United States: Diplomatic Papers, 1945.* Vol. 9. Washington, D.C.: GPO, 1963.

———. *Foreign Relations of the United States: Diplomatic Papers, 1951.* Vol. 2. Washington, D.C.: GPO, 1979.

———. *Foreign Relations of the United States: Diplomatic Papers, 1952–54.* Vol. 4. Washington, D.C.: GPO, 1983.

———. *Foreign Relations of the United States: Diplomatic Papers, 1955–57.* Vol. 6. Washington, D.C.: GPO, 1987.

———. *Treaties and Other International Agreements of the United States of America, 1776–1949.* Vol. 9. Washington, D.C.: Department of State Publications, 1972.

MANUSCRIPT COLLECTIONS

Immigration and Naturalization Service Records. Files 56135/168, 56135/227. Washington, D.C.

Irwin de Shetler Collection. Archives of Labor and Urban Affairs. Wayne State University, Detroit.

National Archives. Department of State Records. RG 59.

National Archives. Department of State Records. RG 84.

National Archives. Office of Defense Transportation Records. RG 219.

National Archives. War Manpower Commission Records. RG 211.
Querétaro (State of). Archivo del Poder Ejecutivo.
Railroad Retirement Board. Bureau of Law Files, 1942–1955. Chicago.
Railroad Retirement Board. Executive Officer's File, 1942–1955. Chicago.
Secretaría de Relaciones Exteriores. Archivo Histórico. Mexico City.

PERIODICALS

Business Week (1941–1946).
Excélsior (1943–1944).
Interamerican 3–4 (1944–1945).
International Labour Review 45–52 (1942–1945).
Monthly Labor Review 53–57 (1941–1944).
Newsweek (1941–1945).
New York Times (1943–1945).
Railway Age 112–119 (1941–1945).
Railway Engineering and Maintenance 43–45 (1943–1945).
Time (1941–1946).

Index

Transportation *(cont.)*
  for repatriation at end of railroad
    bracero program, 155, 156, 157
  return transportation for braceros,
    116
  supervision of braceros during
    transport, 88
Traqueros. See Track workers
Trejo, Ernesto, 127
Trelkeld Company, 106
Trujillo Gurria, Francisco, 77
Truman, Harry, 165
Tuberculosis testing, 84, 93–94

U.S.–Mexico relations, economic
  agreements, 35, 36
Undocumented immigration
  control by Mexican government, 77,
    78
  deportation of undocumented
    workers, 47, 141
  railroad bracero program and, 97,
    161–163, 171
  railroad industry and, 46, 141
Unión Federal Mexicana, and Pacific
  Electric Railway, 30
Union Pacific
  labor shortage and, 62
  meeting with Central Pacific, 15
  number of braceros working for,
    145
  recruitment by, 64
  wages of, 64
Unions. *See* Labor unions
United Auto Workers, 58
United States. *See also* U.S.–Mexico
  relations; and specific federal
  agencies
  and agricultural bracero program,
    53–59, 68–69
  economic growth in, 3
  governmental relationship with rail-
    road industry, 11

United States *(cont.)*
  governmental role in labor supply, 53
  heavy equipment deal with Mexico,
    35
  land grants to railroads, 4–5
  Mexican consuls in, 70–71, 127, 128,
    129, 139
  Mexican labor inspectors in, 74, 95,
    106–107, 122, 125–127
  Mexican Railroad Worker Project
    and, 160–161
  railroad bracero program adminis-
    tration in, 119–135
  railroad bracero program and gov-
    ernment agencies, 64–65
  railroad bracero program negotia-
    tions with Mexico, 67–74
  railroad bracero program opera-
    tions in, 99–118
  railroad discounts to U.S. govern-
    ment, 5
  and termination of railroad bracero
    program, 152–154
  and wage negotiations, 25–26
U.S. Department of Agriculture
  (USDA)
  and administration of agricultural
    bracero program, 120
  farmworker transportation pro-
    gram, 52
  and funding for agricultural bracero
    program, 57, 92
  and importation of Mexican
    farmworkers, 52–53, 54, 55, 65
  and repatriation at end of railroad
    bracero program, 156
U.S. Department of the Army, 66
U.S. Embassy, 67, 91, 94, 95, 104, 125,
  153, 160, 170
U.S. Employment Service, 54, 112, 120
U.S. Justice Department, 53, 54, 109
U.S. Labor Department, 3, 47, 54, 63,
  155

About the Author

Originally from Boston, Massachusetts, Barbara A. Driscoll
has a Ph.D. in history from the University of Notre Dame,
where she studied with Professor Julián Samora. From 1990
to 1997, she was the coordinator of the United States section
of the Centro de Investigaciones sobre América del Norte, at
the Universidad Nacional Autónoma de México, in Mexico
City. She now holds a tenured research appointment there.

CMAS BOOKS

The Tracks North: The Railroad Bracero Program of World War II was designed by Jace Graf and Víctor J. Guerra. The text was composed primarily in Minion, with Hiroshige used for the title pages and chapter titles. The book was printed and bound by Edwards Brothers, of Ann Arbor, Michigan.